The Animal World of the Pharaohs

Patrick F. Houlihan

The Animal World of the Pharaohs

THAMES AND HUDSON

Page i

Bronze statuette of the god Apis striding forward. The bull bears the special markings of the deity on its hide and wears the sun disk and uraeus between its horns. This object served as a votive offering where Apis was worshiped. Late Dynastic Period. KESTNER MUSEUM, HANNOVER.

Page ii

This painted limestone relief scene comes from the tomb-chapel of the mastaba of Ti (no. 60) at Saqqara and shows a naked cowherd carrying a new-born calf on his shoulders across a stream or canal. The terrified young animal looks back and cries out forlornly to its mother, who follows close behind them. The shallow water is cleverly suggested by a pattern of zigzagging lines cut in the relief. Fifth Dynasty.

Page iii

Monumental pink granite statue of a recumbent Lion, one of a pair originally set up as guardian figures before an edifice of King Nectanebo I. In ancient Egypt, the Lion was considered the epitome of vigilance and guardianship. Thirtieth Dynasty. MUSEO GREGORIANO EGIZIO, VATICAN.

Page vi

Detail of a head of a lioness from a large ritual couch discovered in the tomb of Tutankhamun (no. 62) in the Valley of the Kings. The figure is in gilded wood, inlaid with blue and black glass. Eighteenth Dynasty. THE EGYPTIAN MUSEUM, CAIRO.

First published in Great Britain in 1996
by Thames and Hudson Ltd, London

First published in the United States of America in 1996 by Thames and Hudson Inc.,
500 Fifth Avenue, New York, New York 10110

British Library Cataloguing-in-Publication Data
A catalogue record for this book is available from the British Library

ISBN 0-500-01731-X

Library of Congress Catalog Card Number 96-60237

Printed in Egypt by Elias Modern Press

To Susan

And remembering the vital contributions of the
Egyptian Wildlife Service and the Brooke Hospital
for Animals to the well-being of the modern
Egyptian animal world

Contents

Acknowledgments

I would like to extend my sincere thanks to all those who in any way helped and encouraged me in writing this book. I am especially grateful to the many individuals around the world who arranged for the prompt delivery of outstanding photographs and gave me permission to reproduce them in this work. Their courtesy is acknowledged on page 219. Princeton University Press has kindly allowed me to cite J. A. Wilson's translations of Egyptian texts appearing in J. B. Pritchard's *Ancient Near Eastern Texts Relating to the Old Testament*, and the University of California Press has done the same for excerpts from M. Lichtheim's *Ancient Egyptian Literature: A Book of Readings*. Dr. J. F. Borghouts, Dr. H. te Velde, and Dr. R. A. Caminos also granted me permission to include several passages from their respective publications. The staff of the Rare Books and Special Collections Library of the American University in Cairo gave me assistance during my summer trips to Egypt. Prof. R. Stadelmann kindly allowed me to peruse Ludwig Keimer's private papers, housed in the Deutsches Archäologisches Institut, Cairo. I must also duly acknowledge the officials of the Egyptian Museum, Cairo, and the Egyptian Antiquities Organization (now the Supreme Council for Antiquities) for their friendly cooperation since 1973, and for graciously providing me with necessary permits to visit and photograph in museums and monuments. May Trad and Dr. Dia' Abou-Ghazi, in particular, were of considerable assistance in facilitating my work at the Egyptian Museum.

My sister, Mary Beth Wheeler, read an early draft of this work and offered numerous useful comments and observations. Arnold C. Tovell, director of the American University in Cairo Press, and R. Neil Hewison, my editor at the Press, have been enormously helpful in guiding this book from its inception to its final form and fruition. The book has also profited from a close reading of the completed manuscript by two readers selected by the American University in Cairo Press, and I would like to extend my thanks to them for their astute comments and suggestions. What errors remain are my own. I am grateful to the Werner Forman Archive, London, for their kind assistance with many of the color illustrations. Robert T. Wheeler, Pierre Zogg, and Hazel assisted in a number of ways with the black-and-white photographs.

I also gratefully acknowledge the assistance my parents have given me over the years in my endeavors. And above all, I wish to thank my wife Susan, to whom this book is dedicated, for her unfailing encouragement, forbearance, and assistance at every step of this project.

Preface

*T*he animal world was an extremely important and pervasive element in the lives of the ancient Egyptians. Amid the wide range of daily contact with animals, some creatures served the Egyptians as invaluable sources of food, others were harnessed as beasts of burden for tillage, cartage, and as pack animals.

They offered companionship as beloved household pets, they were quarry for the hunt, denizens of the sky flew overhead, vicious predators were feared, and the life-giving waters of the River Nile were home to a vast array of wildlife. Furthermore, a great many animals also had vital associations with gods and goddesses in the pharaonic pantheon. Anyone who has had the good fortune to visit the monuments of ancient Egypt or who has studied its art must have been struck by the dazzling display of animal images that were an integral component of Egyptian iconography.

A range of mammals, birds, fishes, amphibians, reptiles, invertebrates, and other lesser creatures also figured very prominently in the Egyptian hieroglyphic script. The aim of this book is to provide an up-to-date, amply illustrated survey of the animal world of the pharaohs that is accessible to the inquiring, educated, general reader without detailed knowledge of the country but is also interesting to those with previous background in the study of ancient Egypt. In attempting to do this, I have sought wherever possible to emphasize the relationship that existed

Faience figurines of a jerboa and a frog from a vaulted brick tomb discovered at al-Matariya, near Heliopolis. The precise function of these small objects in a human burial is not clearly understood, but they probably had magical attributes. Twelfth or Thirteenth Dynasty. Actual size. THE FITZWILLIAM MUSEUM, UNIVERSITY OF CAMBRIDGE.

between animals and people all those centuries ago. In addition, I have concentrated on those animal species that are most frequently portrayed in representations of everyday life executed on the walls of tomb-chapels and temples, and that are therefore more familiar to the non-specialist. For a more comprehensive treatment of bird life in ancient Egypt than the scope of this volume allows, the reader is referred to my *Birds of Ancient Egypt*.

The source material upon which this volume is based is spread over more than three thousand years of ancient Egyptian civilization. Pertinent information about the animal world of the pharaohs has been gleaned not only from the extremely rich pictorial record but also from textual references, mummified animals, food offerings placed in burials, and bone remains recovered from trash heaps at settlement sites. This area of study is, to a certain extent, still a growing picture. Zooarchaeological investigations in recent years, in addition to

specialized studies by Egyptologists, have thrown new light on this fascinating field, and fresh findings are still appearing from current excavations in Egypt. It is my fervent hope that this book will stimulate in the reader enough interest in the natural history and culture of ancient Egypt to follow up these subjects by reading some of the publications listed in the selected bibliography of general works at the end of the volume.

Finally, a brief note on the taxonomic nomenclature followed in this study. For the domestic animals, an area where little agreement exists among specialists on how to label them, I have relied heavily upon Clutton-Brock 1993. For other mammals, I have closely consulted Osborn and Helmy 1980, and Nowak 1991. The avifauna corresponds to that used by Houlihan 1986, and Goodman and Meininger 1989. Reptiles and amphibians, for the most part, follow Marx 1968. For the fishes, I have in general followed Boulenger 1907, and Brewer and Friedman 1989.

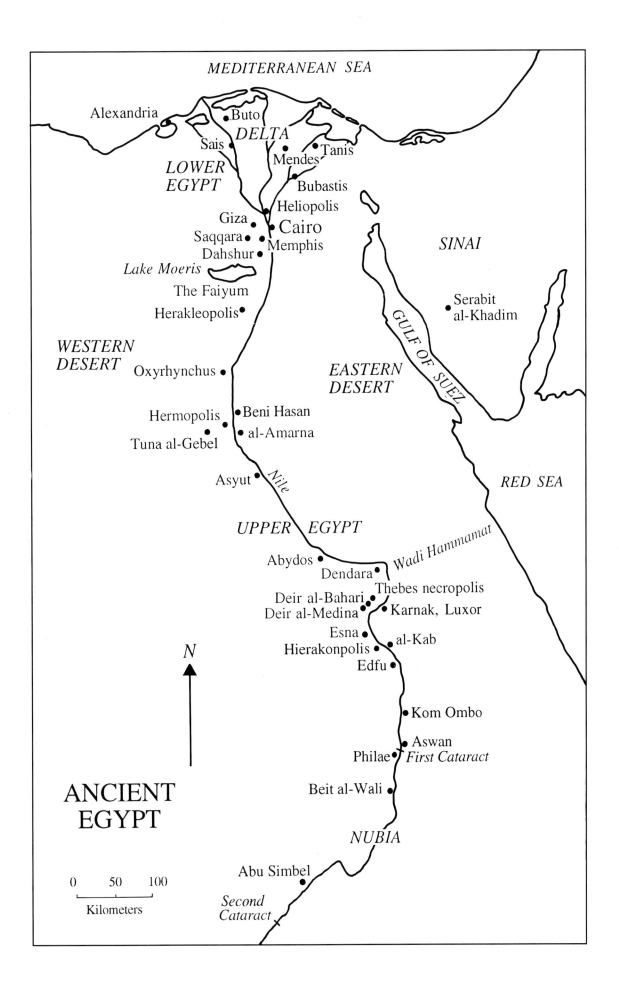

MEDITERRANEAN SEA

Alexandria

Buto

DELTA

Sais

Mendes

Tanis

LOWER
EGYPT

Bubastis

Heliopolis

Giza

Cairo

Saqqara

Memphis

Dahshur

SINAI

Lake Moeris

The Faiyum

Herakleopolis

Serabit
al-Khadim

WESTERN
DESERT

Oxyrhynchus

EASTERN
DESERT

Hermopolis

Beni Hasan

al-Amarna

Tuna al-Gebel

Asyut

Nile

GULF OF SUEZ

RED SEA

UPPER EGYPT

Wadi Hammamat

Abydos

Dendara

Thebes necropolis

Deir al-Bahari

Deir al-Medina

Karnak, Luxor

N

Esna

al-Kab

Hierakonpolis

Edfu

Kom Ombo

Aswan

Philae

First Cataract

ANCIENT
EGYPT

Beit al-Wali

NUBIA

0   50   100

Abu Simbel

Kilometers

Second
Cataract

Chronology of Ancient Egypt

The ancient dates used in this volume generally follow those proposed by John Baines and Jaromír Málek in their *Atlas of Ancient Egypt*, pp. 36–37. All dates are B.C. unless otherwise indicated and, before the rise of the Twenty-sixth Dynasty (664 B.C.), should be considered approximate. Only those monarchs mentioned in the pages of this book are listed below.

PALEOLITHIC PERIOD
500,000–5500

Lower Paleolithic
500,000–100,000

Middle Paleolithic
100,000–30,000

Late Paleolithic
30,000–10,000

Epipaleolithic
10,000–5500

PREDYNASTIC PERIOD
5500–2920

Badarian
5500–4000

Amratian (Naqada I)
4000–3500

Gerzean (Naqada II)
3500–3100

Late Predynastic (Naqada III)
3100–2920
  King 'Scorpion'

EARLY DYNASTIC PERIOD
2920–2649

First Dynasty
2920–2770
  Narmer (=Menes?)
  Aha
  Djet (Uadji)
  Den
Second Dynasty
2770–2649

OLD KINGDOM
2649–2134

Third Dynasty
2649–2575
  Djoser 2630–2611
Fourth Dynasty
2575–2465
  Snofru 2575–2551
  Cheops 2551–2528
  Radjedef 2528–2520
  Chephren 2520–2494

Fifth Dynasty
2465–2323
  Userkaf 2465–2458
  Sahure 2458–2446
  Raneferef (Neferefre) 2419–2416
  Niuserre 2416–2392
  Wenis 2356–2323

Sixth Dynasty
2323–2150
  Teti 2323–2291
  Pepy II 2246–2152

Seventh/Eighth Dynasties
2150–2134

FIRST INTERMEDIATE PERIOD
2134–2040

Ninth/Tenth Dynasties
2134–2040

Eleventh Dynasty (Theban)
2134–2040
  Wahankh Intef II 2118–2069

MIDDLE KINGDOM
2040–1640

Eleventh Dynasty (all Egypt)
2040–1991
  Mentuhotep IV 1998–1991

Twelfth Dynasty
1991–1783
  Amenemhat I 1991–1962
  Sesostris I 1971–1926
  Amenemhat III 1844–1797

Thirteenth Dynasty
1783–after 1640

Fourteenth Dynasty

SECOND INTERMEDIATE PERIOD
1640–1532

Fifteenth Dynasty (the Hyksos)

Sixteenth Dynasty (the Lesser Hyksos)

Seventeenth Dynasty
1640–1550
  Kamose 1555–1550

NEW KINGDOM
1550–1070

Eighteenth Dynasty
1550–1307
  Ahmose 1550–1525
  Tuthmosis I 1504–1492
  Tuthmosis III 1479–1425
  Hatshepsut (queen) 1473–1458
  Amenhotep II 1427–1401
  Tuthmosis IV 1401–1391
  Amenhotep III 1391–1353
  Akhenaten (Amenhotep IV) 1353–1335
  Tutankhamun 1333–1323
  Horemhab 1319–1307

Nineteenth Dynasty
1307–1196
  Seti I 1306–1290
  Ramesses II 1290–1224
  Siptah 1204–1198
  Tausert (queen) 1198–1196

Twentieth Dynasty
1196–1070
  Ramesses III 1194–1163
  Ramesses XI 1100–1070

} Ramesside Period

THIRD INTERMEDIATE PERIOD
1070–712

Twenty-first Dynasty
1070–945
  Psusennes I 1040–992
  Siamun 978–959

Twenty-second Dynasty
945–712
  Takelot II 860–835

Twenty-third Dynasty
828–712
  Osorkon IV 777–749

Twenty-fourth Dynasty
724–712

Twenty-fifth Dynasty (Nubia and Theban area)
770–712
  Piye 750–712

LATE DYNASTIC PERIOD
712–332

Twenty-fifth Dynasty (Nubia and all Egypt)
712–657
   Taharqa 690–664

Twenty-sixth Dynasty
664–525
   Amasis 570–526

Twenty-seventh Dynasty (Persian)
525–404

Twenty-eighth Dynasty
404–399

Twenty-ninth Dynasty
399–380

Thirtieth Dynasty
380–343
   Nectanebo I 380–362

SECOND PERSIAN PERIOD
343–332

GRECO–ROMAN PERIOD
332 B.C.–A.D. 395

Macedonian Dynasty
332–304
   Alexander the Great 332–323
   Philip Arrhidaeus 323–316

Ptolemaic Period
304–30
   Ptolemy II Philadelphus 285–246
   Ptolemy III Euergetes I 246–221
   Ptolemy VIII Euergetes II (Physkon)
   170–163, 145–116
   Ptolemy XII Neos Dionysos (Auletes)
   80–58, 55–51
   Cleopatra VII Thea Philopator 51–30
   Ptolemy XV Caesarion 44–30

Roman Period
30 B.C.–A.D. 395

BYZANTINE OR COPTIC PERIOD
A.D. 395–640

ARAB CONQUEST OF EGYPT
A.D. 640

Chapter One

The Divine Bestiary

*O*ne of the most extraordinary and intriguing aspects of ancient
Egyptian civilization is the religious significance that was attached
to the animal world—the divine bestiary. This important element of Egyptian
culture has aroused the curiosity of both ancient and modern observers and has
caused considerable confusion among them. Foreigners visiting the Nile Valley
during the Late Dynastic and Greco–Roman periods, including some who had
settled there, were fascinated by the flourishing and seemingly ubiquitous animal
cults current in Egypt during these final stages of its ancient history. Educated

Greek and Roman writers were stirred to
express their amusement, puzzlement,
and/or contemptuous mocking of this alien
and completely misunderstood aspect of
popular ancient Egyptian religious expression. Many interpreted the native practices
as merely the worship of household and
farmyard animals. The famous Greek
scholar and traveler Herodotus, who jour-
neyed to Egypt as a tourist about the middle
of the fifth century B.C., remarked (II, 65)
that all animals in Egypt were held to be
sacred. While he was mistaken on this point,
as certainly not every species was viewed
this way, his observation does reflect the
respected position of a great many beasts at
this time in Egyptian history.

The Christian luminary Clement of Alexandria (c.A.D. 160–215), in his work

Paedagogus, was anything but subtle on the
subject of the Egyptians' brand of animal
worship. He scornfully described Egyptian temples and their gods in the following way:

> Their propylaea and outside courtyards,
> their sacred woods and meadows are
> adorned, and the inner courts are sur-
> rounded by very many pillars. The walls
> shine with stones from foreign parts, and in
> no way are they backward in the techniques
> of writing. The temples sparkle with gold,
> silver, and mat gold, and flash with colored
> stones from India and Ethiopia. The sanctu-
> aries are overshadowed by cloths studded
> with gold. If, however, you enter the interior
> of the enclosure, hastening towards the sight
> of the almighty, and look for the statue
> residing in the temple and if a *pastophoros* or
> another celebrant, after having solemnly

*Fig. 1. (opposite) Gray
granite bust of the lioness-
headed goddess Sekhmet,
whose name means literally
'the Powerful One.' She
embodied the destructive
aspects of the sun's heat, and
also possessed healing
powers. This piece was no
doubt originally part of a
seated figure of the goddess.
Many hundreds of these
statues, each averaging over
two meters in height, were
dedicated by Amenhotep III
to Sekhmet in the temple of
the goddess Mut at Karnak.
From Thebes. Eighteenth
Dynasty. PHOEBE HEARST
MUSEUM OF ANTHROPOLOGY,
UNIVERSITY OF CALIFORNIA AT
BERKELEY.*

looked round the sanctuary, singing a song in the language of the Egyptians, draws back the curtain a little to show the god, he will make us laugh aloud about the object of worship. For we shall not find the god for whom we have been looking inside, the god towards whom we have hastened, but a cat, or a crocodile, or a native snake, or a similar animal, which should not be in a temple, but in a cleft or a den or on a dung heap. The god of the Egyptians appears on a purple couch as a wallowing animal.[1]

The outsider approaching Egyptian art, the hieroglyphic script, and the Egyptians' complex mythology and religious thought for the first time is initially confronted with what can seem to be a bewildering repertoire of faunal images. From a very remote age, a host of ancient Egyptian deities manifested themselves in the appearance of a specific animal type: falcon, ibis, ram, cow, cobra, crocodile, fish, Hippopotamus, and others. Attributes admired or feared in the animal kingdom were thought to be directly linked with the divine—for example, the fierceness of the Lion, the deadly sting of the scorpion, or the strength and power of the wild bull. Nevertheless, the underlying motives behind the choice of some sacred animals and the reason for their close association with certain gods remains today largely unknown. Later on, beginning in the Second Dynasty, the gods were often portrayed with human bodies yet retained the heads of their special creatures (figs. 1, 2). The reverse also occurred (though this was much less common) wherein the god possessed an animal's body, but bore the head of a human being. These somewhat startling and uncanny combinations of human and beast do not show what the true appearance of the deity was thought to be, nor do they hold any strange or deep mysterious meaning. What is illustrated is an attribute of the divinity that characterizes its being. Animal-headed creations are the result of the hieroglyphic nature of Egyptian art, and they can be 'read' accordingly.

Almost every nome, town, and village in ancient Egypt possessed its own local, revered animals—for instance, the Griffon Vulture and the Lappet-faced Vulture were sacred to the goddess Nekhbet at al-Kab, the high-flying falcon to the god Horus at Edfu, and the Nile Crocodile to the god Sobek in the Faiyum. Some divinities had more than one species of animal concurrently linked with them, even though the two forms do not appear to share any characteristics that are immediately apparent to us, such as Thoth, for whom both the Sacred Ibis and the baboon were representatives, and the great god Amun, for whom the ram and the Egyptian Goose were chosen animal forms. Conversely, the same animal was regularly associated with different deities at various localities in the country. Bulls, for example, were the focus of a number of cults throughout the Nile Valley. For this reason we can usually only be certain that an animal image represents a particular god or goddess if there is a caption to inform us, or if some other specific visual clues are included. Furthermore, although an animal considered sacred in one part of the country may have been protected by taboos that prevented its kind from being eaten as food there, elsewhere it could be readily consumed.

There remains today a widely held misconception that the pharaonic Egyptians practiced zoolatry, the worship of animals. This was certainly not the case. Animals linked with Egyptian deities received adoration because it was believed that a particular species, or a number of individuals of the species, were uniquely beloved by a particular god, and thus served as the god's symbol and earthly manifestation. Some sacred animals, such as rams and bulls, also delivered oracles from the gods to which they were closely attached. It was not the creature per se that was important, but the divine power it contained, referred to as the *ba* of the deity. The ordinary Egyptian devotee would presumably have been able to distinguish readily between the god and its animal associate. Thus it is unjustified and an oversimplification of ancient Egyptian

Fig. 2. This brilliantly painted wooden statuette represents Anubis, god of embalming, as a jackal-headed man. He is shown standing on a rectangular base with his left leg placed forward, as though about to take a step. Ptolemaic Period. PELIZAEUS-MUSEUM, HILDESHEIM.

religious practices to maintain that the Egyptians worshiped animals; more correctly, they venerated a wide pantheon of gods and goddesses, many of whom had intimate connections with certain members of the animal world. Whether this concept developed from an earlier 'primitive' view during remote prehistory, in which the animals themselves were the focus of religious devotion, can only be speculated upon.

Fig. 3. A striding Leopard carved from wood and coated with a black resin varnish, with a gilded statuette of Tutankhamun wearing the white crown of Upper Egypt and holding a flail and staff in his hands, borne on its back. This is one of two such figures included in the burial of the monarch. The Leopard may have served the boy-king in the netherworld as a protector. Similar wooden Leopards, in various states of preservation, have been discovered among the funerary equipment of other pharaohs in the Valley of the Kings. From the tomb of Tutankhamun (no. 62), Valley of the Kings. Eighteenth Dynasty. THE EGYPTIAN MUSEUM, CAIRO.

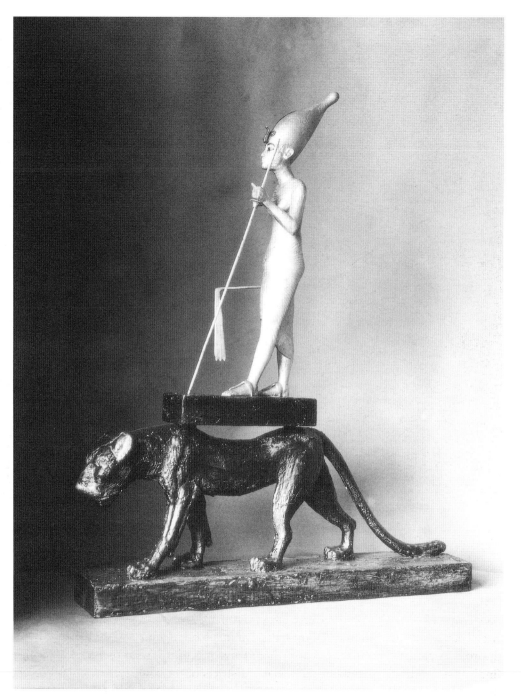

Certainly by the late Gerzean Period (Naqada II), some Egyptian animals were being ritually buried in cemeteries and were occasionally even provided with grave goods of food and drink for the beyond. Recent excavations in an area of the Late Predynastic (Naqada III) royal cemetery (HK-6) at Hierakonpolis have uncovered the existence of an animal precinct. Zooarchaeological findings have thus far identified cattle, Nile Crocodile, Hippopotamus, African Elephant, gazelle, dog, and baboon interred there. The late Michael A. Hoffman, the American excavator of Hierakonpolis, reported that preliminary evidence also indicates rudimentary mummification of the creatures; he also believed that there had been a deliberate effort to bury some of these creatures to correspond with their symbolical functions. The ba-

boons, for instance, associated with the dawn, were located on the eastern periphery of the cemetery. At the early First Dynasty funerary complex of King Aha at Abydos, bone remains of cattle, Lions, baboons, and two species of geese have likewise been discovered in association with the royal burial. In both these cases the findings suggest, without much doubt, that the animals were sacrificed at the time of the king's death for religious reasons, probably to join him in the netherworld. These examples, and many others, seem to adduce some evidence of sacred animal cults already firmly established in Egypt during the Late Predynastic and Early Dynastic periods. This material further suggests a belief already present in Egypt that animals could also share life in the hereafter, that it was not exclusive to human beings. If additional proofs were needed for the religious significance of animals, we could easily point to their prominent place in the iconography of this early epoch. The first known images of mummified sacred animals date from the First Dynasty as well. From this era we also find emblems of animals borne on standards, probably totems or fetishes, representing the various districts of the country, carried in processions on ceremonial slate palettes and maceheads. Many finely carved *ex voto* figurines of animals have been found in early temple sanctuaries too.

Originally a deity was thought to manifest itself in a single, specially selected representative of a given species. This chosen revered creature lived a pampered life, housed in a temple precinct until its natural death. This tradition is best exemplified by the age-old and powerful Memphis cult of the Apis bull, a beast that was regarded as

Fig. 4. This jewel-like blue faience statuette represents Amenhotep III in the form of a traditional sphinx, with human head, arms, and hands, and the hindlegs and body of a Lion. The king is depicted wearing the nemes-headdress and proffers two small jars of wine to a deity. Eighteenth Dynasty. THE METROPOLITAN MUSEUM OF ART, NEW YORK.

Fig. 5. This round-topped limestone stela is dedicated to "the good ram" of the god Amun by the foreman Baki, an inhabitant of the artisans' village of Deir al-Medina, situated in the Theban necropolis. On the upper half, two rams with recurving horns and wearing plumed headdresses are portrayed standing on shrines, shaded by large fans. Below, the owner offers a hymn to Amun-Ra. From Deir al-Medina. Nineteenth Dynasty. MUSEO EGIZIO, TURIN.

sacred to the creator-god Ptah (see chapter 2). Each new Apis was picked by priests from all the young bulls in the land, recognized by certain physical marks it bore on its body. Upon identification and installation in the temple, the bull became the living embodiment of Ptah and received all due honor. A new development in this thinking, however, was introduced during the Eighteenth Dynasty, a period that also witnessed a general expansion in the importance of animal cults throughout Egypt. Numerous individuals of the same species came to be regarded as sacred to the god, rather than a sole representative. Rams, Nile Crocodiles, Sacred Ibises, Egyptian Geese, baboons, and possibly other animals began to be maintained within temple precincts during the New Kingdom and were apparently subject to mummification and burial in animal cemeteries upon death. The flourishing appeal of sacred animals in popular religion in the late New Kingdom is also abundantly evident from their prominent place in iconography, particularly witnessed on private stelae and burial chamber wall decoration (fig. 5), where they are the subject of special invocation and veneration.

With the coming of the Late Dynastic Period, the religious practices relating to sacred animals rapidly proliferated and achieved widespread acceptance among the Egyptian populace, and they were to reach even greater heights during the Ptolemaic Period. The tremendous upsurge in the popularity of these animal cults in Egypt beginning in the Twenty-sixth Dynasty (664 B.C.) has traditionally been explained as a response of the country to the emancipation from foreign control. Some animal cults, such as that of the revered Apis bull at Memphis, were actively encouraged and received considerable financial support from the state. The cults were promoted as a national symbol of cultural revival as well as economic policy.

It was at this time, however, near the close of pharaonic history and later, that the devotion to sacred creatures increased to sometimes truly fanatical levels. On the one hand, acts of piety toward living animals were probably common and could even be equated with charity offered to needy human beings. For instance, on a

stela dating from the end of the Late Dynastic Period, the deceased owner proudly boasts: "I gave bread to the hungry, water [to] the thirsty, clothing to the naked; I gave food to the ibis, the falcon, the cat, and the jackal."[2] On the other hand, the Egyptians' fervor was occasionally so intense that it led to bizarre behavior, such as the lynching of a Roman citizen for having unwittingly killed a cat: the Greek traveler Diodorus Siculus records a vivid eye-witness account (I, 83) of a Roman delegation visiting Alexandria in about 59 B.C., and the misfortune that befell one of its members:

> So deeply implanted also in the hearts of the common people is their superstitious regard for these animals and so unalterable are the emotions cherished by every man regarding the honor due to them that once, at the time when Ptolemy [Ptolemy XII Neos Dionysos, or Auletes] their king had not as yet been given by the Romans the appellation of "friend" and the people were exercising all zeal in courting the favor of the embassy from Italy which was then visiting Egypt and, in their fear, were intent upon giving no cause for complaint or war, when one of the Romans killed a cat and the multitude rushed in a crowd to his house, neither the officials sent by the king to beg the man off nor the fear of Rome which all the people felt were enough to save the man from punishment, even though his act had been an accident. And this incident we relate, not from hearsay, but we saw it with our own eyes on the occasion of the visit we made to Egypt.

During the Late Dynastic and Greco–Roman periods, an impressive range of local Egyptian fauna, but predominantly Sacred Ibises, several species of falcons, household cats, and Nile Crocodiles, were domestically bred and raised on a massive scale in sanctuaries connected with the temples for the celebration of the cult of certain gods, scattered throughout Egypt. The particular species farmed at a temple depended on the animal held sacred to that divinity. Thus at locations where Thoth was worshiped, Sacred Ibises and baboons would be maintained, while for the god-

Fig. 6. *Two ornately decorated cartonnage coffins and lids of sacred animals, one of a cat the other of a falcon, the latter still containing the mummy of the bird. These small coffins are painted and covered with inscriptions and representations of winged Sacred Scarabs holding the sun disk. Late Dynastic Period.* THE UNIVERSITY OF PENNSYLVANIA MUSEUM OF ARCHAEOLOGY AND ANTHROPOLOGY, PHILADELPHIA.

dess Bastet, cats would be required. A highly organized industry developed around these centers, geared to the production, mummification, and sale of sacred animals and figurines of them to pilgrims, in a phenomenon unique to this age. After being dispatched, usually at a young age, and often by having their necks wrung or strangled, the animals were crudely embalmed by an army of busy undertakers. They were then intricately wrapped many times in linen bandages, some even lavishly decorated, placed in costly wooden, stone, or *cartonnage* coffins (fig. 6), and finally offered as votive presentations to the particular god by temple devotees. Through the process of mummification the animal was thought to live again and serve as an intermediary agent between the gods and humankind. It was believed that such prepared animals were capable of transmitting the prayers of the pious pilgrims who had purchased them and who wished to petition the deity or offer thanks for benefactions already delivered. In this way, the animal mummies provided the ordinary ancient Egyptian worshiper with an instrument for direct access to the divine. Eventually, the overflowing hordes of mummies were collected from the temple and interred by the priests *en masse* in nearby sacred animal necropolises. These sometimes consisted of vast subterranean galleries or catacombs.

Other animals routinely used at cult temples and identified from mummified remains include rams, baboons, dogs, shrews, mongooses, snakes, fishes, beetles, gazelles, cattle, and possibly even Lions, although no Lion mummies have actually been found (see chapter 4). Quite literally, untold millions of creatures lost their lives in this way, in what has aptly been termed a massacre of animals. The estimated four million mummified Sacred Ibises at Saqqara, placed in pottery jars and neatly stacked, row upon row, and several million more of them entombed at Tuna al-Gebel, speak to the vast energy invested in this activity, which may even, as some authorities have suggested, have hastened the demise of certain wild species in the country. Yet as we have seen, the accidental killing of a single cat might be construed as grounds for the ultimate penalty to a human being—death!

The ancient Egyptians' general attitude toward the animal world was always a very positive one indeed. The excesses of the Late Dynastic Period and beyond may perhaps be viewed as proper intentions gone sadly awry. The multitude of charmingly expressed and sympathetic renditions of animals found decorating the walls of temples and tomb-chapels over many centuries clearly reflect a caring and respectful relationship with them. Here, animals are frequently portrayed in a loving fashion at the side of people, both at home and on the farm. In addition, as we have seen, the very gods themselves could appear in the guise of an animal. In the ancient Egyptian view, humankind did not command as superior a position in creation over the animal kingdom as, for example, in the Judeo–Christian tradition. Instead there existed a 'partnership,' as Erik Hornung has sensitively characterized it, between Egyptian and animal. Both were created by the gods, and both were bearers of life. Therefore, animals were entitled to respect and care. In the following chapters, we will examine that long and deeply complex relationship to better understand and appreciate animal and humankind in Egyptian civilization.

Chapter Two

Animals in Service

*I*n a culture where the secular and sacred spheres of life were often indissolubly linked, the ancient Egyptians established profound and vital relationships with animals, relationships which endured for more than three thousand years. Perhaps in no other civilization in human history has the association between humans and animals been as intimate or intense as in pharaonic Egypt. The important position accorded to the animal world and its

religious significance cannot be emphasized enough. As a pastoral people, the Egyptians clearly reflected this in their attitude toward their domestic farmyard beasts, those enlisted into the service of humankind.

An illuminating record of an ideal, bucolic life during the passing seasons in ancient Egypt has been bequeathed to us, preserved in picturesque scenes carved or painted on private tomb-chapel walls from virtually every period in history, and from painted wooden tomb models of daily life. Contained within these is a revealing look at the various animal husbandry and agricultural practices on the great estates of wealthy landowners and those on royal domains. These pastoral scenes feature farmhands carrying out their duties of earthly life for the benefit of the deceased tomb-owner in the hereafter. This fundamental, but highly selective, visual source

of information is supplemented by varied textual materials, and of course by physical remains of the animals themselves, recovered from archaeological excavations, some wrapped for eternity as mummies. This great body of evidence provides a window onto the utilization and care of domestic livestock and the busy day-to-day activities involved; and further, it bespeaks the Egyptians' love of these animals and acute knowledge of their characteristics. In this chapter, we survey the principal creatures used by the ancient Egyptians—those exploited for domestic stockbreeding, those used as beasts of burden, and those employed as draft animals for tillage and cartage—and briefly explore the role each played in the religious beliefs of their owners.

Esteemed for their array of valuable products (meat, milk, fat, blood, hide, bone, sinew, dung, and horn), not to mention their utility for all manner of hard work, common domestic cattle *(Bos taurus)* were of paramount economic importance in ancient Egypt. Adequate pasture land for grazing them would have been found along the entire length of the Nile Valley but was most abundant in the broad fertile green marshes and meadows of the Nile Delta, which was always the center of cattle breeding activities in antiquity.

Prior to the New Kingdom, only long-horned varieties (with very prominent, lyre-shaped horns; fig. 7) and short-horned types are attested in Egyptian art and hieroglyphs. Some of these cattle were also polled (de-horned), while others appear to have had their horns intentionally deformed, a practice still current in some African cattle-herding cultures. The earliest firm evidence for Zebu or Indian Humped Cattle *(Bos indicus)* in Egypt comes from the Eighteenth Dynasty, when they can be recognized from paintings in Theban tomb-chapels, working in the fields as draft animals and occasionally being delivered as tribute or trade by Syrian merchants. The beast was introduced comparatively late in history and therefore played a considerably less significant part in the Egyptian farmyard.

Today it is almost universally accepted among zoologists that the progenitor of all domestic cattle was the now extinct Aurochs *(Bos primigenius)*. Wild herds of these huge, long-horned cattle still roamed the Egyptian wetlands and desert margins bordering both sides of the Valley late into the New Kingdom and beyond. There is ample pictorial and textual documentation that this powerful and awesome creature was much sought after as big game by professional hunters, monarchs, and nobles alike, who brought them down with their arrows or captured them alive using lassos (see chapter 3). Without doubt, the most celebrated wild bull hunt in Egyptian art is preserved in a grand relief composition on the rear of the first pylon of the Twentieth Dynasty mortuary temple of Ramesses III at Medinet Habu, Thebes: it represents the king in a chariot, brandishing a long spear, charging valiantly into a reed swamp in pursuit of his bounding prey.

In the present state of our understanding it remains rather uncertain whether

Fig. 7. A block of limestone relief showing herdsmen bringing four prize long-horned oxen for slaughter as an offering to the deceased. Over the animals' backs are written short labels: yewa, 'ox.' From Saqqara (?). Fifth Dynasty. THE BROOKLYN MUSEUM.

Fig. 8. Detail of relief depicting a protesting long-horned cow being restrained with a rope and milked by two peasants. The creature's milk flows in two steady streams into a bowl on the ground. From the tomb-chapel of the mastaba of the vizier Kagemni (LS 10) at Saqqara. Sixth Dynasty.

domestic cattle in ancient Egypt were descended from the endemic population of Aurochs or if the first herds were introduced from western Asia at a remote date. In any case, cattle were probably the earliest domestic animal to be raised in Egypt. Fred Wendorf and his colleagues have suggested that they were already present in the Western Desert oases of Egypt as early as about 7700 B.C. If this is correct, it would lend support to the possibility that cattle pastoralism may have originated independently in Africa. The extensive Neolithic settlement site of Merimda Beni Salama on the southwestern fringe of the Nile Delta, which had an initial occupation in the early part of the fifth millennium B.C., provides some of the oldest domestic cattle remains known from Egypt in a cultural context. Zooarchaeological findings from the village indicate that the subsistence activity of its inhabitants included extensive herding

of cattle, as well as sheep *(Ovis aries)*, goat *(Capra hircus)*, and pig *(Sus domesticus)*. Clay models of apparently domesticated long-horned cattle have been found placed in some human graves dating from Amratian (Naqada I) times.

Already in the Late Predynastic Period (Naqada III), the potent image of the wild bull was linked to the majesty of the king. On the famous dark schist Narmer Palette, a ceremonial votive object dating from the very beginning of the First Dynasty and now in the Egyptian Museum, Cairo, a detail shows the victorious king, symbolized by a large raging bull with its head lowered and attacking a fortified town, trampling and goring his fallen foes. We are reminded that during the New Kingdom, pharaohs continued to identify themselves with the awesome bull, and sometimes bore epithets such as 'Strong Bull, Great of Strength' or 'Bull of Horus.' During the Predynastic and Early Dynastic periods, kings probably controlled enormous herds of domesticated cattle, which testified to their wealth, power, and prestige. For example, one side of the early First Dynasty commemorative or votive Libya Palette, also in Cairo, is carved with relief decoration featuring three registers with processions of domestic cattle, donkeys (*Equus asinus*), and rams, representing great numbers of animals obtained by an Egyptian king through trade, tribute, or booty from Libya, a locale that continued to be a source for farmyard beasts later in history: in the Fifth Dynasty mortuary temple of Sahure at Abusir, for instance, 123,440 cattle, 233,400 donkeys, 232,413 goats, and 243,688 sheep are enumerated as having been obtained from Libya alone during the monarch's conquest of it. Ramesses III of the Twentieth Dynasty proclaims he captured about 42,700 cattle, horses, donkeys, goats, and sheep from these Libyan lands. And on the early First Dynasty ceremonial macehead of Narmer, now in the Ashmolean Museum, Oxford, a record of four hundred thousand cattle and 1,422,000 goats is mentioned. This assertion has usually been interpreted as livestock acquired by the king as booty from military action, but the figures may indicate the total wealth of the Delta; in any case, the count seems highly inflated. Some of the well-to-do private individuals of this time also held great herds of domestic cattle, or aspired at least to magically take such herds into the beyond. The magnificent First Dynasty tomb of a high official (S 3504) from the reign of King Djet (Uadji) at Saqqara, for example, was equipped with a long row, arranged on a low bench around the tomb, of approximately three hundred steers' heads modeled in clay and provided with long pairs of genuine horns.

Scenes from the life of the humble cattle herdsmen abound in tomb-chapels from every period and are often touchingly conveyed. Among the recurring motifs are: men milking cows, or calves suckling (figs. 8, 9); drovers assisting cows with the delivery of their calves (fig. 10); cattle fording canals with crocodiles lurking and herdsmen reciting a protective water charm to ward them off (pl. VIII); great bulls locked in mortal combat (fig. 11); cattle being ferried in cargo ships on the Nile to their grazing grounds; bulls and cows mating; and large, ponderous beeves that can barely walk

Fig. 9. This pastoral vignette in sunk relief from the limestone sarcophagus of the princess Kawit features a farmer milking a large polled cow, who has her young calf tethered to her left foreleg. Touchingly, the mother cow sheds a tear of sorrow at the loss of her milk that was destined for her offspring. From Deir al-Bahari. Eleventh Dynasty. THE EGYPTIAN MUSEUM, CAIRO.

13

Fig. 10. A painted wooden figure of a piebald cow giving birth to her calf, assisted by an experienced pair of cowherds. This model captures the very moment of the delivery, and we view the newborn's head, shoulders, and forelegs just emerging from its mother. This theme is frequently encountered in scenes of country life on tomb-chapel walls, but this is the only example in the round presently known. Said to come from Meir. Middle Kingdom. ROYAL ONTARIO MUSEUM, TORONTO.

being crammed with food by cowherds in stalls. If we gauge from tomb scenes, offering lists, and actual finds of victuals deposited in tombs from virtually every era, prosperous ancient Egyptians seem to have been especially fond of beef and wished to feast on it throughout eternity. An almost indispensable episode in the decorative program of tombs includes the proffering and ritual sacrifice of some choice cattle to the owner (figs. 7, 14). Teams of busy butchers are depicted cutting the carotid artery of the bound, prostrate steer with a broad flint knife, slicing off the right foreleg (the prized *khepesh* cut), extracting the heart, removing the head, and collecting the blood in a large basin. The select joints of meat would then be presented to the deceased or

hung in butchers' shops to dry, before being potted with salt. (Recent examination of some dried beef victual samples from New Kingdom Theban tombs under a scanning electron microscope with an element identifier has apparently proved that the ancient Egyptians used salt to preserve foods, which previously had been in question.) Occasionally, during the Old and Middle kingdoms at least, the slaughtered animal would have been examined and certified ritually fit for human consumption by a supervising official who bore the title 'Doctor and *Wab*-Priest.' As shown in the tomb-chapel of the Fifth Dynasty mastaba of Ptahhotep II (D 64) at Saqqara, to judge the meat this official would smell the creature's blood on the fingers of one of the butchers and pronounce

14

"it is pure." These officials were certainly not veterinary practitioners, as is sometimes claimed, but priests of the goddess Sekhmet, whose duties included inspecting cattle destined for offerings. There is some limited evidence that cattle housed on temple grounds may have received specialized medical attention, perhaps from the priests of the temple. Generally, however, the experienced hand of the herdsman saw to the care and welfare of the beasts under his charge. Since beef formed such an important part of the daily food offerings laid on altars before the gods, temple complexes probably maintained substantial numbers of cattle and quartered some of them in sheds nearby. A fragment of a papyrus roll from the Fifth Dynasty temple archives of the king Raneferef (Neferefre) mentions that, on the occasion of a feast, thirteen oxen were slaughtered each day for ten consecutive days.

The Petrie Museum of Egyptian Archaeology, University College London, possesses a fragmentary but unique papyrus roll from Kahun, dating from the late Twelfth Dynasty, that has been described as a veterinary manual for the care of sick cattle. Due to the damaged condition of the document, it is uncertain whether other species were included in it or not. In any event, the preserved text relates three prescriptions for the medical treatment of domestic cattle. The first part of one reads:

> Prescription for treatment of a bull suffering a cold fever [?]. If I see [a bull suffering] a cold fever [?], its condition being that its eyes water, its temples are heavy, the roots of its teeth are reddened, and its neck is stretched out, one reads for it: it is to be placed on one of its sides, and it is to be sprinkled with cold water, and its eyes and its flanks and all its limbs are to be rubbed with bundles of reeds.[3]

Although several suggestions and interpretations have been offered by veterinarians and Egyptologists alike, the exact nature of the bovine malady described in the passage remains quite mysterious, as does the treatment!

The counting and recording of the numbers of cattle in order to assess the tax due was an important event on great cattle-owning estates in ancient Egypt. So much so that during the Old Kingdom the official tally of domestic cattle formed the basis for dating the years of a king's reign. The in-

Fig. 12. This large and extraordinarily realistic painted wooden model portrays the counting and recording of a great herd of long-horned cattle belonging to the estates of the chancellor Meketre, who is shown seated, viewing the proceedings from a pavilion.

The cowherds drive the animals before the great man and his scribes tally their numbers. The purpose of this funerary model was to ensure Meketre a continuance of the wealth and bounty of his cattle herds for eternity. From the early Twelfth Dynasty tomb of Meketre (no. 280) at Thebes. THE EGYPTIAN MUSEUM, CAIRO.

spection, review, and counting of the herds of cattle was also a frequent theme in Egyptian iconography (pl. XXII). Occasionally, scenes illustrating the subject have accompanying captions, giving the names, numbers, or perhaps other descriptions of the animals involved. Rakhaefankh, a Fifth Dynasty (or later) mortuary priest of the pyramid of King Chephren, boasts in his rock-cut tomb at Giza (G 7948) that he owned 835 long-horned cattle, 220 hornless cattle, 2,235 goats, 760 donkeys, and 974 sheep. More likely than not, however, this wealth of livestock belonged to the estates over which he had some official control and may be wishful thinking on his part. The same can be said of the vaunting claim of a late Fifth or Sixth Dynasty court official and mortuary priest, the achondroplastic dwarf Seneb (who every student of Egyptian art knows from the charming painted limestone statue group of him and his family from Giza, now in the Egyptian Museum, Cairo)—we are informed in inscriptions on the false door from his mastaba, also in the Cairo collection, that he possessed 62,540 head of various farmyard beasts! On the other hand, in the early Eighteenth Dynasty rock-tomb of Renni (no. 7) at al-Kab, the mayor of the town states the inventory of his livestock as 122 head of cattle, one hundred sheep, twelve hundred goats, and fifteen hundred pigs, which seems to be a more truthful account of a high nobleman's holdings. Nowhere

has the inspection and review process been more vividly or memorably captured than in the now famous painted wooden model of the cattle count from the early Twelfth Dynasty tomb of the chancellor Meketre (no. 280) at Thebes (fig. 12). Here we see cowherds parading a group of nineteen long-horned cattle, mostly piebald and skewbald, in a yard before the great nobleman, who is seated under a colonnaded portico, overseeing the activities from the shade, while four scribes in his service are on task, counting and writing down the numbers of his herds.

Despite the many references to the extreme bountifulness of domestic cattle in ancient Egypt, their meat was, by and large, a luxury food that the average Egyptian citizen could rarely afford: beef was a prerogative of the wealthy. To prevent thefts of these valuable beasts and to distinguish individuals in pasture, cattle herds on large farming estates were sometimes marked by branding. Cattle-branding scenes appear in several New Kingdom tomb-chapels at Thebes. As rendered in the Eighteenth Dynasty tomb-chapel of the police captain Nebamun (no. 90) at Thebes, branding may have taken place at the time of recording the numbers of the herds. A few branding irons from ancient Egypt are now housed in museum collections. One of these irons from the Eighteenth Dynasty, said to come from al-Amarna and now in the Staatliche Sammlung Ägyptischer Kunst,

Munich, would have left a mark on the animal's hide that probably should be read as "living and perfect."

In addition to supplies reared at home, a stream of foreign cattle flowed into the Nile Valley as part of trade, tribute, or the spoils of warfare and conquest from abroad (pl. xv). We have already mentioned considerable numbers of cattle obtained from Libya. The Palermo Stone reports that Snofru, the first king of the Fourth Dynasty, carried out a raid in Nubia that resulted in the capture of some two hundred thousand head of cattle. In the Eighteenth Dynasty 'annals' of Tuthmosis III at Karnak, the powerful warrior king records the acquisition of very significant quantities of cattle from western Asia, Punt, and Nubia. And colossal numbers were needed: during the course of his long thirty-one year reign in the Twentieth Dynasty, Ramesses III (so the great Harris papyrus tells us) endowed the Theban temples alone with some 421,659 head of various cattle.

Cattle, especially castrated males of the long-horned variety, were the traditional draft animals in ancient Egyptian agriculture. From earliest times, teams of stout oxen were employed to help till the soil, and scenes featuring them laboring in the fields became a standard element of tomb decoration throughout the Dynastic period. Characteristic is a splendid detail in painted relief from the renowned Fifth Dynasty mastaba of Ti (no. 60) at Saqqara (fig. 13). We observe two naked farmhands, one wielding a short stick to drive the span of yoked long-horned cows, the other manning the plow. The spotted beasts drag the wooden scratch-plow, attached by a rope to the base of their horns, through the field to create the deep furrows needed for planting the seeds. Small groups of working cattle were likewise routinely used at the harvest on the threshing floor, treading the ripe grain with their hooves in order to separate the seed from the husk. A vignette of threshing with cattle in the Eighteenth

Fig. 13. A detail of painted relief from an agricultural scene in the tomb-chapel of the Fifth Dynasty mastaba of Ti (no. 60) at Saqqara, showing a pair of spotted long-horned cows hitched to a wooden scratch-plow. A naked fieldhand wields a long stick to drive the animals forward.

Dynasty rock-cut tomb of Paheri (no. 3) at al-Kab, features a boy urging his long-horned cattle around and around with a whip, as he sings a simple but charming country song: "Thresh ye for yourselves, thresh ye for yourselves, oh cattle! Thresh ye for yourselves, thresh ye for yourselves! Straw to eat, and barley for your masters—Let not your hearts be weary, for it is cool."[4]

The New Kingdom tale *The Two Brothers* offers us a fictionalized glimpse of the very close relationship of one small farmer with his working cattle. Bata, the hero of the story, spent his days in the fields with his beasts, plowing, sowing, reaping, and milking them. At night he even slept in the stable among them. But Bata's cattle also talked to him! They told him where to find the best grass for them to graze, as well as warning him of his brother's plot to do him harm. Under his superior care, we are told,

Fig. 14. Painted limestone relief of a pair of butchers cutting up a large, bound sacrificial steer lying on the ground. The left foreleg of the slaughtered animal is tied securely to both its hind legs, and the men are busy slicing off the right foreleg. A third butcher stands just to the left sharpening his knife on a whetstone attached to his belt. From the tomb-chapel of the mastaba of the princess Idut at Saqqara. Sixth Dynasty.

the cattle "became exceedingly fine and they increased their offspring considerably."

Beginning with a small picture of a wheeled catafalque in the Thirteenth Dynasty rock-tomb of Sobeknakht (no. 10) at al-Kab, pairs of oxen are also occasionally encountered in Egyptian art drawing vehicles, a detail that may have been influenced by the recent introduction of the chariot into Egypt by the Hyksos. Almost unique is a fragment of relief from the Eighteenth Dynasty tomb-chapel of Duauneheh (no. 125) at Thebes, now in the Metropolitan Museum of Art, New York. In a bucolic scene, a team of the newly imported humped Zebu appear pulling a plow. Above this is a detail of a two-wheeled ox-cart in a harvest field being utilized to transport the crop to the threshing floor. The first recorded use of wagons drawn by

oxen during military operations comes from the Eighteenth Dynasty, during the reign of Tuthmosis III. While he was campaigning in northern Syria, the king had oxen haul boats loaded in sections on wagons to the city of Carchemish on the Euphrates river. During the Nineteenth Dynasty, Ramesses II also employed teams of oxen on his military campaigns, and they can be seen pulling baggage carts in gigantic relief compositions of the famous battle of Kadesh in his temple at Abu Simbel and elsewhere. Later in the Ramesside Period there is also a report mentioning that teams of oxen were used to pull ten wagons full of supplies to support a quarrying expedition to the Wadi Hammamat in the Eastern Desert.

The use of oxen to draw wheeled vehicles, however, is generally more often associated in Egyptian art with foreign peoples. Oxen served the Hittites for the same purpose at Kadesh. In the Eighteenth Dynasty tomb of Nebamun (no. 17) at Thebes, Syrians are shown with oxen pulling two-wheeled carts; while in the Eighteenth Dynasty tomb of Huy (no. 40), also at Thebes, a Nubian princess rides in a chariot pulled by a span of oxen. On a pylon of the Twentieth Dynasty mortuary temple of Ramesses III at Medinet Habu, Thebes, amid a great battle composition against the 'Sea Peoples,' the women and children of these foreigners appear in wagons with wooden or wickerwork bodies drawn by humped Zebu oxen.

In Egyptian funerary processions routinely represented on tomb-chapel walls and in vignettes on papyri, the mummy of the deceased is often laid on a wooden sledge and dragged to the final resting place by teams of long-horned oxen. And a fragment of rock relief now in the Egyptian Museum, Cairo, dating from the beginning of the Eighteenth Dynasty from the quarries of Maasara–Tura, represents the hauling of a large block of limestone (estimated to weigh about five tons) upon a wooden sledge drawn by three pairs of yoked Zebu oxen, guided by three probably foreign overseers wielding short batons. This small scene demonstrates that oxen were sometimes used as draft animals for transporting stone during building construction in ancient Egypt.

As sacred animals, both the cow and the bull were the subject of special veneration in ancient Egypt. The cow was closely associated with several female deities, including the goddesses Isis and Nut, but was surely most widely known as the customary earthly manifestation of the sky-goddess Hathor of Dendara (pl. xxxiv). Renowned for her motherly care and fertility, Hathor protected the ruler and suckled the infant king with her divine milk (pl. xix). She was also a prominent funerary goddess in the Theban necropolis, as well as the mistress of love, music, dance, and alcohol.

There were three major cults of bulls in ancient Egypt. The Apis bull was worshiped at Memphis, connected with the gods Ptah and Osiris; the Mnevis bull was the sacred animal of the sun-god of Heliopolis; and the Buchis bull of Armant was equated with the gods Ra and Montu. The Apis bull was far and away the most important, influential, and long-lasting of all the animal cults in Egyptian history, although it achieved its greatest prominence during the Late Dynastic and Ptolemaic periods. First attested at the beginning of the First Dynasty, the cult of the Apis bull survived until at least 362 A.D. The image of the Apis is widely known from a multitude of outstanding dedicatory monuments fashioned of stone and bronze in various sizes (see the figure on page i) and votive stelae, most of which date from the later centuries of Egyptian civilization. The Apis also regularly appears during this time prominently painted on the foot end of humans' wooden coffins, sometimes carrying the deceased on its back into the netherworld (fig. 15). Upon the death of a holy Apis bull, a successor was selected from all the male calves in the land, according to certain physical signs it was required

Fig. 15. Painting on the foot end of the inner wooden coffin of the lady Tabakenkhonsu, representing the Apis bull carrying the mummy of the deceased on its back into the netherworld. From Deir al-Bahari. Twenty-sixth Dynasty. THE METROPOLITAN MUSEUM OF ART, NEW YORK.

to display on its hide, principally a light triangular marking on its forehead and a certain patterning on its back; other distinguishing features, we are told by several Classical writers, were double hairs in the tail and a mark resembling a Sacred Scarab beetle on the tongue. Originally regarded as a potent symbol of fertility, the Apis bull came gradually to represent many different attributes and was linked with deities other than Ptah and Osiris. The significance of this national cult is revealed by the impressive tombs constructed for the embalmed bodies of the bulls in the vast subterranean galleries of the Serapeum at Saqqara. (The oldest burial of the beast thus far known dates from the Eighteenth Dynasty, during the reign of Amenhotep III.) Some idea of the splendor and expense lavished on the state funeral of an Apis during the Late Dynastic Period can be had from an inscription on a commemorative

stone stela from the Twenty-sixth Dynasty, now in the Musée du Louvre, Paris:

In the year 23 [= 547 B.C.] on the 15th day of the 9th month of the time of His Majesty, the King of Upper and Lower Egypt, Amasis, may he be given eternal life, the god [Apis] peacefully withdrew to the beautiful west [= the world after death]. He was laid to rest in his tomb in the necropolis at the site which His Majesty prepared for him. Never before since the beginning had anything alike been made. All ceremonies were performed on him in the house of purification, because His Majesty remembered how Horus had cared for his father Osiris. A great granite sarcophagus was cut, and His Majesty deemed well to let this be done of more precious stone than was ever used before. A shroud was made from secret materials obtained from the sacred site of Sais to give him protection. His jewelry was made of gold and all sorts of precious stones, more elaborate than ever before. For His Majesty adored Apis more than any previous king.[5]

Fig. 16. A long file of overlapping horned rams and ewes in carved relief. This flock of sheep is being employed by farmers to tread the freshly sown grain seed into the muddy ground. The text above the animals is the famous 'sower's song.' From the tomb-chapel of the mastaba of Ti (no. 60) at Saqqara. Fifth Dynasty.

Nor was this account mere hyperbole. From the middle of the Twenty-sixth Dynasty, the sacred Apis bulls were buried in truly massive sarcophagi carved out of single blocks of stone, mostly granite, and weighing up to seventy tons each, to house and protect the bejeweled mummies. Some bulls were even equipped with magical bovid-headed *shabti* figurines to serve their needs in the next life. Some special cows too, those that were revered because they were the mothers of divine bulls, received elaborate entombments in animal cemeteries. The burial place of the mothers of the Apis bull, the Iseum, for example, was discovered at north Saqqara near the Serapeum not too long ago. These sanctified cows were regarded as a manifestation of the goddess Isis.

The enterprising team of French zoologists Louis C. Lortet and Claude Gaillard, around the turn of the present century, studied a number of 'bull' mummies of Greco–Roman date from a cattle cemetery at Abusir. The intricately wrapped and decorated mummies, with hundreds of yards of fine linen bandages arranged in a series of geometrical patterns, belied the complete disarray Lortet and Gaillard discovered within—a jumble of various non-articulated bones, each mummy containing the remains of more than one animal. Rather than being pampered divine Apis bulls, these were probably the remains of ordinary working oxen, which may even have been butchered and consumed before being mummified, which would account for the mix of bones. A similar state of internal disorder was encountered during the recent examination of a pair of large 'bull' mummies of late Ptolemaic date housed in collections of the Smithsonian Institution, Washington, D.C., and a specimen from the same period now in the Staatliche Sammlung Ägyptischer Kunst, Munich. Quite obviously, then, the Egyptian undertakers bestowed their utmost attention only on the special sacred bulls, and other mummified cattle were treated with much less care. Some researchers have pointed to a passage in the work of Herodotus (II, 41) that may explain these composite cattle mummies:

> Oxen that die are dealt with in the following way:—Cows are cast into the river, bulls are buried by each city in its suburbs, with one or both horns uncovered for a sign: then, when the carcass is decomposed, and the time appointed is at hand, a boat comes to each city from the island called Prosopitis.... Many go about, some to one town and some to another, and dig up the bones, which they then carry away and bury all in one place.

Another valued and longtime member of the ancient Egyptian circle of farmyard animals was the sheep. Since all African sheep are descended from an Asian progenitor, the western Asiatic Mouflon (*Ovis orientalis*), flocks of this domesticated animal must have first reached Egypt from abroad. Evidence of the common domestic sheep in the country can be traced back to the early part of the fifth millennium B.C. at Merimda Beni Salama. Remains have also been identified from a score of other Predynastic settlement sites and cemeteries in the Nile Valley. Sheep can be readily recognized in the art of the Gerzean Period (Naqada II), painted on pottery vessels and fashioned on zoomorphic schist cosmetic palettes.

A traditional scene in tomb-chapel decoration, especially during the Old Kingdom, represents the sowing of grain and the treading of the seed into the ground by mixed flocks of horned rams and ewes (fig. 16). Typically, one or more sowers is portrayed encouraging the flock of reluctant sheep forward with handfuls of grain, fed to those in the lead, and as this procession slowly makes its way through the field, the animals trample the newly scattered seed with their small hooves into the rich, muddy, black earth. Taking up the rear, there are several herdsmen brandishing long whips of twisted rope, driving the file of beasts from behind. Sheep were also occasionally employed during the harvest on the threshing floor, to tread out the ripe grain.

As we have noted above, royal and privately-owned flocks of sheep in Egypt could easily number into the hundreds and flocks were sometimes imported from Libya and western Asia. But the orthodox dead, to keep themselves ritually pure, apparently did not indulge in eating mutton in the beyond. Sheep are not mentioned in the extensive offering-list menus inscribed in tombs of the privileged classes, nor can they be distinguished amid the profusion of victuals presented to and heaped before

the deceased. All this seems to point to some prohibition against sheep as food. Nevertheless, it seems highly likely that while some of the elite may have abstained from mutton in funerary situations, a significant number of the living who could afford such luxurious fare probably relished it on their tables. While the use of woolen fabrics never seems to have achieved much popularity in ancient Egypt, recent investigations into Egyptian textiles suggest greater use than was previously thought to be the case. However, raising sheep and goats for wool only became extensive in Egypt during the later Greco–Roman Period.

The ancient Egyptians reared two very distinct breeds of sheep on their vast agricultural estates. The original stock, a fleeceless variety, was characterized by the length of its tail and long, horizontal, corkscrew-shaped horns (fig. 16). A fat-tailed wool-producing sheep, with horns curling around its ears (fig. 5), was introduced to the Nile Valley from western Asia during the Middle Kingdom. The two forms apparently lived side by side for a short while. A large flock consisting of both breeds is represented in a herding scene in the Twelfth Dynasty rock-tomb of the nomarch Khnumhotep III (no. 3) at Beni Hasan. By the beginning of the New Kingdom, the woolly sheep had become the prevailing form and the older type disappeared from the Egyptian farmyard. In spite of the fact that it no longer lived in the country, though, the beast continued to figure as a standard hieroglyphic sign, for reasons of tradition. Its long corkscrew horns also remained an element of the iconography of certain crowns of kings and were still worn by some deities for centuries to come (pl. XXVIII). Further, we see some composite creatures that spuriously display both sets of horn types simultaneously (fig. 17).

The ram played an important role in ancient Egyptian religious beliefs. Always regarded as a potent symbol of fertility, the ram was closely connected with several

Fig. 17. A pair of striding rams on a limestone votive plaque or, less likely, a sculptor's study. The rams are imaginatively executed, sporting two sets of horns on their heads. Said to come from Qena. Ptolemaic Period. THE WALTERS ART GALLERY, BALTIMORE.

key deities in the Egyptian pantheon. At Elephantine Island and Esna, the ram was considered the emblem of Khnum, the god who fashioned humankind on his potter's wheel and created the animal world. It was worshiped at Herakleopolis as the manifestation Herishef, and was likewise sacred at Mendes in the Delta. The ram also had close associations with Ra, the sun-god (pl. XXVIII). The chief god of Thebes, the great Amun, could also appear in the guise of a ram. He was almost without exception pictured in the form of the more recently introduced breed, sporting the recurving horns on the side of the head (fig. 5). During the New Kingdom, the sovereign was

Fig. 18. This small limestone relief episode pictures a flock of goats at pasture, grazing on the foliage and branches of a Sycamore Fig tree. In the lower right, a goat is giving birth and a curious or preying dog is awaiting the emerging kid. From the tomb-chapel of the mastaba of Akhethotep at Saqqara. Fifth Dynasty. MUSÉE DU LOUVRE, PARIS.

occasionally portrayed on temple wall reliefs wearing the same set of horns as the Amun ram, which symbolized his divine nature, and much later Alexander the Great wore them too. Long rows of ram-headed sphinxes, or criosphinxes, were sometimes used to flank the processional avenues to major temples in the New Kingdom and later, as for example at the temple of Karnak. Michela Schiff Giorgini's excavations have seemingly demonstrated that under the Eighteenth Dynasty a flock of Amun's sacred rams was maintained on the grounds of Amenhotep III's beautiful temple at Soleb in Upper Nubia.

Untold numbers of rams were mummified throughout the course of Egyptian history. The earliest known image of an embalmed sacred ram reaches all the way back to the time of the First Dynasty. Particularly during the Late Dynastic and Greco–Roman periods, some sacred rams were elaborately wrapped in bandages, decorated with headpieces, placed in gilded wooden coffins and stone sarcophagi, and interred in special cemeteries connected with the cults of the various ram-gods. These burial places have been located at Elephantine Island, Tihna, Tebtunis, and Mendes. The visitor to the antiquities museum on Elephantine today can inspect mummified sacred rams found in tombs near the temple of Khnum on the island.

Like sheep, the domestic goat is descended from a western Asiatic progenitor, the Scimitar-horned Goat *(Capra aegagrus)*. And this common livestock species too was introduced to the Egyptian farmyard at a remote age. The goat is known to have reached the country by the early part of the fifth millennium B.C., being well attested at the Neolithic site of Merimda Beni Salama. That the Predynastic Egyptians shepherded flocks of goats is amply demonstrated by the bone remains recovered at a range of other archaeological sites, including Toukh, Hierakonpolis, Maadi, and Heliopolis. The familiar silhouette of the goat, easily told by its distinctive horns and beard, can first be identified in art painted on a number of pottery vessels during the Gerzean Period

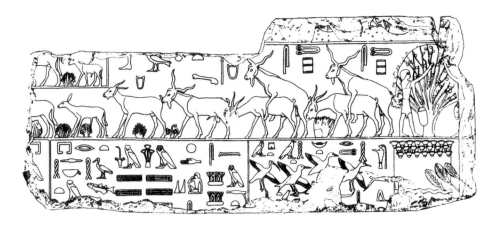

Fig. 19. A drawing of a scene on a block of limestone relief from the so-called 'chamber of the seasons' in the sun temple of Niuserre at Abu Ghurab. The decoration adorning the walls of this fascinating chamber has been described as a visual hymn to the beneficence of the sun-god. The top register of our fragment displays the harvesting of fruits of either a Sycamore Fig or a Persea tree (Mimusops laurifolia), and several billy goats mounting receptive females. Below, some migratory birds are on the wing near the Papyrus swamplands. Fifth Dynasty. ÄGYPTISCHES MUSEUM, BERLIN.

(Naqada II). The goat's widely known foraging habits allow pastoralists to graze flocks on marginal land, since it will eat types of vegetation that cattle and sheep will not. This makes the animal especially well suited to the desert margins bordering both sides of the Nile Valley, though if not controlled, grazing goats can severely damage fragile landscape and cause desertification.

During the Dynastic period, flocks of goats certainly continued to be kept in Egypt, and we have already referred to the considerable size of some of these. Scenes representing goatherds tending their charges appear as a frequent theme in tomb-chapel decoration from the Old Kingdom onward. A notable and recurring motif is a flock of goats in the wild at pasture, the animals browsing in trees. Delightfully rendered in a relief from the tomb-chapel of the Fifth Dynasty mastaba of Akhethotep at Saqqara, five adult goats gnaw on a leafless tree and climb in its lower branches (fig. 18). At the lower right, a curious vignette shows one of them in the process of giving birth and a hungry dog about to prey upon the emerging kid. (Just out of the frame an alert shepherd is about to strike the mischievous hound with his upraised staff and drive it away.) This setting sometimes also features a man with a knife in his hand, gutting and skinning the carcass of a goat hanging by its hind legs from a branch of a tree, probably in preparation for a fine meal.

Goats are also depicted in Egyptian art mating during the rutting season (fig. 19), and they are occasionally met with in tomb scenes housed in paddocks and feeding from mangers (pl. XIII), sometimes being forcibly fed by hand, to fatten them up prior to slaughter. An almost unique detail on a fragment of wall painting from the First Intermediate Period tomb of Ita at Gebelein, now in the Museo Egizio, Turin, depicts an offering-bearer bringing a goat. Their appearance in the tomb-chapels of the well-heeled clearly indicates that goat flesh was sometimes eaten by those of high rank, and was not confined to the tables of those of humble station. Goatskins were surely used for a variety of utilitarian purposes, including widespread use as containers for carrying water, but to what degree goat and sheep dairy products were enjoyed in ancient Egypt has yet to be fully elucidated.

It is nowadays generally presumed among zoologists that the local breed of domestic pig in ancient Egypt was descended from an indigenous ancestor, the Wild Boar (*Sus scrofa*). This wetlands-dwelling species was once rather abundant in the country and had a fairly extensive range in the Nile Valley, the Delta, the Faiyum, and Wadi Natrun. It became locally extinct in Egypt around the turn of the present century due to overhunting and loss of its prime habitat. Remains of the Wild Boar have been

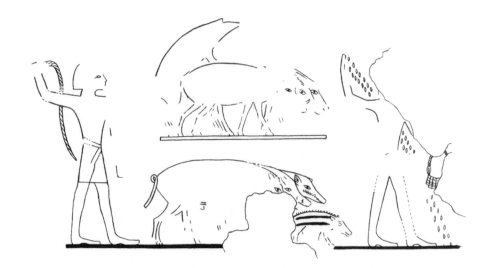

Fig. 20. This drawing of a damaged detail of wall painting from the Theban tomb-chapel of Nebamun (no. 24) depicts a herd of pigs being driven to trample newly sown grain seed into the damp earth with their hooves, and a boar and sow copulating. Eighteenth Dynasty.

identified from Late Paleolithic levels in a context suggesting the creature had been exploited as a game animal for food. The oldest domestic pig bones thus far known in Egypt have been found in very significant quantities at the Neolithic settlement site of Merimda Beni Salama, which had an initial occupation in the first part of the fifth millennium B.C. This osteological evidence proves that the beast was reared here in considerable numbers. That herds of common swine were kept, and that pork formed an element of the diet of at least some Predynastic Egyptians, is corroborated by the presence of pigs at a range of other archaeological sites: Maadi, al-Badari, the Faiyum, al-Omari, Hierakonpolis, Hammamiya, Abydos, and Armant, to name a few. Nevertheless, the image of the pig is rarely attested in Egyptian iconography prior to the rise of the pharaonic period. The Ägyptisches Museum, Berlin, possesses a most curious ceramic statue of what has been called a "pig deity," which is dated to the Amratian Period (Naqada I). Otherwise we have very little evidence that the pig was considered sacred to any god in ancient Egyptian culture. A handful of exceptional faience sow figurines from the First Dynasty, perhaps *ex voto* objects, were discovered at early temple sanctuaries at Abydos, Hierakonpolis, and Elephantine Island. The Brooklyn Museum possesses

an ivory cylinder seal, dated to the First Dynasty, that displays figures of bristling pigs carved on it, and they are featured on other seals of this age as well.

Notwithstanding some authorities' insistent claims to the contrary (see fig. 55), the pig was never portrayed in Egyptian temple or tomb-chapel decoration during the Old Kingdom, though it does appear as a rare hieroglyph determinative in the word 'pig.' Its complete absence from scenes in the great tombs of the privileged classes, and the apparent strict avoidance of mentioning the pig in their long offering-list menus, seems to indicate an extensive prohibition against eating pork in the Old Kingdom. Pigs were evidently regarded as unclean food for the pious dead who sought to keep ritually pure in the next world. The origin of this taboo is obscure, but the pig's legendary association with grubbing, dirt, and filth may have prompted its generally low status in the eyes of the ancient Egyptians. In any case, the strength of the taboo seems to vary over time, and it was probably never absolute. It appears to have escalated to a much higher level during the Late Dynastic Period and later. So much so that, according to Herodotus (II, 47), "if an Egyptian touch a hog in passing by, he goes to the river and dips himself in it, clothed as he is; swineherds, native born Egyptians though they be, are alone of all men forbidden to enter any Egyptian temple." Nevertheless, pigs were almost certainly consumed by the living during the Old Kingdom, as they were in all subsequent periods, at least by the lower rungs of society.

Herds of swine probably continued to be maintained just as in prehistoric times, even if supporting evidence is rather slender until the New Kingdom. In the early Fourth Dynasty tomb-chapel of the high official Metjen (LS 6) at Saqqara, now in the Ägyptisches Museum, Berlin, the deceased owner states that the bequest he received from his father included "people, small livestock, and pigs." The Eleventh Dynasty rock-cut tomb of the nomarch Khety (no. 17) at Beni Hasan is adorned with a small painting showing a herd of seven wiry pigs, quite likely domestic ones. In any event, they are the first of their kind in Egyptian art since the First Dynasty. During the Middle Kingdom there are also several textual references to keeping swine. Herding pigs is briefly mentioned in a passage in the autobiographical text of Hornakhte from his Eleventh Dynasty tomb (D 3128) at Dendara, now in the Egyptian Museum, Cairo, and in the well-known

Twelfth Dynasty moralizing story *The Tale of the Eloquent Peasant*, pigs are listed in the inventory of goods and farmyard animals owned by Djehutynakht. On the Twelfth Dynasty painted limestone stela of the steward Montuwosre from Abydos, now in the Metropolitan Museum of Art, New York, he proudly tells us: "I served as overseer of cattle, overseer of goats, overseer of donkeys, overseer of sheep, and overseer of swine." The impression one arrives at from this body of written sources is that the pig was viewed in the Middle Kingdom as just another livestock species. Yet apart from the scene in Khety's tomb, pigs are conspicuously absent from scenes of everyday life on Middle Kingdom tomb walls.

With the coming of the New Kingdom, our information on the place of the pig in Egyptian animal husbandry dramatically expands. We have previously noted that at the beginning of the Eighteenth Dynasty the mayor of al-Kab, Renni, relates that he owned a herd of fifteen hundred of them. In the tomb-chapels of several Theban notables from the first half of the Eighteenth Dynasty, swine are openly depicted alongside the other domestic farmyard beasts of

Fig. 21. Tempera facsimile detail of a preliminary drawing from an unfinished wall composition of the Book of Gates in the sarcophagus chamber of the tomb of Horemhab (no. 57), Valley of the Kings. The vile pig of the god Seth flees in a bark before the enthroned Osiris and is driven away by a monkey (probably representing the god Thoth), wielding a long stick. Eighteenth Dynasty.

Fig. 22. Faience statuette of a large sow nursing her litter of piglets, with a dedicatory inscription on the base naming the goddess Nut. Such figurines were intended to endow their owners with fecundity. Late Dynastic Period. THE BRITISH MUSEUM, LONDON.

their estates. In at least two of these tombs, herds of pigs are shown in agricultural scenes, being driven over newly sown fields, treading the seed into the damp black soil (fig. 20), just like the sheep described above. This practice was still current in Egypt a thousand years later when Herodotus (II, 14) visited the country. During the Eighteenth Dynasty, a temple of Amenhotep III at Memphis was endowed with some one thousand pigs and one thousand piglets, and in the Nineteenth Dynasty, during the reign of Seti I, large herds of swine were maintained on the domains of his mortuary temple at Abydos. Also in the Nineteenth Dynasty, but under Ramesses II, herds of pigs are mentioned in

a report on the wealth of the god Amun of Thebes. It is well established through zooarchaeological findings and inscriptions on ostraca (pottery shards or limestone flakes) that the inhabitants of the artisans' village at Deir al-Medina during the Ramesside Period occasionally indulged in meals of pork. Recent excavations conducted by the Egypt Exploration Society at the site of the workers' village of Akhenaten's short-lived capital city at al-Amarna, dating from the Eighteenth Dynasty, have disclosed a pig farm. The pigs were housed in specially constructed pens; their bones have been identified from the village trash heaps. Pig breeding continued to be a relatively important economic activity in Egypt through the Greco–Roman Period.

The ancient Egyptians seem to have held deeply ambivalent feelings about the pig. On the one hand, the animal was considered by some people impure and an abomination, at least in funerary or mythological circumstances, but it was highly valued as a food animal by others. Already during the Middle Kingdom, in Spell 157 of the *Coffin Texts*, the pig was linked with the Typhonian god Seth, the arch-enemy of the god Horus. Here it is said that "the pig is detestable to Horus." Thus the pig came to be regarded as a powerful symbol of evil. In addition, by the late Eighteenth Dynasty, the *Book of Gates* includes an episode featuring Seth having assumed the form of a black pig. A detail from the judgment scene of this funerary composition in the sarcophagus chamber of the late Eighteenth Dynasty tomb of King Horemhab (no. 57) in the Valley of the Kings illustrates a pig in a bark (fig. 21), fleeing before Osiris and being driven away by a monkey with a stick. At the great Ptolemaic temple at Edfu, Horus is pictured on a wall relief ritually destroying Seth, who again has adopted the appearance of a pig. Conversely, during the Late Dynastic Period, charming statuettes and amulets in the shape of a fat sow nursing her litter of piglets were popular and had associations with the sky-goddess Nut and the goddess Isis. These charms were thought to bring their owners fertility and good luck (fig. 22).

Even before the dawn of recorded history, the domestic donkey *(Equus asinus)* was already firmly in the service of the Predynastic Egyptian farmer, tirelessly toiling in the fields from dawn until dusk: at Predynastic archaeological locales in the Nile Valley, such as at Maadi in Lower Egypt, the donkey has been identified amid the assemblage of domestic farmyard animals. Though there is as yet no firm proof, zoologists now generally believe that ancient Egypt was the site of the earliest domestication of the common donkey. Its progenitor was the African Wild Ass *(Equus africanus)*, whose original distribution, although it is probably now extinct in Egypt, must have included large expanses of the country. The African Wild Ass is occasionally seen among the variety of wild game pictured in ancient Egyptian scenes of the desert hunt, especially during the New Kingdom (see chapter 3). A superb example can be found on the spectacular 'painted box' from the Eighteenth Dynasty tomb of Tutankhamun (no. 62) in the Valley of the Kings, now in the Egyptian Museum, Cairo, where the youthful king is depicted about to slay a small free-ranging herd of African Wild Asses from a speeding chariot with bow and arrow.

One side of the finely decorated dark schist ceremonial or votive Libya Palette, dating from the very beginning of the First Dynasty, now in the Egyptian Museum, Cairo, features a register filled with four donkeys, displaying their characteristic shoulder stripe, brought as tribute or booty from Libya. The palette therefore strongly suggests that considerable numbers of donkeys were imported into the country even at this distant age. The donkey's early economic importance along the banks of the Nile is further indicated by the numbers of their burials within close proximity of the tombs of human beings, doubtless so the beasts might accompany and continue to serve their owners in the next world. These have been discovered at several Early Dynastic Period cemeteries, including Tarkhan, Helwan, and Abusir.

The sturdy but infamously obstinate donkey was the principle beast of burden throughout the history of ancient Egypt, and continues to play a valuable role in rural Egypt to this day (donkey carts are still a frequent sight even in some sections of Cairo). Beginning early in the Fifth Dynasty, donkeys are routinely encountered in the scenes of everyday life on great farming estates figured on the walls of the splendid tomb-chapels of the Egyptian elite,

Fig. 23. This fragment of limestone relief shows a well composed herd of overlapping donkeys being driven toward the harvest field, making for a highly spirited and busy little scene. From a private tomb-chapel at Saqqara. Fifth Dynasty.
RIJKSMUSEUM VAN OUDHEDEN, LEIDEN.

where they are closely associated with the various activities relating to the harvest field. The animal was particularly useful in transporting heavy bundles of cut grain from the field to the threshing floor, and the herding of great numbers of donkeys together for this laborious task was a frequent theme in the art of the Old Kingdom (fig. 23). Amid shouts and jeers directed at the beleaguered donkeys, fieldhands are represented in the reliefs and paintings trying to steady the stubborn and defiant animals by tugging on an ear or tail, lifting or pulling a leg, or even applying a headlock to the poor beast. In the Fifth Dynasty tomb-chapel of the mastaba of Ti (no. 60) at Saqqara, a drover bellows out at a group of donkeys with a long stick upraised: "Hey! I will whack you right on the rump." Other men then busily tie the sheaves in large panniers or sacks hung in pairs over the backs of the donkeys (fig. 24, pl. XIII). Prodded by stiff blows delivered by farmers brandishing long, heavy sticks, the train of donkeys finally trots off in a cloud of choking dust, carrying their burdensome loads. In a handsome limestone relief composition from the tomb-chapel of the Fifth Dynasty mastaba of Neferirtenef (D 55) at Saqqara, once they

arrive at the threshing floor a small herd of seven donkeys is driven to mill around in a circle, threshing out the grain, probably Emmer wheat *(Triticum dicoccum)*, with their pointed hooves (fig. 25). One donkey has paused and lowers its head to nibble some cereal, and another is pictured with its head upraised, perhaps uttering a loud, boisterous bray (and note, by the way, that the number of donkey legs shown is insufficient for the number of individuals depicted). Every large agricultural estate in ancient Egypt owned many hundreds of these hard working donkeys. An inscription carved in Neferirtenef's mastaba, for instance, mentions a donkey herd of some 2,300 beasts, and we have previously alluded to other substantial numbers of them controlled by both royal and private hands. The ancient Egyptian peasant was not averse to using the rod on the backside of recalcitrant donkeys: a fragment of wall painting from the First Intermediate Period tomb of Ita at Gebelein includes a vignette of a donkey transporting a field crop to the granaries, in which the painter has meticulously included the bloody, open sores on the animal's hindquarters, the result of the cruel, heavy hand of its driver (pl. XIII).

In contrast to their modern descendants, ancient Egyptians apparently opted not to ride on the back of the donkey. At least this is the conclusion one reaches from the extant pictorial and textual records. The reason for this avoidance can only be speculated upon—but perhaps it was simply viewed as undignified to do so. If the donkey was ridden at all regularly during antiquity, the practice was very likely confined to the lower strata of Egyptian society. Nevertheless, there are a few rare depictions of it. The Fifth Dynasty rock-tomb of Khuwiwer (LG 95) at Giza and the Fifth Dynasty mastaba of Niankhkhnum and Khnumhotep at Saqqara contain unusual renderings of donkeys transporting humans (fig. 26). In each of these details, the deceased tomb-owner is portrayed riding in a wooden palanquin that has been strapped on the backs of a pair of stout donkeys.

Otherwise in Egyptian iconography only foreigners were depicted on the backs of donkeys. Asiatic princes are shown riding donkeys side-saddle on three Egyptian stelae of Twelfth Dynasty date from Serabit al-Khadim in Sinai, and some Asiatic Bedouin children ride on a donkey in the rock-tomb of the Twelfth Dynasty nomarch Khnumhotep III (no. 3) at Beni Hasan. A scarab, dated on stylistic grounds to the Fifteenth Dynasty, now in the Ägyptisches Museum, Berlin, also bears an image of an Asiatic prince seated on the back of a donkey. Donkey burials have been discovered in front of human tombs at Tell al-Dabaa near the eastern edge of the Nile Delta dating from the Hyksos domination, and these foreigners from western Asia living in Egypt probably rode them. At the temple of Sanam in Upper Nubia, dating from the reign of King Taharqa in the Twenty-fifth Dynasty, a group of non-Egyptians (probably Kushites) is rendered riding on donkeys that have elaborate saddle-cloths on their backs. Some blocks from this scene are now in the Ägyptisches Museum, Berlin. In the Eighteenth Dynasty, Tuthmosis III's historical stela from Gebel Barkal describes how, after their defeat at the battle of Megiddo in Palestine, the local princes were forced to ride off on donkeys, the victorious king having seized their valu-

Fig. 24. A detail of painted limestone relief displaying a female donkey transporting sheaves of cut grain in panniers to the threshing floor, her charming youngster trotting along just ahead. From the tomb-chapel of the mastaba of Ti (no. 60) at Saqqara. Fifth Dynasty.

Fig. 25. In this limestone relief a naked field worker is pictured wielding a stick aloft, forcing a group of seven donkeys, one obviously a male, around and around on the threshing floor. The caption above the asses refers to the act of driving them around. From the tomb-chapel of the mastaba of Neferirtenef (D 55) at Saqqara. Fifth Dynasty.
MUSÉES ROYAUX D'ART ET D'HISTOIRE, BRUSSELS.

able horses, an obvious blow to their pride. Beyond question, the best known reference to a foreigner riding a donkey—certainly the most humorous—comes from the splendid Eighteenth Dynasty mortuary temple of Queen Hatshepsut at Deir al-Bahari, where a short caption written above a little saddled donkey on a fragment of wall relief, now in the Egyptian Museum, Cairo, identifies the poor creature as the mount of the famous Queen of Punt, Ati. The queen was obviously in no condition to walk, owing to her tremendous obesity—whether a symbol of her royal station in Puntite culture or a symptom of a disease. In any event, what a miserable life for that unfortunate beast!

Donkeys were also employed in pharaonic Egypt for long-distance travel, as pack animals going off to war, and in desert expeditions to carry water and equipment. An inscription from Sinai mentions such an expedition to the area utilizing five hundred donkeys. In his Sixth Dynasty rock-cut tomb (no. 8) at Aswan, Harkhuf, the governor of Upper Egypt, records in his wonderful autobiography several journeys

he undertook deep into the tropical Nubian hinterlands. On one of these trips his caravan consisted of some three hundred donkeys, which returned to Egypt laden with valuable exotic products, including incense, Ebony *(Dalbergia melanolxylon)*, Leopard and Cheetah pelts, and elephant's tusks.

Notwithstanding its considerable usefulness and widely acclaimed endurance in all manner of difficult work, the mundane donkey seemingly came to be despised by the ancient Egyptians. As early as the Middle Kingdom, the creature became one of several real and mythological animals associated with the god Seth. And when ancient Egyptians cursed one another, they might have used a vile expression that enjoyed widespread use from the late New Kingdom onward: "May a donkey violate him, may a donkey violate his wife, may he not bequeath his (official) post to his children."[6] This vernacular curse may have inspired the maker of an obscene faience figurine now in the Ägyptisches Museum, Berlin, showing a donkey copulating with a woman from behind. The idea of sexual intercourse with a virile donkey, coupled with its Sethian links, must have struck the Egyptians as a particularly base and abhorrent evil.

The ingredients of medical prescriptions in ancient Egypt were quite often, in addition to numerous herbs and the like, derived from a wide range of animal products. The donkey figures prominently in a great many of these potions, which might consist of "the urine of a male donkey that has begotten another," or donkey fat, liver, hoof, blood, dung, ear, teeth, skull, or testicles.

Whereas the humble donkey was often reviled in ancient Egypt, the domestic horse (*Equus caballus*) was seen as a noble creature of eminent rank, worthy of royal praise and affection. This new and exciting exotic creature arrived in Egypt from western Asia comparatively late in pharaonic history. The invading Hyksos are generally credited with the introduction of the horse and chariot into the country. Two equine molars have been recovered during the course of archaeological excavations by the Austrian team working at Tell al-Dabaa (now generally accepted to be the Hyksos capital of Avaris) in the northeastern Nile Delta, in levels that suggest horses were kept there from the beginning of the early Hyksos Period (c.1640 B.C.). Earlier evidence still for the horse in ancient Egypt may come from the Thirteenth Dynasty. A skeleton of a horse was discovered at the fortress of Buhen in Upper Nubia, in a Middle Kingdom context, and was dated by its British excavators to c.1675 B.C. Unfortunately, the bones could not be radiocarbon-dated, and consequently some Egyptologists have preferred to remain skeptical of the proposed dating of the Buhen horse, suggesting that it may have been an intrusive. Fresh light may be thrown on the early use of the horse in Egypt by the very recent discovery, announced in the Egyptian press and elsewhere, of a horse skeleton in a cemetery in the Nile Delta at Tell al-Kibir, purportedly dated to c.1750

B.C., a time when Asiatic settlers, the forerunners of the Hyksos, were already present. If the identification and the dating are correct, these horse remains would be the oldest thus far known from the Nile Valley. Further details about this interesting find are anxiously awaited.

The first known written mention of the horse in ancient Egypt comes from the reign of Kamose in the late Seventeenth Dynasty, and this reference is quickly followed by a few inscriptions and representations at the very beginning of the Eighteenth Dynasty. Shortly after this, the horse must have become a rather familiar sight in Egypt and it routinely appears in art hitched to chariots, is often mentioned in texts, and even occurs as a standard hieroglyphic sign. Artisans rapidly adapted to the beast and used it to create some of the most stirring and memorable images in the Egyptian animal genre (fig. 27). Especially admirable are the prancing and rearing horses created during the Amarna interlude (reign of Akhenaten), which display consummate skill and a realism seldom achieved in stone.

Possessing and owning a horse in ancient Egypt was a symbol of considerable prestige and pride and because of the high costs of ownership was always the privilege and luxury of the king, the core aristocracy, and the military. The Egyptians took an immediate love to the fiery horse and to its training and handling for use with two-wheeled chariots. The practice of horseback riding seems to have been very limited. While a handful of isolated representations in art during the New Kingdom show Egyptians riding on the back of their trusty mounts (fig. 28), these are military scouts and messengers, and it is extremely doubtful whether the ancient Egyptian military machine ever possessed a mounted cavalry. In any event, no Dynastic Egyptian king, or any notable for that matter, is ever pictured on horseback. The well-known western Asiatic goddess Astarte, who appears in Egypt during the Eighteenth Dynasty, rides bareback on a horse

Fig. 26. Drawing of a now destroyed detail of carved relief featuring the deceased tomb-owner in a wooden palanquin borne on the backs of a pair of donkeys. From the rock-cut tomb of Khuwiwer (LG 95) at Giza. Fifth Dynasty.

Fig. 27. This small fragment of limestone relief portrays the richly caparisoned and bridled heads of a span of two horses. A Nubian (?) groom seeks to steady the fiery chargers, which would have been harnessed to draw a light chariot. Probably from a late Eighteenth or Nineteenth Dynasty tomb-chapel at Saqqara. ROYAL MUSEUM OF SCOTLAND, EDINBURGH.

in depictions of her. It is interesting to note that a short passage of an inscription on the war chariot of Tuthmosis IV from the Eighteenth Dynasty, found in his tomb (no. 43) in the Valley of the Kings and now exhibited in the Egyptian Museum in Cairo, praises the monarch as being "valiant on horseback like Astarte." This text may indicate that the king occasionally rode, as some authorities have suggested, but this interpretation is by no means certain. Several gigantic Ramesside Period battle reliefs carved on temple walls include details of the enemy fleeing in great haste on horse-

back from the triumphant Egyptian forces. Riding on horses for pleasure or otherwise may not have become popular in antiquity before the Ptolemaic Period.

The Egyptians' brand of horsecraft became part of the tradition of the 'sportsman-king'; texts frequently vaunt the king's physical prowess and chariot-driving skills. Paintings and relief compositions displaying various kings in their chariots behind teams of rearing steeds are commonplace. A seemingly genuine interest in horses is captured in a thrilling episode in the life of the young crown prince Amenhotep II, a

34

formidable athlete, recorded on an Eighteenth Dynasty limestone stela erected near the colossal Sphinx at Giza:

> Now when he was [still] a lad, he loved his horses and rejoiced in them. It was a strengthening of the heart to work them, to learn their natures, to be skilled in training them and to enter into their ways. When [it] was heard in the palace by his father [Tuthmosis III] . . . , the heart of his majesty was glad when he heard it, rejoicing at what was said about his eldest son . . . . Then his majesty said to those who were at his side: "Let there be given to him the very best horses in my majesty's stable which is in Memphis, and tell him: 'Take care of them, instill fear into them, make them gallop, and handle them if there be resistance to thee!'" Now after it had been entrusted to the King's Son to take care of horses of the king's stable, well then, he did that which had been entrusted to him . . . . He trained horses without their equal: they would not grow tired when he took the reins, nor would they sweat [even] at a high gallop. He would harness with the bit in Memphis and stop at the rest-house of Harmakhis [the Sphinx], [so that] he might spend a moment there, going around and around it and seeing the charm of this rest-house of Khufu [Cheops] and Khaf-Re [Chephren], the triumphant . . . .[7]

Surely the most touching royal document regarding the horse, attesting to a real passion and sensitivity for the care of these costly animals, is a short passage on the granite victory stela of King Piye of the Twenty-fifth Dynasty from Gebel Barkal, now in the Egyptian Museum, Cairo. It relates how after King Namart surrendered the besieged city of Hermopolis, Piye inspected the stables of his defeated foe and expressed his deep grief at the sight of the starving horses. Namart was censured (he was lucky to escape with his life) for allowing the horses to suffer from hunger during the siege: "His majesty proceeded to the stable of the horses and the quarters of the foals. When he saw they had been [left] to hunger he said: 'I swear, as [Ra] loves me, as my nose is refreshed by life: that my horses were made to hunger pains me more than any other crime you committed in

your recklessness!'"[8] This same monarch carried his affection for his own valiant chargers to the degree that he had four of them interred, richly caparisoned with silver trappings and strings of ornate beads, beside his tomb at al-Kurru in Upper Nubia. No doubt these horses were sacrificed at the time of the king's death so they could accompany him into the netherworld. Similar graves of fine horses have been discovered at al-Kurru dating from later in Kushite history as well. There is really no such comparable treatment of royal horses known from Egypt proper. Even though chariots were included in the royal tombs during the New Kingdom, the horses that drew them were not.

Those private, well-to-do ancient Egyptians fortunate enough to have owned and loved a horse may also have provided their favorite steed with a fine burial, but only two instances of such interments are known from Egypt. During excavations in the Theban necropolis in 1936, the Metropolitan Museum of Art's Egyptian Expedition came upon a horse belonging to that most illustrious courtier of the Eighteenth Dynasty, Senenmut, chief spokesman of Queen Hatshepsut. Elaborately interred in front of Senenmut's tomb-chapel (no. 71), this prize horse, probably a mare, had been buried with full honors, its body wrapped in many yards of fine linen bandages (but apparently not mummified) and placed in a large wooden coffin two and a half meters long. Protecting its back was a fine linen and leather saddle-cloth or blanket, with long tapes for securing it around its body, and its short mane had been tied in tufts with strips of leather. The horse's age at death was estimated at five or six years. It was a small animal, about the size of a modern pony, having a shoulder height of only about 14 hands (142 centimeters). Both the horse from the fortress of Buhen and Senenmut's mare would in life probably have closely resembled the fine-limbed, compact ponies still found in Egypt and Arabia today. The other example of an elaborate horse burial comes from Saqqara, where three horses were uncovered in a reused tomb. The body of one had reportedly been mummified and was found wrapped in cloth in a massive painted wooden coffin. The skeleton and coffin are now in Cairo's Agricultural Museum. Unfortunately, this burial could not be precisely dated and may come from any time between the Twentieth Dynasty and the Ptolemaic Period.

Innumerable lively scenes from the New Kingdom capture the elite of Egyptian society in light chariots drawn by teams of spirited horses speeding at full gallop (pl. XVII). Hunting desert game from chariots was an especially popular activity with these notables (see chapter 3). They engaged in other pursuits as well and these may even have included racing their chariots. A long, straight desert track approximately four kilometers in length and 120 meters wide, at Kom al-Abd near the site of Amenhotep III's Theban palace complex at Malkata, dating from the Eighteenth Dynasty, has been interpreted as an area for chariot exercising, an activity not otherwise documented from ancient Egypt. The site was complete with a rest-house and a large, flat-topped, brick platform, perhaps the grandstand for viewing races. Excavations carried out at al-Amarna, the site of Akhenaten's short-lived capital city during the Eighteenth Dynasty, revealed a military post with extensive stabling for horses.

The high status accorded the horse in ancient Egypt and elsewhere in the ancient Near East can be appreciated from the Amarna letters, a royal archive of 382 cuneiform clay tablets, diplomatic correspondences between sovereigns, dating from the Eighteenth Dynasty and found at al-Amarna late in the last century by local diggers. The standard salutations of the letters include wishes for the welfare of a king's horses and his chariots, indicative of the intense pride and prestige invested in these valuable beasts. Horses were also a part of the gifts of friendship among this elite group. Another indication of the high regard in which horses were held is the fact that their owners often gave them names. During the Nineteenth Dynasty, for instance, Ramesses II called the pair of magnificent horses that pulled his war chariot at the famous battle of Kadesh 'Victory at Thebes' and 'Mut is Content.'

There is a wealth of pictorial and written evidence that the ancient Egyptians imported, by means of booty, trade, or tribute, a large number of horses during the New Kingdom, especially from western Asia (pl. XV). The acquisition of horses was one of the priorities of the Egyptian army when fighting overseas. During Tuthmosis III's western Asiatic campaigns, for example, the spoils of the city of Megiddo in Palestine alone included 2,041 mares, 191 foals, six stallions, and 924 chariots. On another of this monarch's daring military expeditions into northern Syria—so we are told in the autobiographical text in the Eighteenth Dynasty Theban tomb-chapel of Amunemhab (no. 85)—the king of Kadesh employed a brilliant defensive tactic against the Egyptian forces utilizing a mare in season. Having realized that the Egyptian war chariots were pulled by stallions, he sent the mare running into the Egyptian horses to break the rank of the chariots. The ruse ended in failure, however, and Amunemhab saved the day for Egypt; he pursued the mare and slew her, cut off her tail, and presented it to the grateful Tuthmosis III.

Eventually, Egypt itself became known for breeding and exporting magnificent horses. During the Twenty-first Dynasty, for instance, possibly in the reign of Siamun, King Solomon of Israel purchased horses from Egypt. In the Old Testament (1 Kings 10:28–29), we read that "the horses which Solomon had were brought out of Egypt; and the king's merchants received them in droves, each drove at a price. And a chariot came up and went out of Egypt for six hundred shekels of silver, and an horse for

an hundred and fifty: and so for all the kings of the Hittites, and for the kings of Syria, did they bring them out by their means." Also, during the Twenty-third Dynasty, according to Assyrian annals, King Osorkon IV of Egypt had delivered to King Sargon II of Assyria a splendid diplomatic present of twelve fine Egyptian horses, which the latter proudly boasted were "without their equals in the land [of Assyria]."

While the image of the horse is closely associated in Egyptian iconography with pomp, power, and warfare, it was also used as a symbol of the beloved one in love poetry in the New Kingdom: "O that you came to [your sister swiftly]! Like a horse of the king; picked from a thousand steeds of all kinds, the choicest of the stables. It is singled out in its feed, its master knows its paces; when it hears the sound of the whip,

there's no holding it back. There's no chief of charioteers who could overtake it. Sister's heart is aware: He is not far from her!"[9]

The ancient Egyptians also occasionally employed teams of another valued equid to draw their chariots. This engineered hybrid has been identified probably correctly by Juliet Clutton-Brock as not a mule but a hinny, that is, the offspring of a male horse and a female donkey. The creature is found rendered on the walls of several New Kingdom Theban tomb-chapels, where pairs of them appear harnessed to chariots in scenes related to the harvest. Surely the best known of these is executed on a wonderful fragment of wall painting from the unlocated Eighteenth Dynasty tomb-chapel of the scribe Nebamun at Thebes (fig. 29). The upper register depicts a groom restraining a span of nervously

Fig. 28. An unusual illustration on a block of limestone relief showing a mounted Egyptian scout galloping into a military camp to report to his superiors. The rider holds the reins and a short stick in his hands. The rare subject matter is made all the more interesting by the lively and convincing rendering of the running steed. From the tomb-chapel of the general (later pharaoh) Horemhab at Saqqara. Eighteenth Dynasty. MUSEO CIVICO, BOLOGNA.

Fig. 29. Fragment of wall painting from the unlocated tomb-chapel of the scribe Nebamun at Thebes, displaying in the upper register a groom or driver restraining a span of nervous horses hitched to a chariot. Below, a closely observed team of hinnies is shown, also attached to a chariot, but much more relaxed. One of the animals is drinking or feeding from a trough in the shade of a tree. Eighteenth Dynasty. THE BRITISH MUSEUM, LONDON.

energetic stallions while beneath, in sharp contrast, a pair of fine hinnies, painted a grayish-blue, is shown so docile that their attendant can relax in the cab of the chariot. The hybrid is similarly handled in a relief composition in the Eighteenth Dynasty tomb-chapel of Khaemhet (no. 57) at Thebes. How widespread the use of the hinny was in ancient Egypt, and whether the Egyptians also used the mule, remain largely uncertain.

The Dromedary *(Camelus dromedarius)*, the one-humped camel, is probably the animal that modern Westerners most often associate with contemporary Egypt. It has achieved worldwide fame for its unique adaptation to the intensely hot, dry, desert environment, and has played an extraordinary role in history as a vital beast of burden in establishing long-distance trade routes over vast, arid, desert tracts and in enabling human habitation in otherwise uninhabitable areas. But when compared with the extremely long history of many domestic species in the service of humankind in Egypt, the camel must be viewed as a relative newcomer.

The date at which this fascinating domestic animal first appeared on Egyptian soil has stirred considerable lively debate among scholars. Over the past hundred

years or so an assortment of finds have been made in Egypt that have been claimed to be camel bones, camel hair products, or representations of camels, ranging in date from the late Neolithic to the close of the pharaonic period. Even that brilliant student of the natural history of ancient Egypt, Ludwig Keimer, suggested that the camel was known fleetingly to the ancient Egyptians, from the Predynastic Period onward. In recent years, however, the supposed evidence has come under the close scrutiny of informed specialists, who have almost unanimously concluded that most of the material is highly ambiguous or has nothing to do with the camel, and thus cannot be used to substantiate contentions of its early introduction.

The oldest currently reliable date for the domestic camel in the Nile Valley comes from samples of its dung recovered from Napatan levels at the site of Qasr Ibrim in Lower Nubia, radiocarbon-dated to approximately 740 B.C. The camel may well have arrived in Egypt only during the Third Intermediate Period. From textual sources, we are informed that King Takelot II of the Twenty-second Dynasty sent the king of Assyria, Shalmaneser III, an offering of some unusual animals, which included a couple of Bactrian Camels *(Camelus bactrianus)*, the two-humped camel. These creatures were themselves, no doubt, already rare exotic imports into Egypt, since this species made its home in the mountainous areas of central Asia. The invading camel-using Assyrian army under King Esarhaddon in 671 B.C. in turn probably further familiarized the ancient Egyptians with the beast. The increased importance of the Western Desert oases of Egypt after the Persian invasion in 525 B.C. may be connected with the introduction and use of the camel in these areas. In any event, camels did not become well known in Egypt until the Ptolemaic Period. In Ptolemy II Philadelphus's grand procession in Alexandria a number of camels appeared, both the Dromedary and the Bactrian, some in harness, others carrying hundreds of kilograms of costly spices on their backs. It is quite likely, however, that the Dromedary became a common sight on farms along the Nile only in the Roman Period, when it was widely employed as a draft animal.

Chapter Three

The Thrill of the Hunt

*F*ive thousand years ago, at the dawn of pharaonic civilization, Egypt
was a land replete with indigenous animal life—very different from
the present day. The climate and the environment were different, too. We know
from the evidence of copious Predynastic rock drawings emblazoned on cliff faces
along the edge of the Nile Valley and in the deserts of Upper Egypt and Lower
Nubia, from hunting scenes carved and painted on the walls of Old Kingdom
temples and tomb-chapels, and from archaeological, zooarchaeological, and paleo-
botanical findings that the deserts surrounding the Nile Valley were not always

*Fig. 30. Rock drawing
featuring a grand procession
of game animals. An
Ostrich, an African
Elephant, a two-horned
rhinoceros, and perhaps a
Scimitar-horned Oryx and a
Soemmering's Gazelle, are
chased by a bold hunter with
bow and arrows. Near Silwa
Bahari, between Edfu and
Kom Ombo, in Upper Egypt.
Probably from the Amratian
(Naqada I) Period.*

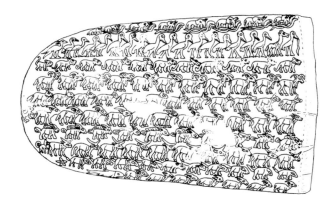 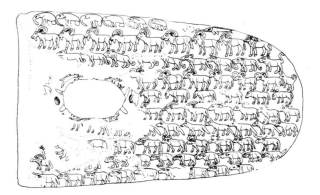

as stark and inhospitable as they are today. Throughout prehistoric times and well into the Old Kingdom, the low desert lands that fringe either side of the Nile flood plain enjoyed more rainfall than they do now, and there were localized sources of water: vast tracts of savanna-like vegetation bounded almost the entire length of the prehistoric Nile Valley, providing a fertile setting for a wide range of game animals, a veritable hunters' paradise. Over a long period of time, from the Late Paleolithic to the Predynastic Period, fauna less well adapted to dry conditions had been drawn from the increasingly arid neighboring semidesert lands to these better-watered areas, and the trees, tall grasses, low shrubs, and other vegetation teemed with an array of wildlife. Here, long ago, sizable herds of African Elephant (*Loxodonta africana*), rhinoceros (Rhinocerotidae), and Giraffe (*Giraffa camelopardalis*) once browsed, eagerly sought after as quarry by some of the first ancient Egyptians wishing to obtain food on the hoof (figs. 30, 31). Today one needs to venture very far south, deep into the modern republic of Sudan, to find conditions and wildlife to compare with prehistoric Egypt.

The hunting of wild animals was one of the most important necessities of life for the earliest Egyptian people, and it was still widely practiced even after the appearance of domesticated plants and animals with the coming of the Neolithic revolution in Egypt around 5500 B.C. (at the beginning of what Egyptologists call the Predynastic Period). The Egyptians hunted not only to procure meat but to obtain all manner of needed animal by-products, such as bone, feathers, gut, horn, ivory, leather, and shell, and also to protect themselves from ferocious animals that shared their environment, like the Lion and Hippopotamus. The large species of game animals such as African Elephant and Giraffe were more than likely completely eradicated north of Aswan by the close of the Early Dynastic Period: their demise from the Egyptian landscape was predominantly the result of human disturbances, particularly intensive hunting pressures, but was also closely related to the increasing desiccation of Egypt from the time of the First Dynasty, the result of continuing climatic change.

The host of remaining creatures flourished in the favorable riverine setting. The key species identified from ancient Egyptian art and hieroglyphs include: Addax (*Addax nasomaculatus*) (fig. 40), Scimitar-horned Oryx (*Oryx gazella dammah*) (figs. 30, 31, 34, 36–38, 126, pl. I), Roan (*Hippotragus equinus*), Bubal Hartebeest (*Alcelaphus buselaphus buselaphus*) (figs. 34, 39–41, 150), Dorcas Gazelle (*Gazella dorcas*) (figs. 34, 74, pl. II), Soemmering's Gazelle (*Gazella soemmeringii*) (fig. 30), Nubian Ibex (*Capra ibex nubiana*) (figs. 31, 34, 35, 42–44, pl. I), Barbary Sheep (*Ammotragus lervia*) (figs. 31, 34, 45, pl. I), Aurochs (*Bos primigenius*) (figs. 31, 34, pl. I), deer (Cervidae) (figs. 35, 46), African Wild Ass (*Equus africanus*), Com-

Fig. 31. Drawing of the rich decoration carved on either side of an ivory handle of a flint knife probably belonging to a great hunter, featuring a bestiary of game animals recorded in minute detail, row upon row, with the utmost skill and care. Some 227 individual creatures are represented on the knife handle. Without much difficulty we can distinguish African Elephants trampling intertwined serpents, the now locally extinct Saddlebill Stork (Ephippiorhynchus senegalensis), Giraffe, Lion, African Wild Ass, Barbary Sheep, Scimitar-horned Oryx, Nubian Ibex, North African Porcupine, Aurochs, and others. From Abu Zaidan, south of Edfu. Late Predynastic Period (Naqada III). THE BROOKLYN MUSEUM.

mon or Golden Jackal *(Canis aureus lupaster)*, Red Fox *(Vulpes vulpes aegyptiaca)* (pl. XXI), Striped Weasel *(Poecilictis libyca libyca)* (fig. 32), Honey Badger *(Mellivora capensis)*, Common Genet *(Genetta genetta)* (fig. 84, 95, pl. XXIV), Striped Hyena *(Hyaena hyaena)* (figs. 35, 48, pls. XI, XVII), Lion *(Panthera leo)* (figs. 1, 4, 31, 34, 53, 65–67, 146, 150, pls. I, XXXII), Leopard *(Panthera pardus)* (figs. 3, 34, 66, pls. I, XVI), Caracal *(Caracal caracal)*, Cape Hare *(Lepus capensis)* (figs. 51, 52, pl. XVII), North African Porcupine *(Hystrix cristata)* (figs. 31, 33), jerboa *(Jaculus sp.)* (figure on page ix), hedgehog (Erinaceidae) (figs. 49–51), Ostrich *(Struthio camelus)* (figs. 30, 120), and many others. This rich faunal community represented a valuable resource in ancient Egypt, both for the table and for recreation. While hunting in the Dynastic period was no longer the significant life-supporting activity it had been in former times as the principal means of securing food, the pursuit of game continued nevertheless to be important and was to be a recurrent theme in art throughout the Dynastic and Ptolemaic periods. For the well-heeled, the chase became as much a sport as a way to augment their diet. And for the lower rungs of Egyptian society, hunting small game was a vital supplemental source of nourishment, since their access to domestic livestock animals was limited.

The Egyptians' deep appreciation of animals is clearly evinced in the remarkable fidelity of nature, vitality, and exuberance of the images produced by the ancient artisans. When portraying animals, Egyptian artisans were somewhat less restricted by the representational conventions that governed much of their other work. Consequently, there is often a freedom in the animal scenes not readily observed elsewhere. This is perhaps nowhere more evident than in the many depictions of the hunt. The thrill of the desert hunt, either on foot or (in later periods) from light, two-wheeled, horse-drawn chariots racing at breakneck speeds, developed into a tremendously popular sporting pastime in ancient Egypt, enjoyed by the monarch and members of the privileged classes. The motif of the chase became an integral part of the standard repertoire of scenes executed in both royal and private funerary monuments from the Old Kingdom onward. For the well-to-do, the desert hunt frequently took place in well-stocked confined areas, the animals being corralled together. The earliest prototype for this spirited theme seems to be the large wall scene in the Fifth Dynasty mortuary temple of Sahure at Abusir. The monarch is portrayed standing outside the walls of an extensive, fenced-off enclosure, forming a

Fig. 32. This detail of painted limestone relief from the 'chamber of the seasons' in the sun temple of Niuserre pictures two Striped Weasels giving birth on the sparsely vegetated, gently rolling surface of the desert margin. From Abu Ghurab. Fifth Dynasty. ÄGYPTISCHES MUSEUM, BERLIN.

kind of hunting park or reserve, into which a great concourse of wild desert animals has been driven by attendants. He fires a rain of arrows at the mêlée of fleeing wildlife, slaying many, while his dogs are in full pursuit of others. In this and other depictions we see the frantic movements of great swarms of hunted wild animals that had often been driven by beaters or lured by food and water into the vast enclosures fenced in by tall, strong, spanning nets and occasionally surrounded by deep ditches. Here the hunt was carefully managed, virtually guaranteeing kings and courtiers a lavish yield of prize trophies (fig. 34). Sometimes rare and exotic creatures were released into these reserves for increased hunting thrills (fig. 35). Interestingly enough, a royal hunting park of precisely this kind has been located near the splendid Eighteenth Dynasty jubilee temple of Amenhotep III at Soleb in Upper Nubia. A series of small holes for the tall forked poles that supported the long spanning nets have been traced on the ground, revealing its overall plan. This reserve formed a vast, oval enclosure, about three hundred by six hundred meters, and would have served for the king's hunting pleasures

when teeming with exotic Nubian wild game. The park's close proximity to the temple could indicate that it was used in conjunction with a ceremonial rite.

The vibrant, decorative hunting compositions probably served several crucial functions. Through the power of picture and word, these artistic works could magically provide the tomb-owner with quantities of fresh game that could be drawn upon forever by continuing these recreational pursuits after death. This bounty would be further preserved in the afterlife through the representation of beasts mating, giving birth (some females drop their young during the hunt out of sheer panic), or suckling their offspring—presumably reproducing to ensure an endless supply of their kind for all time. Another important aspect of these hunting scenes was their ritualistic significance: the symbolic destruction of adverse forces and evil that might somehow threaten the welfare or rebirth of the deceased. For the ancient Egyptians, the stark desert environment was also the haunt of fabulous mythical monsters, notably the serpo-feline and the griffin, and these creatures are sometimes included in scenes of the desert chase from

Fig. 33. Fragment of painted limestone relief from a desert hunting composition, showing a number of inhabitants of this environment including a very rare depiction of a North African Porcupine and a small to medium-sized feline whose identification remains uncertain. In the lower register a hunting dog wearing a collar sinks its teeth into the neck of a jackal. From the tomb-chapel of the mastaba of Pehenuka (D 70) at Saqqara. Fifth Dynasty. ÄGYPTISCHES MUSEUM, BERLIN.

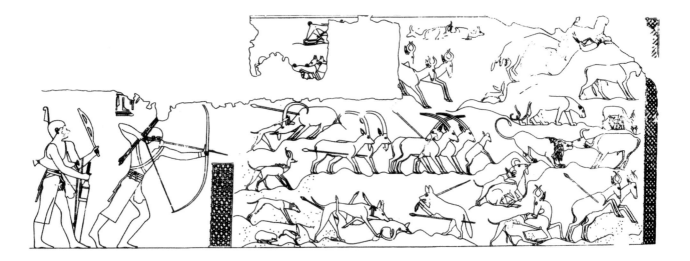

Fig. 34. Drawing of an extraordinarily lively desert hunting scene in carved relief. The tomb-owner stands outside the walls of a fenced enclosure, shooting with his bow at a multitude of fleeing game, including Scimitar-horned Oryx, Nubian Ibex, Striped Hyena, Dorcas Gazelle, Bubal Hartebeest, Barbary Sheep, Cape Hare, hedgehog, and Leopard. Also, note the Lion attacking an Aurochs. Many of the hunter's arrows have already found their mark and his trained hunting dogs are in hot pursuit. From the rock-cut tomb of the nomarch Senbi (B. 1) at Meir, in Middle Egypt. Twelfth Dynasty.

the Late Predynastic Period through the Middle Kingdom (pl. I). For Egyptian monarchs, the annihilation of quarry was a feat of valor, equated with their success in battle against Egypt's traditional enemies or other malignant powers, and illustrated their personal triumph over disorder. While hunting may have been a pleasurable activity, there was a decidedly religious meaning underlying the royal slaughter, and these illustrations should not be interpreted as merely demonstrating a passionate love of sporting activities or outdoor life.

While the king was rendered hunting with bow and arrow on monuments during the Old Kingdom, this weapon does not appear in private tomb-chapels until the end of this age. Before this time, hunting was carried out by teams of highly skilled professional huntsmen, accompanied by trained and fearless greyhound-like dogs, who trapped and lassoed wild bovids and other beasts on the rolling, scrub terrain adjacent to the Nile Valley. The aim of the hunt in these instances seems to have been to secure the animals alive, and the beasts were taken into captivity to supplement and give variety to the diet of the privileged classes, and for use as important sacrificial offerings to the gods and the dead.

Reliefs and paintings executed on tomb-chapels walls, particularly during the Old Kingdom, occasionally include intriguing vignettes of the force-feeding of appar-

ently tamed hyenas, gazelles, ibex, and antelopes, and their feeding from mangers within fenced paddocks. These scenes have been interpreted as either experiments to bring these animals within the orbit of complete domestication (experiments which ultimately ended in failure), or as cases of semi-domestication, the beasts being under human control but probably not freely breeding in captivity. It must remain an open question to what extent the ancient Egyptians ever achieved, or indeed ever sought, captive propagation of these creatures. The extant pictorial and textual records do not provide us with a clear answer and are open to more than one interpretation. It seems most likely that the scenes merely show the management of previously captured wild animals, perhaps now tamed, and the operation of fattening them prior to slaughter, though in the Eleventh Dynasty rock-tomb of the nomarch Baket III (no. 15) at Beni Hasan, small herds of Dorcas Gazelle and Scimitar-horned Oryxes are shown together with their young under the charge of a keeper, which may support the view that some captive breeding success was achieved.

A considerable number of the accurately portrayed wild animals in the scenes on ancient temples and tombs have either long since vanished from the Egyptian landscape or are now extremely rare. Even in the mid-fifth century B.C., Herodotus (II,

Fig. 35. Drawing of a relief composition portraying the nomarch Ukhhotep I drawing his bow on a variety of game animals, including an exceptional representation of a Giraffe and a deer. From his rock-cut tomb (B. 2) at Meir. Twelfth Dynasty.

65) remarked that "though Egypt has Libya on its borders, it is not a country of many animals." Indeed, his observation is substantially correct, for an enormous change had taken place in the Egyptian animal world over the nearly three millennia since the beginning of the pharaonic civilization. By Herodotus's day, Egypt's former endemic wild fauna had already been appreciably depleted. Some of the species that had inhabited the country when the Egyptian state was formed had become locally extinct, especially the larger mammals, which had once freely roamed the countryside. Some of this decimation can be attributed to the increasing desertification of Egypt, which continues to this day. But human activity has largely been at the center of this profound change. Since as early as the Old Kingdom, the expansion of cultivation, domestic livestock grazing, the draining of swamplands, excessive wood gathering, overhunting, and the intentional slaying of dangerous animals or crop pests have all contributed to an irreversible change in the Egyptian landscape and fauna.

The elegant Scimitar-horned Oryx, one of the most perfectly adapted large mammals to desert wastelands, is able to live without water for several weeks at a time. It is today virtually extinct from its former range in Egypt, a modern-day victim of unregu-

lated and senseless overhunting with sophisticated firearms. As recently as a hundred years ago it was still quite plentiful in the Sahara Desert, and in antiquity its numbers and distribution must have been much greater. It is little wonder, then, that this antelope was the single most important desert-dwelling species known to the ancient Egyptians, valued for its high-quality meat, horns, and hide. It also played a very significant role in the performance of certain sacrificial rites.

The oryx, with its highly distinctively shaped horns, can first be recognized during the early Predynastic Period on Amratian (Naqada I) painted pottery and later in the form of small slate palettes used for grinding malachite. The celebrated tomb 100, the 'decorated tomb' of the Gerzean Period (Naqada II) at Hierakonpolis in Upper Egypt, was adorned with a magnificent wall painting that contained several fascinating desert animal motifs. Fragments of this famous work are now in the Egyptian Museum, Cairo, but are in very poor condition. One detail clearly shows the taking of a group of gazelles and what seems to be an oryx. The motif shows five individuals caught in a single, small wheel-trap fashioned of pointed pieces of wood or palm-leaf spikes. The large number is surely exaggerated (this kind of device allows only one beast to be caught at a time), but it is interesting to note that this is precisely

Fig. 36. This fragment of wall painting from the time of the pyramids records the presentation of an offering of desert animals to the tomb-owner. We view two retainers wearing short kilts bringing six Scimitar-horned Oryxes with collars around their necks. From the tomb-chapel of the mastaba of Metjetji at Saqqara. Fifth Dynasty. MUSÉE DU LOUVRE, PARIS.

Fig. 37. (opposite) Relief of an offering-bringer with a Scimitar-horned Oryx and a Common Crane, which has its long, sharp bill securely tied to its long neck. From the tomb-chapel of Paatenemhab at Saqqara. Eighteenth Dynasty. RIJKSMUSEUM VAN OUDHEDEN, LEIDEN.

the method sometimes used to trap this type of game in Egypt today.

The Scimitar-horned Oryx eventually became a standard member of the Dynastic faunal repertoire. Its image was incorporated in objects of utilitarian function, such as cosmetic dishes (fig. 38), and there is hardly an extant hunting scene in Egyptian art that does not contain at least one of these nimble-footed creatures racing along the undulating slopes of the desert margin. The compositions often feature dramatic details of terrorized oryxes being savagely attacked by lunging dogs or dying in agony from wounds inflicted by marksmen's arrows (figs. 34, 35). Nor is it unusual for pairs of oryxes to be pictured in these works mating. Sometimes the objective of the desert chase, especially during the Old Kingdom, was to capture game animals alive, using traps, lassos, or other means. Numerous tomb-chapels of this period depict the presentation of hunting spoils—

coaxed forward in processions—to the deceased as offerings, and the oryx is nearly always included here (figs. 36, 37).

Many years ago, the distinguished German zoologist Max Hilzheimer, who had a considerable interest in the natural history of ancient Egypt, aptly observed that the ancient Egyptians "were complete masters of the art of domestication, and tamed a large number of animals which were not so elsewhere."[10] One of the creatures he had in mind must have been the Scimitar-horned Oryx. From early in the Fifth Dynasty, these antelopes can regularly be observed on tomb-chapel walls (as for instance in the painted Twelfth Dynasty rock-tomb of Khnumhotep III (no. 3) at Beni Hasan) in captivity on the country estates of great landowners, kept along with farmyard animals, wearing collars and tethered, and being force-fed or feeding from mangers. The oryx also routinely appears thrown to the ground, its legs bound with

Fig. 38. Cosmetic dish of glazed steatite fashioned in the shape of a Scimitar-horned Oryx bound with cord. Eighteenth Dynasty. THE TOLEDO MUSEUM OF ART.

cord; it is then dispatched and cut up by teams of busy butchers wielding broad flint knives, who deliver the choicest cuts to the deceased owner. We can be reasonably certain that this antelope continued to be a prized dish served up at great tables for many centuries; nor was it confined to Old and Middle kingdom tastes, for it is depicted being brought by offering-bearers on tomb and temple walls through the New Kingdom and beyond. It is prominently mentioned in the endowment lists of the Fifth Dynasty sun temple of King Niuserre at Abu Ghurab, which suggests it must have been pleasing to the gods too.

The Scimitar-horned Oryx appears frequently in religious contexts. In the Twentieth Dynasty, Ramesses III appointed archers to capture wild oryxes in the desert for sacrifice and presentation to the *ka* of the god Ra on every feast day. Also, the great Harris papyrus records that Ramesses III donated 367 male oryxes to various temples in the land. Sacred to the god Sokar, oryxes were sacrificed and their heads offered to him during the New Kingdom. This explains the iconography of the divine bark of Sokar, which had a large oryx's head mounted facing backward on its upturned prow. In the Eighteenth Dynasty,

during the reign of Amenhotep III, the king is rendered on a wall of the Luxor temple ritually killing a live oryx by cutting its throat with a long knife. Similarly, in the Nineteenth Dynasty, Ramesses II is pictured in a wall relief at the temple of Karnak sacrificing a bound oryx in the presence of the divine Theban triad.

The seemingly benign character of the species belies the fact that by the end of the New Kingdom it was regarded as a potent symbol of evil. Since the god Seth was connected with the hostile desert, and the oryx was viewed as the desert animal *par excellence*, the creature became closely associated with Seth and was therefore subject to slaughter in religious rites at temples. On the so-called *cippi*, or magical stelae, of 'Horus on the crocodiles,' the youthful god is usually portrayed (on Ptolemaic examples at least) grasping in his hands such noxious desert beasts as serpents, Lions, scorpions, and the now Sethian Scimitar-horned Oryx (fig. 126).

Two other species of oryx seem to have been known in ancient Egypt. On a wall of the Nineteenth Dynasty rock-cut temple of Ramesses II at Beit al-Wali in Lower Nubia, the king is depicted receiving the spoils of war and Nubian tribute, including exotic

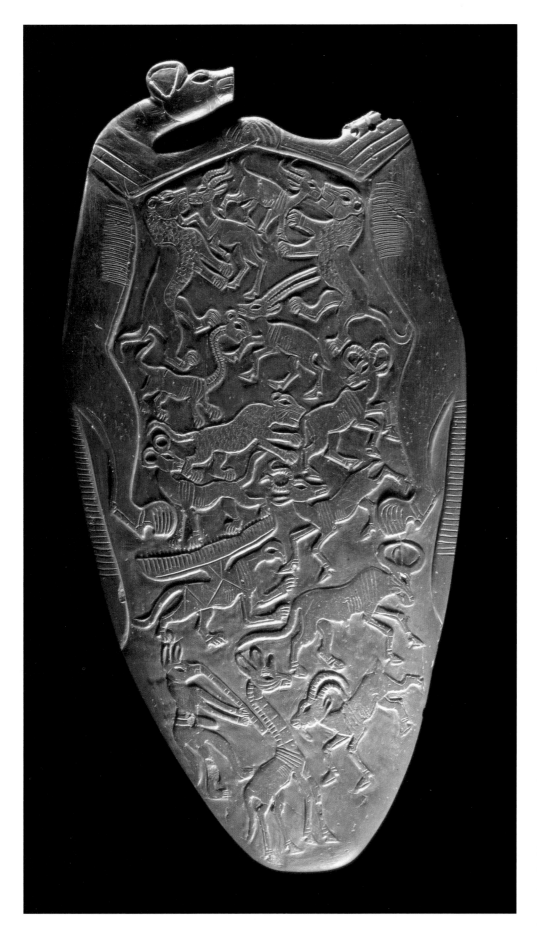

Pl. I. This monumental votive or ceremonial palette with relief decoration depicts, on this side, a mêlée of real and fabulous desert animals in conflict, bordered by two large heraldic Cape Hunting Dogs. Amid this odd mix of animal life we can easily recognize Lion, Leopard, Giraffe, Nubian Ibex, Scimitar-horned Oryx, Barbary Sheep, Aurochs, and gazelle, as well as mythical creatures such as a serpent-necked feline and the griffin. Also note the enigmatic figure of a jackal on two legs playing a flute—or is it a hunter wearing a jackal's head and tail? For the ancient Egyptians, the sun-baked deserts flanking the Nile Valley were not only home to a vast array of game but were also the domain of strange monstrous beasts and represented chaos. Within the symmetrically sculpted rampant Cape Hunting Dogs, the creatures present a confusion of forms, the very picture of disorder. Green schist. From Hierakonpolis. Late Predynastic Period (Naqada III). THE ASHMOLEAN MUSEUM, OXFORD.

Pl. II. (opposite) Black steatite disk carved in relief, with pink calcite inlay, probably used in a table game. The decoration shows two sleek greyhound-type hunting dogs attacking and dispatching a pair of Dorcas Gazelles. This gaming disk, one of forty-five made of various materials and adorned with a variety of motifs (see fig. 109), was found at Saqqara in the First Dynasty tomb of Hemaka (S 3035), a high official during the reign of King Den. The piece is pierced in its center, presumably so that it could be spun, allowing the animals to chase round and round. THE EGYPTIAN MUSEUM, CAIRO.

Pl. III. This brilliantly painted pair of Red-breasted Geese, ambling slowly to the right, form a detail on a fragment of wall painting from the tomb-chapel of the mastaba of Nefermaat and his wife Atet at Meidum. The whole frieze of six geese, known today as the 'Geese of Meidum' (see fig. 100), is one of the most treasured objects of the Cairo Museum. The deep reddish hue of this species' striking plumage has been admirably duplicated in these beautiful portraits. Early Fourth Dynasty. THE EGYPTIAN MUSEUM, CAIRO.

Pl. IV. From the tomb-chapel of the mastaba of Neferherptah at Saqqara comes this detail of a master drawing from unfinished wall decoration, depicting an almost unique scene in ancient Egyptian iconography, the trapping of doves (less likely, pigeons) with a clap-net. We view an immense flock of doves, some at repose, caught in the net, many others on the wing, having escaped with their lives. This is by all means a busy and lively scene. Not included in our picture, several fowlers are shown nearby placing some of the captured birds into crates for transport. Other birds immediately face their fate and have their necks wrung. The deceased tomb-owner would surely have enjoyed these doves on his table in the beyond. Fifth Dynasty.

Pl. v. This enormously appealing block of limestone relief, on which only the slightest traces of pigment are now preserved, is from the mortuary temple of King Userkaf at Saqqara, and is unquestionably the work of a master artisan. The fragment depicts part of a Papyrus swampland scene, perhaps one that featured the king engaged in the pleasures of fowling with throwsticks, with some of the bird life of the thicket roosting on and winging above the stems and umbels. The general form and detailing of the birds is unrivaled in Old Kingdom relief. This enables us to confidently identify some of the birds: Purple Gallinule, Kingfisher, Pied Kingfisher, Bittern, Hoopoe, and what is probably a Sacred Ibis. Note that the Pied Kingfisher is realistically poised fluttering in midair, just seconds before its dart down to the surface of the water. Fifth Dynasty. THE EGYPTIAN MUSEUM, CAIRO.

Pl. VI. Detail of a painted limestone relief from the tomb-chapel of the mastaba of Ti (no. 60) at Saqqara, showing one of the deceased's retainers, an achondroplastic dwarf, leading Ti's pet Green Monkey. The man carries a small truncheon, one end of which terminates in an open hand. Servants with physical abnormalities, at least under the Old and Middle Kingdoms, were sometimes given charge of the family pets and are seen following their masters on tomb-chapel walls. Fifth Dynasty.

Pl. VII. This Nilotic fishing scene, in painted limestone relief, appears in the tomb-chapel of the mastaba of the princess Idut at Saqqara. Two fishermen are pictured plying their trade from a small Papyrus raft. One angler closely inspects the line he has cast, which has multiple hooks on it. He is shown with a small wooden mallet in his left hand, ready to dispatch the fish (one of them a Synodontis catfish) that are nibbling on the hooks below. His companion is bent over, dipping a hand-held net into the water. Sixth Dynasty.

Pl. VIII. This painted limestone relief scene is an outstanding example of an almost standard motif in Old Kingdom tomb-chapel decoration: cowherds with cattle fording a canal. Some of the herders travel across the water by means of a Papyrus raft. A balding man has hold of the forelegs of a young calf, its head turning anxiously for reassurance back to its mother, who follows closely behind with the rest of the herd. Another herder stands on the raft with his right arm upraised and may be reciting a magical 'water spell' to prevent the stealthy crocodile, who carefully watches while submerged below, from attacking the vulnerable beasts as they struggle to cross the stream. From the tomb-chapel of the mastaba of the princess Idut at Saqqara. Sixth Dynasty.

animals and products, one of which is an oryx, more than likely the Beisa Oryx *(Oryx gazella beisa)* of eastern Africa. There is also some textual evidence from the Ramesside Period indicating that captive oryxes entered Egypt from Nubia. The ancient Egyptians also seem to have been acquainted with the Arabian Oryx *(Oryx gazella leucoryx)*, but only as a rare, exotic import during the New Kingdom (see chapter 8).

For many affluent ancient Egyptians, their eternal banquet in the hereafter included meat from two other species of large antelope, the Addax and the Bubal Hartebeest. The shape of their horns is diagnostic, and both can easily be recognized and traced back to the oldest series of Predynastic rock drawings scrawled by hunters on cliff faces along the edge of the Nile Valley and adjacent deserts. On the early First Dynasty ceremonial macehead of King Narmer, now in the Ashmolean Museum, Oxford, a curious detail shows three Bubal Hartebeest in what has been interpreted by some as a paddock, suggesting that this species was being controlled to some degree very early in Egyptian history. Judging from the profusion of

their appearances in all subsequent periods, the Addax and Bubal Hartebeest were probably quite abundant and enjoyed an extensive range in ancient Egypt. Today, however, both have been thoroughly eradicated from their former distributions in the country, and the Bubal Hartebeest is now thought to be completely extinct.

The image of a newborn Bubal Hartebeest was a standard hieroglyphic phonetic sign, and, like the Scimitar-horned Oryx, both the Addax and the Bubal Hartebeest were stock items that skilled artisans included in the traditional desert chase motif in art from the earliest times (fig. 34). Here the scampering wild animals fell prey to hunters' intrepid hounds or were the target of their piercing arrows, often while penned within the large game enclosures. As with the oryx, the Addax and the Bubal Hartebeest are sometimes rendered mating or giving birth (fig. 39). In the decorative program of tomb-chapels during the Old Kingdom, these two antelopes are regularly featured in the file of wild desert fauna brought home from the hunt (fig. 40). Once housed in captivity, they are occasionally depicted wearing collars, be-

Fig. 40. Detail of painted relief depicting a retainer bringing on leashes an offering of a Bubal Hartebeest (left) and an Addax. These animals would have enriched the menu of the deceased. From the tomb-chapel of the mastaba of two senior officials, the two brothers Niankhkhnum and Khnumhotep at Saqqara. Fifth Dynasty.

ing forcibly fed, or eating food from mangers, all to ensure a plump and succulent table dish for the deceased owner of the tomb. Even in the Eighteenth Dynasty, the Bubal Hartebeest was occasionally kept by wealthy Egyptians, presumably for consumption. A fragment of a limestone manger recovered from the area of the north palace at al-Amarna, for example, shows a pair of hartebeest carved in sunk relief, standing before a manger containing fodder, almost certainly indicating that some of their kind were maintained at the site (see chapter 8).

Amid the amazing record of hunting life that has come down to us from ancient Egypt, the Nubian Ibex, still found today in small populations in the Eastern Desert and Sinai, figures as a valued game animal throughout history. The identification of this species presents little difficulty, even

to the untrained eye, with the great circular sweep of its long horns, the long and pointed beard on its chin, and its short tail. In the wealth of Predynastic rock drawings from the Nile Valley, the Nubian Ibex is clearly attested as a desired quarry of early hunters. Its profile can also readily be discerned in long files embellishing ceramic vessels dating from the Gerzean Period (Naqada II), sometimes juxtaposed with equally long painted rows of Greater Flamingoes (*Phoenicopterus ruber*) (fig. 42). In compositions of the pursuit of wild desert animals during the pharaonic period, the Nubian Ibex received special attention (figs. 34, 35). In the tomb-chapel of the Fifth Dynasty mastaba of the prince Raemkaj (no. 80) at Saqqara, for example, a splendid scene in carved relief, now in the Metropolitan Museum of Art, New York, shows huntsmen capturing a small herd of ibexes with lassos on the tawny desert hills, which

Fig. 41. Slab of limestone with sunk relief figures of young Bubal Hartebeests frolicking. This piece was once part of a grand wall scene, probably illustrating the traditional chase of desert game. As such, these young animals may have been among the quarry of the king. From an edifice of Akhenaten at al-Amarna, found at Hermopolis (al-Ashmunein). Eighteenth Dynasty. THE BROOKLYN MUSEUM.

are dotted with bushes. The ibex probably entered the circle of kept animals in ancient Egypt in this way, but the species never became truly domesticated. During the Old Kingdom the animal appears, along with other captive beasts, wearing a collar, being fed by hand, and being led before the deceased as offerings. The ibex was apparently prized enough to be imported occasionally as well. In the Twelfth Dynasty rock-tomb of the nomarch Khnumhotep III (no. 3) at Beni Hasan, a wall painting celebrates the arrival of a group of gaily dressed Asiatic Bedouin, and among the gifts they present is a Nubian Ibex. Likewise, men from the African land of Punt proffer a choice Nubian Ibex to the tomb-owner in the Eighteenth Dynasty tomb-chapel of the vizier Rekhmire (no. 100) at Thebes.

Ibex flesh continued to be a much appreciated delicacy well into the New Kingdom, and the ibex, in addition to being the focus of the chase, was occasionally still kept on estates belonging to the aristocracy. A pair of wonderful Nubian Ibexes is portrayed on a fragment of a limestone manger discovered at the north palace of Akhenaten's short-lived capital city, Akhetaten, at the modern site of al-Amarna, which dates from the Eighteenth Dynasty (fig. 43). These captive animals are shown standing before a trough of fodder themselves, probably indicating that animals just like these were housed on the palace grounds. There is some textual evidence

from the Ramesside Period indicating that supplies of captive ibexes were also imported from Nubia (see chapter 8).

During the Eighteenth Dynasty, the image of a recumbent or kneeling Nubian Ibex developed into a very prolific decorative device, its form gracing, among other things, toilet articles such as cosmetic dishes and combs (fig. 44). This pose is reminiscent of the submissive attitude adopted by a weak ibex to a stronger and more dominant male, and it has been suggested that this image may have been regarded as something of a good-luck charm. The sides of a magnificent wooden armchair discovered in the small tomb (no. 36) of Yuia and Thuya, the parents of Queen Tiye, in the Valley of the Kings, and now housed in the Egyptian Museum, Cairo, are also ornamented with these humbled animals. A small number of sensitive and delightful vases in pottery and alabaster, fashioned like crouching ibexes, can be seen in several museum collections, the finest in the Musée du Louvre, Paris, depicting a fawn nestled against the body of its mother. These containers were probably used for storing cosmetic substances.

Within historical times, the Barbary Sheep probably had an extensive distribution in Egypt. At one time it may have ranged throughout most of the Eastern and part of the Western deserts. In modern Egypt, however, the species is now extremely rare or

perhaps even extinct. First recognized from the white painted decoration on pottery wares from the Amratian Period (Naqada I) (fig. 45), the Barbary Sheep continues to be met with occasionally in Egyptian scenes of the desert hunt from the Old Kingdom to the very close of the Dynastic period (figs. 31, 34, 45, pl. 1). Under the Old Kingdom, the Barbary Sheep can also be counted among the beasts in the traditional file of desert animals presented to the tomb-owner, sometimes simply labeled "young sheep." It would have been a welcome addition to the funerary table. Although the species is somewhat common in these compositions, it is generally used as a decorative space filler, always cast in a rather unassuming role. During the Ramesside Period, though, the Barbary Sheep experiences a brief prominence in Egyptian iconography. A small limestone figured ostracon, for example, originally from the artisans' village at Deir al-Medina in the Theban necropolis and now in the Egyptian Museum, Cairo, features a pair of large males, head-to-head, crashing horns in heated combat, precisely as they do in the wild. In fact, the Barbary Sheep was apparently regarded by this community of workers as a manifestation of the great god Amun, and a small group of limestone ostraca from this vicinity are known to have been used as votive offerings to the powerful deity, bearing images of this very distinctive creature.

There is an abundance of pictorial evidence indicating that the ancient Egyptians were familiar with two native species of gazelle and represented them in art and hieroglyphs: the Dorcas Gazelle and Soemmering's Gazelle. They may also have known the Persian Gazelle (*Gazella subgutturosa*) from western Asia, but only as an extremely rare import (see chapter 8). Famed for their nervous energy, graceful movement, and beauty, these handsome, medium-sized antelopes formed an important exploitable food and sportive resource in antiquity. They also had symbolic significance and were occasionally even befriended and raised as household pets (see chapter 4). Of the two, the slender Dorcas Gazelle—distinguished by its more or less S-shaped horns—is by far the more routinely encountered in art, and is known from scores of examples from all ages. The Dorcas Gazelle continues to remain comparatively plentiful in modern Egypt but is now seriously threatened by unregulated hunting with firearms. The Soemmering's Gazelle was very rarely depicted in the iconography and may always have been uncommon in Egypt in ancient times. It has never been documented in modern Egypt, and it is not known when it became extinct.

Fig. 42. (opposite) This pottery vessel with deep red painted decoration against a light buff-colored ground, features a motif of a long file of Nubian Ibexes and, below, a row of Greater Flamingoes. The precise significance of these designs remains obscure. Gerzean Period (Naqada II). THE METROPOLITAN MUSEUM OF ART, NEW YORK.

Fig. 43. Fragment of a limestone manger displaying a pair of deftly executed Nubian Ibexes in sunk relief standing before a feeding-trough full of fodder. From al-Amarna. Eighteenth Dynasty. THE TOLEDO MUSEUM OF ART.

Fig. 44. An acacia-wood comb with a handle decoration of a kneeling Nubian Ibex. Eighteenth Dynasty. MUSÉE DU LOUVRE, PARIS.

One indisputable example of this species is clearly portrayed in the file of desert animals in the tomb-chapel of the Fifth Dynasty mastaba of Ptahhotep II (D 64) at Saqqara.

There is already proof of gazelle trapping during the Gerzean Period (Naqada II), evidenced by the famous wall painting in tomb 100 at Hierakonpolis. It is still largely a matter of conjecture whether or not the early Predynastic Egyptians hunted gazelles using desert 'kites' (large stone corral traps into which animal herds were driven), as a number of writers have maintained, and the confirmation of their use during the Dynastic period is even more tenuous. Some have claimed that one of these structures is depicted on the monumental First Dynasty palette of King Narmer, now in the Egyptian Museum, Cairo, but the small sign in question is open to other interpretations. A number of Predynastic cemeteries contained burials of gazelles, presumably intended to serve as food offerings for the human beings interred nearby. Other burials have been described as pets or sacred animals; some of these gazelles were wrapped in mats and even provided with grave goods. All

Fig. 45. White-on-red decoration on a tall pottery vessel showing a group of horned animals. These painted figures are difficult to identify, but the larger beast, told by the shape of its horns and long hair, is almost certainly a Barbary Sheep. From Naqada, in Upper Egypt. Amratian Period (Naqada I).

ASHMOLEAN MUSEUM, OXFORD.

Fig. 46. This detail of carved limestone relief exhibits a deer, with a large rack of antlers, being led forward by two attendants in the file of desert animals represented in the tomb-chapel of the mastaba of Ti (no. 60) at Saqqara. The caption above the beast's back identifies it: hnn, 'deer.' Fifth Dynasty.

Fig. 47. (below) A unique electrum diadem that once belonged to a queen or princess. The band of the piece is decorated with four rosettes and four gazelles' heads, two of each placed on either side of a large, central element of a deer's head with a tall rack of antlers. From the eastern Delta. Fifteenth Dynasty (Hyksos Period)?

this seems to suggest some management of this wild species. But bone remains previously thought to be gazelle from at least one site, Wadi Digla, have now been shown to be kid and/or lamb, so perhaps there should be some question about the identification of the other finds.

From the Early Dynastic Period through the Middle Kingdom, Dorcas Gazelles regularly appear in tomb scenes of the chase, with fierce hunting dogs grappling them or nipping at their hind legs as they flee, just as they are about to be brought down

(figs. 34, 35, pls. II, XVIII). Both the Dorcas Gazelle and the rarer Soemmering's Gazelle are also pictured at this time in processions of wild desert game delivered by hunters to the deceased on tomb-chapel walls, and they were taken into captivity and raised on the agricultural estates of the wealthy, where they appear wearing collars, being force-fed by attendants, or eating fodder from troughs in stalls.

An Eleventh Dynasty rock inscription in Wadi Hammamat in the Eastern Desert relates an auspicious event that occurred

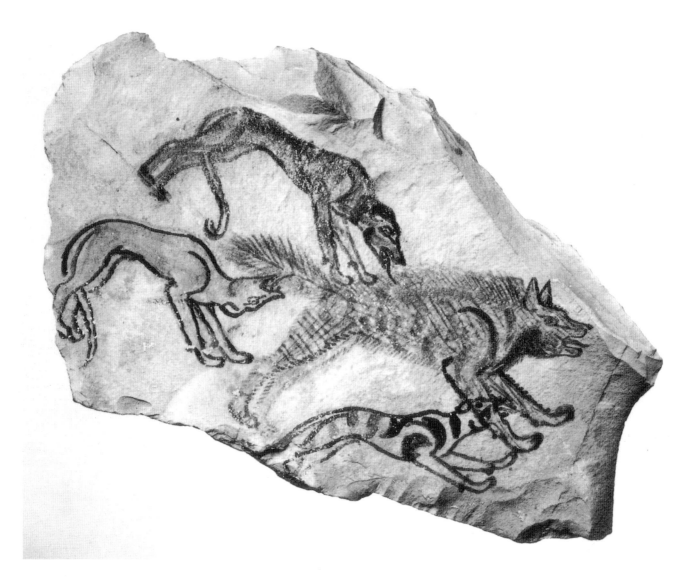

nearby: during a quarrying expedition for a sarcophagus for King Mentuhotep IV, the sarcophagus lid was selected from a great block of stone on which a gazelle gave birth while the gang of workmen looked on in awe. In the painted decoration of the large Middle Kingdom rock-tombs at Beni Hasan, images of gazelles abound: being forcibly fed, in small herds under the charge of keepers brandishing sticks, being brought by offering bearers, and of course as a ubiquitous element of every desert hunting composition. In the Twelfth Dynasty tomb of the nomarch Khnumhotep III (no. 3), a group of Asiatic Bedouin present what appears to be a Dorcas Gazelle, though it

may be a foreign species. On the Nineteenth Dynasty rock-hewn temple of Ramesses II at Beit al-Wali in Lower Nubia, the monarch is pictured receiving what is probably an exotic gazelle as part of Nubian tribute, and gazelles are also listed in accounts of tribute or booty from Nubia in Ramesside texts.

During the New Kingdom, the Dorcas Gazelle certainly continued to be among the more popular creatures of the desert pursuit (pl. XVIII), and its form developed into a widespread decorative motif (see chapter 4). It was also one of the wild creatures of the desert represented in scenes greeting the rising sun at dawn, 'dancing' on its hind

Fig. 48. This figured limestone ostracon, approximately the size of a human hand, bears a superb red and black ink drawing of three hunting dogs savagely attacking a fleeing Striped Hyena. The sense of terror and panic of the pursued beast—the fur of its coat standing erect and its long red tongue extended—has been admirably conveyed by the artisan. From Deir al-Medina. Ramesside Period.
MUSÉE DU LOUVRE, PARIS.

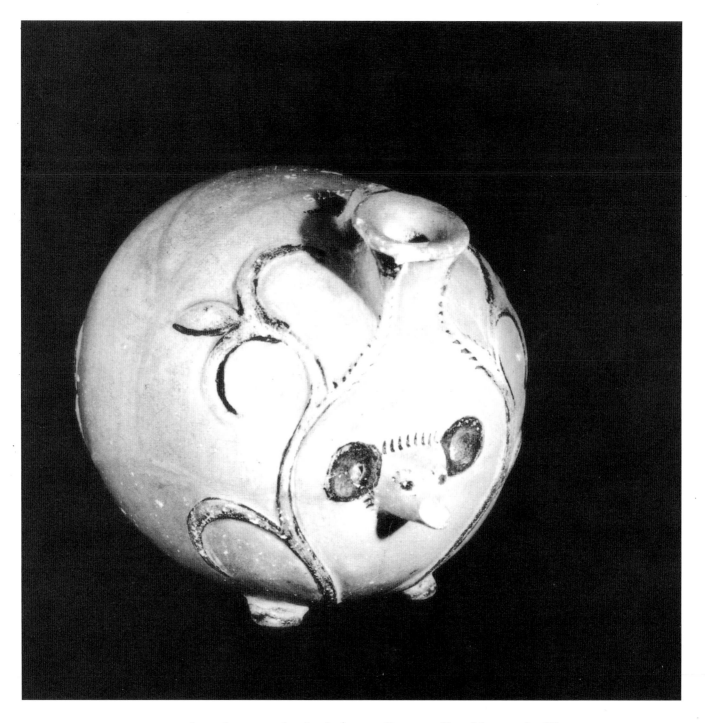

legs. As a sacred animal, the gazelle was regarded as the earthly manifestation of the huntress Anukis, a goddess of the divine triad of Elephantine Island, near the First Cataract. During the Late Dynastic and Greco–Roman periods, gazelles were ritually mummified: cemeteries containing great numbers have been discovered at several locations, including Dendara, and an especially extensive one has been uncovered at Kom Mer, south of Esna.

The image of a speeding gazelle fleeing from the hunt is recalled poignantly in a love poem from the New Kingdom: "O that you came to your sister [i.e., lover] swiftly, like a bounding gazelle in the wild; its feet reel, its limbs are weary, terror has entered its body. A hunter pursues it with his hounds, they do not see (it in) its dust; it sees a resting place as a (trap?), it takes the river as road. May you attain her hiding-place, before your hand is kissed four times; as you pursue your sister's love, the Golden gives her to you, my friend!"[11]

Among the great many representations of wild animals in ancient Egyptian art, no more than thirty-five or so can be confidently identified as deer. Readily recognized by the characteristic large rack of antlers of the male, their appearances range in date from the Late Predynastic Period (Naqada III) down through the mid-Eighteenth Dynasty. The Egyptian monuments then maintain a complete silence, after which they vanish until the last quarter of the fourth century B.C., just prior to the Ptolemaic Period, when two beasts are shown being brought as offerings in the grand tomb-chapel of Petosiris at Tuna al-Gebel. Generally, deer are confined to scenes of the desert hunt and files of captured game delivered to the deceased on tomb-chapel walls, particularly in the Old and Middle Kingdoms (figs. 35, 46). A notable exception to the foregoing is a remarkable and skillfully fashioned electrum diadem, perhaps from the Fifteenth Dynasty (the Hyksos Period), on which the central animal head is represented in the form of a great deer's head is flanked by four gazelle heads and rosettes (fig. 47). It must be noted, however, that the dating of this piece is not entirely certain and it could also be of Egyptian manufacture, merely showing western Asiatic influence. By the reign of Tuthmosis III in the Eighteenth Dynasty, deer were apparently so rare in ancient Egypt that this warrior pharaoh had recorded in his 'annals' at the temple of Karnak the arrival in year thirty-eight of his reign of a foreign specimen as tribute or trade from Syria.

The identification and source of the deer species in ancient Egyptian art have been the subject of considerable discussion over the years. This is because, with the exception of the Barbary Red Deer (*Cervus elaphus barbarus*), which occurs in Tunisia, and possibly the European Fallow Deer (*Dama dama*

dama), which inhabited parts of Libya, Tunisia, and Algeria until late in the last century, deer are not generally regarded as indigenous to the African continent. There are currently no wild deer in Egypt, though there is some evidence that a possibly introduced population of fallow deer was known here during the sixteenth century A.D., and it is quite likely that this population continued to live in the Wadi Natrun into the nineteenth century. Since there seems to be a complete absence of fossil evidence for deer in Egypt and no osteological proof of them from Predynastic settlement sites along the Nile Valley, the question has been: where did the deer known to the ancient Egyptians originate? Were deer part of the original faunal community of the country, were they introduced in the Predynastic Period, or were they known to the Egyptians only from exotic imports from western Asia? And what species were they? This mystery cannot as yet be solved conclusively. Since the ancient Egyptians clearly wished to create the impression that deer were part of the landscape, whether naturally occurring or introduced, it is probably not too presumptuous simply to accept their records at face value. The relative scarcity of deer in art, the unfamiliarity displayed by the artisans in reproducing them, and their infrequent mention in texts would seem to speak of their extreme rarity. However, the identity of at least some of the deer appears to have been settled by recent zooarchaeological findings from the royal palace at Piramesse, near Qantir, the Delta residence of the Ramesside kings, where the existence of the Persian Fallow Deer (*Dama dama mesopotamica*) has apparently been firmly established (see chapter 8).

From a twentieth-century Western point of view, perhaps the most surprising animal kept by the ancient Egyptians—and relished as an article of food by some of the aristocracy—was the Striped Hyena. Apparently once abundant in the arid uplands bordering the length of the Nile Valley, the Striped Hyena survives in present-

Fig. 49. (opposite) A delightful pottery vessel fashioned in the characteristic spherical shape a living hedgehog assumes when threatened with danger. The humorous appeal of this vase is heightened by its pointed snout, tiny legs, and overly large ears. From Abydos. Eighteenth Dynasty.
ASHMOLEAN MUSEUM, OXFORD.

Fig. 50. This deep cerulean blue faience figurine amply suggests the thick coat of spines that cover the body of a hedgehog. During the Middle Kingdom, statuettes like this one were occasionally placed in burials, but their purpose is by no means certain. They quite likely held some symbolic meaning. Perhaps the hedgehog's protective spines made the beast a benevolent aid to the deceased. From Abydos. Twelfth or Thirteenth Dynasty. ASHMOLEAN MUSEUM, OXFORD.

day Egypt in vastly reduced numbers and limited range. From remote times, this dog-like carnivore was an enormously popular hunted species in ancient Egypt, and it is a recurrent figure amid the mêlée of wild animals depicted in desperate flight in scenes of the desert chase on both royal and private funerary monuments of every period (figs. 34, 35). Egyptian artisans seem to have felt especially free and creative when portraying hyenas in these compositions. Many include closely observed and animated representations of the creatures bloodied from wounds inflicted by bowmen, writhing in pain and trying to dislodge arrows lodged in their muzzles, leaping wildly, spontaneously defecating in terror, and fleeing with manes erect while packs of eager dogs trail them in hot pursuit (fig. 48).

The height of appreciation for this species on the bill of fare of tomb-owners seems to have been reached during the Old Kingdom. In several tomb-chapels of

notables at Saqqara, such as the magnificent Sixth Dynasty mastaba of the vizier Mereruka, seemingly tame Striped Hyenas are illustrated wearing collars, securely tethered to the ground, and kept along with farmyard animals on Mereruka's agricultural estates. They are shown lying on their backs with their legs bound together with cord, while being forced-fed until they are entirely stuffed (pl. XI). In the Sixth Dynasty tomb-chapel of the mastaba of the vizier Kagemni (LS 10) at Saqqara, hyenas are forced to swallow entire trussed ducks or geese! On other Old Kingdom tomb-chapel walls at Saqqara, Giza, and elsewhere, the Striped Hyena can be seen in the traditional procession of men leading desert animals and proffering them to the deceased, often with captions above them giving their number or simply labeling them as "young hyena." From this considerable body of evidence, it is clear that the ancient Egyptians kept hyenas in captivity and that they were fattened for the funerary table—and presumably eaten in everyday life too—but there is no suggestion of controlled breeding. Most hyenas were caught alive during hunting forays along the desert margins and then held and fed until slaughter. Hyenas were still occasionally taken alive in the New Kingdom, as evidenced by a vignette in the Eighteenth Dynasty tomb-chapel of User (no. 21) at Thebes, where one is borne fresh from the hunt, slung on a pole, by two attendants. That the ancient Egyptians knew the scavenging and opportunist feeding behavior of this carnivore is clearly revealed by the fact that, during the close of the Ramesside Period, when the Egyptian countryside was in the grips of a terrible famine, one year was appropriately dubbed "the year of the hyenas."

Possibly the most extraordinary example of the Striped Hyena that has come down to us from ancient Egypt is to be found in the Eighteenth Dynasty tomb-chapel of Amunemhab (no. 85) at Thebes. This justly well-known and frequently reproduced painting features the valiant tomb-owner, armed with only a long spear and a stick, on a (foreign?) landscape covered with all manner of strange plants and flowers, about to do battle with an enormous, menacing-looking female Striped Hyena. Such one-on-one mortal combats are extremely rare in private tomb decoration, and this occurrence is especially vivid.

It has often been suggested over the years that the ancient Egyptians employed trained hyenas in the pursuit of desert game, just as they used dogs, but this seems highly doubtful, and firm proof is wanting. It has been asserted more than once, for instance, that a composition in the Fifth Dynasty tomb-chapel of Ptahhotep II (D 64) at Saqqara features hyenas performing just this function: but there is no doubt that the huntsman pictured here with some hounds and with captured hyenas on leashes should more correctly be interpreted as part of the traditional file of men bringing the spoils of

the chase to the deceased owner of the tomb. The several hyenas under his charge are food offerings, not his trained helpers. The Egyptians' supposed use of Striped Hyenas as hunting 'dogs' is one of those long-held myths that is difficult to do away with, because it has been so often repeated. Similarly, it is very unlikely that the ancient Egyptians ever employed the Leopard *(Panthera pardus)* or the Cheetah *(Acinonyx jubatus)* in hunting, although it is routinely and rather matter-of-factly stated in both the Egyptological and zoological literatures that they did so. Both of these feline species were occasionally kept in captivity by royalty (see chapters 4 and 8), but they did not serve the ancient Egyptians as helpers to run down desert game.

Two small mammals found as a stock component of practically every extant Egyptian desert hunting scene are the Cape Hare and the hedgehog. They are typically glimpsed scurrying across the undulating scrub terrain, or at repose outside the main action (figs. 34, 35, pl. xvii). The hedgehog's appearance is unmistakable: stubby legs, very short tail, pig-like snout, and a thick coat of spines. This small creature may seem a rather odd game animal for pleasure-seeking sportsmen and others to pursue for a table dish, but wild hedgehogs were captured by Egyptian hunters, and they can sometimes be recognized being carried in cages by offering-bearers on tomb-chapel walls in both the Old and Middle kingdoms. Their peculiar defensive posture, in which they curl themselves up tightly into a ball when threatened by enemies, covering their vulnerable parts with stiff bristles, was well understood by the ancient Egyptian artisans, and is admirably suggested in some representations of them in the round (figs. 49, 50). The image of the hedgehog also seems to have possessed apotropaic powers: the large backward-facing head of a hedgehog appears on the upturned prow of Old Kingdom traveling ships. Perhaps, as a protective

Fig. 51. An appealing faience figurine of a recumbent Cape Hare, its long ears drawn back, resting on a rectangular base. As with the hedgehog model in fig. 50, the precise function of the Cape Hare statuette in a human burial remains unclear. Since the ancient Egyptians ate hares, its purpose may lie in this sphere, or perhaps the species' well-known fertility was hoped for. From al-Lahun. Twelfth Dynasty.
ÄGYPTISCHES MUSEUM, BERLIN.

device, its spiny back could magically prevent the vessel from running aground on sandbanks or dispel other dangers lurking beneath the murky Nile waters. The hedgehog's magical properties may also explain its frequent appearance in the form of vessels, statuettes, scaraboids, and amulets.

Probably the earliest instance of a Cape Hare in Egyptian art is on the elaborately decorated commemorative or votive dark schist Hunters' Palette from the Late Predynastic Period (Naqada III), now in the British Museum, London, where the creature figures in a desert hunting scene. The species also appears as a standard hieroglyphic phonetic sign. During the Middle Kingdom, faience figurines of the Cape Hare were occasionally deposited in tombs, and their presence here probably means the figures had some magical or amuletic significance (fig. 51). Perhaps their legendary fecundity came into play here.

The diverse menu of prosperous ancient Egyptians during all ages was occasionally enriched by hare, bagged by ruling kings and high nobility alike. Particularly during the Eighteenth Dynasty, Cape Hares appear among the multitude of offerings delivered to the deceased by bear-

ers on tomb-chapel walls. An especially well-observed pair of them appear on a fragment of wall painting from the unlocated Eighteenth Dynasty tomb-chapel of Nebamun at Thebes, carried by their long ears by an attendant in a procession (fig. 52). During the New Kingdom, the image of the hare was sometimes used as a decorative motif, particularly on toiletries. As a sacred animal, the Cape Hare was associated with the goddess Wenut ('the Swift One') of Hermopolis, in Middle Egypt. During the Late Dynastic and Ptolemaic periods, there are several finely cast bronze votive statuettes, and a great number of small faience amulets in the shape of Cape Hares, which give an indication of its revered status during these times.

During the New Kingdom, sensational big-game hunting adventures—especially of rhinoceros, elephant, and the quarry valued above all others, the Lion—appear to have been strictly a royal prerogative. These relatively rare animals and other exotics never figure in scenes of the chase in the tomb-chapels of New Kingdom nobles, who seemingly had to be satisfied with the traditional indigenous game beasts.

Although it had been known in Egypt during Predynastic times (figs. 30, 31), the great African Elephant had been entirely exterminated from the country for better than ten centuries by the beginning of the Eighteenth Dynasty. But stalwart warrior kings of this dynamic period, while on arduous military campaigns into western Asia, encountered and seized the opportunity to hunt the now wholly extinct Syrian Elephant (*Elephas maximus asurus*) for sport and to obtain its valuable ivory tusks. Inscriptions inform us that the ancient Egyptians met with herds of the beast in northern Syria, in the ancient land of Niya (Qalat al-Mudikh). The energetic King Tuthmosis III paused from waging war there and indulged in elephant hunting in nearby marshes. He is said to have bagged 120 of them almost single-handedly. In doing so, he was following the earlier example of his grandfather Tuthmosis I, who had also pursued elephants here. Tuthmosis III was aided by his trusted officer Amunemhab, famous for his battle with the Striped Hyena (see above), who relates in the fascinating autobiographical inscription in his Theban tomb-chapel (no. 85) that he distinguished himself by cutting off the trunk of the largest elephant while it was still alive, before the giant could harm the sovereign. For this act of bravery the king suitably rewarded Amunemhab, who eventually rose to the rank of 'Lieutenant-Commander of Soldiers.' An exotic rhinoceros was also taken by Tuthmosis III with bow and arrow while campaigning in Lower Nubia (see chapter 8).

A remarkably detailed account of the hunting of a great herd of wild cattle (Aurochs) along the desert margin by Amenhotep III during the Eighteenth Dynasty is preserved on a series of large, commemorative scarabs issued to mark the monarch's heroic feat. The text inscribed on the scarabs is worth quoting at some length, since it successfully captures the charged atmosphere and operation of the royal chase:

> A wonderful thing happened to His Majesty. A messenger came to tell His Majesty that there were wild cattle upon the desert of the district of Shetep [Wadi Natrun?]; His Majesty thereupon floated down river in the royal dahabiyeh, 'Shining-in-Truth,' at the time of the evening, and after having had a

Fig. 52. Fragment of wall painting illustrating a procession of offering-bearers bringing produce of the fields for the funerary banquet: sheaves of grain, vegetables, a young gazelle, and a pair of Cape Hares. From the unlocated tomb-chapel of the scribe Nebamun at Thebes. Eighteenth Dynasty. THE BRITISH MUSEUM, LONDON.

Fig. 53. This figured limestone ostracon bears a vigorous black and red ink drawing of a king, accompanied by his dog, slaying a charging Lion with a spear. The king wears the red crown of Lower Egypt and is dressed in a tunic with an elaborate kilt. This small piece was found by Howard Carter near the entrance to the tomb of Tutankhamun (no. 62) in the Valley of the Kings, and originally it was thought to depict Tutankhamun himself. On stylistic grounds, however, this drawing is more probably the work of an artisan of the Ramesside Period. The hieratic inscription sings the praises of the unnamed monarch. THE METROPOLITAN MUSEUM OF ART, NEW YORK.

good journey, arrived in safety at the district of Shetep at the time of the morning. His Majesty mounted upon a horse [i.e., in his chariot], and his whole army followed him. The nobles and the *'ankhu* officers of the entire army were marshalled, and the children of the quarter were ordered to keep watch upon these wild cattle. His Majesty thereupon ordered that they should surround these wild cattle with a net and a ditch and His Majesty then ordered that these wild cattle should be counted in their entirety, and the number of them amounted to wild cattle 190. The number . . . which His Majesty brought in by his own hunting in this day was 56. His Majesty rested four days in order to give spirit to his horses; then His Majesty mounted again upon a horse and the number of these wild cattle which were brought to him in hunting was, wild cattle 20 plus 20; making the total number . . . captured 96.[12]

This same illustrious 'sportsman-king' boasted on another series of commemorative scarabs that he brought down with his own arrows 102 savage Lions during the course of his first ten years on the throne. The hunting park where Amenhotep III may have slain such Lions has apparently been located at the site of his jubilee temple at Soleb in Upper Nubia (see above).

Whereas most such tales of the hunt probably actually happened, the best known and most impressive representation of Lion hunting in ancient Egyptian art surely did not. On the extraordinary 'painted box' from the Eighteenth Dynasty tomb of Tutankhamun (no. 62) in the Valley of the Kings, now in the Egyptian Museum, Cairo, the youthful monarch is portrayed in a desert hunting scene in a swift horse-drawn chariot utterly routing a company of Lions. The Lions lie strewn about the landscape, their bodies riddled with the king's arrows, having easily fallen to his overwhelming, apparently superhuman power. Other New Kingdom pharaohs were shown in a simi-larly conventionalized manner battling a Lion. Generally armed with only a single weapon and accompanied by a faithful hound, they thrust a long spear into the body of a fierce, charging Lion (fig. 53) or smite the noble beast with a curved *khepesh*-sword or a mace.

Fig. 54. Ceremonial or votive palette in gray schist with relief decoration, showing, on the side illustrated here, a pack of four heraldic Cape Hunting Dogs surrounding two Giraffes, which flank a tall Date Palm. Both of these African species must have become locally extinct in ancient Egypt before the close of the Early Dynastic Period. Late Predynastic Period (Naqada III). MUSÉE DU LOUVRE, PARIS.

Chapter Four

The Pleasures of Pets

*T*he ancient Egyptians' tremendous fondness for animals can be observed in their age-old and well-documented practice of keeping household pets. They were great pet-fanciers and took considerable delight in portraying these cherished animals in art, close at their sides, a constant source of joy and pleasure in their daily lives. Their love of pets strikes a chord with many of us today, and

helps to narrow the gap of the many millennia that separates our times. The ancient Egyptians seem less remote and more human when portrayed with their favorite household pets close at hand. Through the power of picture and word, the Egyptians believed that by including images of their beloved animal companions with them on the walls of their tomb-chapels and elsewhere, their pets would be able to accompany them and share in the afterlife. In this chapter, we survey a number of the animals from the diverse range of species that were kept as domestic pets: dogs *(Canis familiaris),* cats *(Felis catus),* the Green or Vervet Monkey *(Cercopithecus aethiops),* the Hamadryas Baboon *(Papio hamadryas),* the Olive or Anubis Baboon *(Papio cynocephalus anubis),* the Dorcas Gazelle, the Pintail duck *(Anas acuta),* and the Hoopoe *(Upupa epops)* among others. A few domestic creatures also had powerful symbolical associations, which no doubt led to them being kept as pets, such as the majestic Lion and the ever pugnacious Egyptian Goose *(Alopochen aegyptiacus).*

As much the faithful companion in antiquity as today, the domestic dog was always regarded by the ancient Egyptians as the pet *par excellence,* the subject of special attention and heartfelt affection. Dogs are featured in Egyptian iconography in the company of monarch, aristocrat, and humble field laborer alike, as both pet and worker. There has been a long and highly successful relationship between human and canine. Dogs were the earliest animals to be domesticated: the progenitor of the dog, and ancestor of every breed, was the Common Wolf *(Canis lupus),* whose domestication is thought to have begun at least twelve thousand years ago in western Asia. The link between humans and dogs was forged and evolved as a response to the need for them to become hunting partners, cooperatively working together rather than competing independently for the same food.

The oldest securely dated appearance of the domestic dog in ancient Egypt occurs on a well-known, and frequently reproduced, handsome Predynastic bowl from

Fig. 55. In this relief detail we glimpse a scene of country life. A partially balding peasant sitting in a portable seat made of reed matting is holding in his arms a young puppy, which he is feeding in a curious mouth-to-mouth fashion. A man standing just to the left of the action is holding what is probably a jar of milk. Perhaps the peasant is attempting to wean the puppy with milk placed on his tongue, allowing the dog to gently lick it off. Several writers have maintained over the course of the years that this animal is not a dog but a piglet! However, the fact alone that no image of a pig is otherwise documented from Old Kingdom temple or tomb-chapel wall decoration argues for its identification as a puppy, as indeed most authorities have long maintained. Note too that the animal has paws, not the hoofs of a pig. From the tomb-chapel of the mastaba of the vizier Kagemni (LS 10) at Saqqara. Sixth Dynasty.

the Amratian Period (Naqada I), now housed in the collections of the Pushkin State Museum of Fine Arts, Moscow. The white, painted decoration depicts an Egyptian huntsman carrying a bow and arrows in one hand and holding on to four dogs on leashes with the other. From their characteristic build, their erect, pointed ears, and their short, curled tails, these are clearly a type of greyhound. Two of these hounds are also dramatically pictured on a small, black steatite gaming disk with colored inlays found at Saqqara in the First Dynasty tomb of Hemaka (S 3035), a high official in the reign of King Den. They are vividly depicted attacking and dispatch-

ing a pair of Dorcas Gazelles (pl. II). This sleek and sinewy hunting hound, almost always rendered sporting a collar so that it can be leashed, is the most commonly portrayed type of dog in Egyptian art throughout the Old Kingdom. Some scholars have seen a strong resemblance between this breed and the modern Sudanese basenji.

Other breeds of dog already existed during the Predynastic Period: one had small, floppy ears and a short, straight tail, a variety that continues to be represented during the Old Kingdom. We should note here that the Egyptians of Predynastic times were also well acquainted with a species of wild dog, the Cape Hunting Dog (*Lycaon pictus)*, which should not be confused with the domestic hound. These pack-hunting carnivores are prominently displayed on a number of superbly decorated Late Predynastic Period (Naqada III) dark schist ceremonial or votive palettes (fig. 54, pl. I) surrounding their prey. The Cape Hunting Dog does not appear in the faunal repertoire of artisans during the Dynastic period, and more likely than not had become locally extinct or very rare fairly soon after the rise of the First Dynasty. Today, one would have to go much further south on the African continent to find the Cape Hunting Dog, which now lives mostly on the sub-Saharan savannas.

From its earliest appearance in the country, the domestic dog was primarily employed in the hunt. Presumably, however, it must have filled other roles too, particularly as an aid to herders and farmers, who may have trained their dogs to guard flocks and crops from marauding wild animals. Some Predynastic dogs discovered buried in cemeteries near graves of humans at the sites of Maadi, Wadi Digla, and Heliopolis in Lower Egypt, for example, have routinely been interpreted by archaeologists as watchdogs. The same is true for a greyhound that was uncovered guarding the entrance to a large First Dynasty tomb (S 3507) at Saqqara. One of the first kings of the First Dynasty had his pet dogs interred near his tomb complex at Abydos, each provided with a stone stela bearing its name. These animals were very likely dispatched at the time of the king's death in order that they might accompany him in the netherworld. This practice probably occurred in later times as well: in the intact royal tomb of Psusennes I of the Twenty-first Dynasty discovered at San al-Hagar (Tanis) in the Delta, for example, the French excavator Pierre Montet found the skeleton of the king's favorite dog interred along with him in the burial chamber, watching over the sepulcher for eternity. During the Old Kingdom, one royal watchdog so pleased a king of the Fifth or Sixth

Dynasty that it was rewarded with a fine burial at Giza (G 2188). An inscription carved on a limestone block from the tomb-chapel reads:

> The dog which was the guard of His Majesty. Abuwtiyuw [*'bwtyw*] is his name. His Majesty ordered that he be buried (ceremonially), that he be given a coffin from the royal treasury, fine linen in great quantity, (and) incense. His Majesty (also) gave perfumed ointment, and (ordered) that a tomb be built for him by the gangs of masons. His Majesty did this for him in order that he (the dog) might be honored.[13]

An especially intriguing and much discussed detail of limestone relief, found in the Sixth Dynasty tomb-chapel of the mastaba of the vizier Kagemni (LS 10) at Saqqara, illustrates a pendant-eared puppy being fed in a unique mouth-to-mouth fashion by a farmhand resting in a portable seat (fig. 55), perhaps attempting to wean the young animal with milk placed on his tongue.

From the early Middle Kingdom onward, a wider variety of breeds of dog are portrayed, including a curious type of low-slung dog with erect ears, not identifiable with a specific modern breed but somewhat resembling a dachshund. Other dogs are reminiscent of mastiffs, and even the village mongrels appear. Certainly by the time of the New Kingdom, the renowned saluki was regularly figured (figs. 48, 53, pl. XXXII), especially at the side of royalty or the elite. Scenes executed on tomb-chapel and temple walls, in addition to textual evidence, show that by the time of the New Kingdom the ancient Egyptians also imported considerable numbers of foreign dogs from Punt, Nubia, Libya, and possibly also western Asia, as part of trade, tribute, or the spoils of warfare (pl. XV). Already during the Eleventh Dynasty, King Wahankh Intef II was so proud of his pack of five exotic dogs that he had them recorded near his feet on the lower part of a funerary stela from his tomb-chapel at Thebes (fig. 56). Probably most great landowners in ancient Egypt, as well as the royal family itself, maintained substantial numbers of dogs on their estates, which would have performed a variety of functions and tasks. The excavators of Akhenaten's Eighteenth Dynasty capital city of Akhetaten at al-Amarna uncovered a building they later identified as kennels for the royal hounds, due to the great quantity of greyhound skeletal remains they discovered there.

When not at their masters' sides viewing activities on their estates, venturing out on the desert hunt (figs. 34, 35), accompanying the king into battle, assisting in the policing of the deserts, or helping herdsmen to shepherd flocks, dogs are frequently pictured as everyday household pets sitting, ever alert, under their owners' chairs, especially in the tomb-chapels of the privileged classes (pl. XXXII). During the Old and Middle kingdoms, affluent ancient Egyptians often placed their pets under the charge of a keeper, who was occasionally an achondroplastic dwarf. Accompanying short inscriptions written above them sometimes name these favored dogs. To date, approximately seventy-seven examples of dogs with names are known. Some of these names may provide a hint of the individual's occupation in life. For instance, a handsome pet dog led on a leash by its owner painted on one face of the early Twelfth Dynasty wooden coffin of Khuw, from his tomb (no. 8) at Asyut in Middle Egypt (fig. 57), is labeled with its name: Menyupu, 'He is a Shepherd.' Another hound bore the descriptive name 'the Good Watcher.' Indicative of the dog's comparatively high status in ancient Egyptian thought, and of the Egyptians' attachment to pet dogs as family members, the names given to these pet dogs are also sometimes the same as those given to human beings. Ancient Egyptian animals other than dogs were rarely given personal names of any kind.

Beloved dogs were sometimes honored by their owners with a fine burial in a coffin. A touching epithet inscribed on a small Middle Kingdom wooden coffin made for a pet female, now in the Musées Royaux d'Art et d'Histoire, Brussels, reads:

"The loved of her mistress, Aya [the 'Woofer'?]." The Eighteenth Dynasty tomb of the courtier Maiherperi (no. 36), in the Valley of the Kings, contained a pair of wonderfully crafted wide dog collars of colored and gilded leather, now in the Egyptian Museum, Cairo. One was inscribed with the pet's name: Taentniuwet, 'She of the Town [Thebes].' Since the dogs that wore these finely decorated collars were not included in Maiherperi's burial, they may have served as mementos to remind him of his loyal companions.

During the Late Dynastic and Greco–Roman periods, many hundreds of thousands of Egyptian dogs of differing breeds were mummified and buried en masse. These later dog interments have been discovered in animal cemeteries at a number of sites scattered throughout the country, including Abydos, Hiw, Asyut, Koptos, Speos Artemidos, al-Lisht, and Saqqara. But the animals were not thus treated because they were prized pets, rather because during these later times the dog was vitally connected with the gods Anubis, Wepwawet, and other sacred funerary canine figures. The precise identification of Anubis' sacred beast (sometimes also associated with other deities) has stirred much spirited debate over the years, though it seems clear that Ludwig Keimer came closest long ago when he stated that the representation of Anubis' form was principally fashioned after the Common or Golden Jackal (*Canis aureus lupaster*) but was influenced by other species as well. Always depicted entirely black, a color of resurrection and rebirth, Anubis was the jackal-headed embalmer of the dead and protector of human burials in his role as lord and sentinel of the necropolis (figs. 2, 58, 93). Certainly, the most widely known and deftly executed image of Anubis that has come down to us from ancient Egypt is the powerful recumbent statue of him on top of a gilded shrine from the Eighteenth Dynasty tomb of Tutankhamun (no. 62) in the Valley of the Kings (fig. 59), where the lanky creature acted as a divine watchdog and guarded the entrance to the innermost tomb chamber against any intruder.

In rural Egypt and elsewhere in the Middle East today, packs of half-starved stray and feral dogs sometimes prowl at night along the desert margins, in the fields, the ruins, and in village streets. Unexpectedly meeting up with one of these fierce packs on a lonely desert track without a staff or other form of protection can be a frightening experience. This was apparently also the case in antiquity: in an amusing letter preserved from the Ramesside Period, an Egyptian official complains of the hardships of his post abroad, a godforsaken hellhole where he encounters fierce packs of dogs:

> If ever a flask full of beer of Kedy is opened, and people go out to get a cup (of it), there are 200 large dogs as well as 300 jackals, 500 in all, and they stand in readiness every day at the door of the house as often as I go out through their smelling the liquor when the jar is opened. What if I had not the little jackal of the royal scribe Nhihu here in the

Fig. 56. Detail of carved relief on the famous limestone funerary stela of King Wahankh Intef II from his Theban tomb-chapel, picturing three of the king's five foreign dogs at his feet. The names inscribed above the dogs are Libyan, but in two instances an Egyptian translation is conveniently provided just to the side: the uppermost dog's name is 'Oryx'; the name of the second is not translated, but probably means 'Hound'; and the bottom dog is called 'Black One.' Eleventh Dynasty. THE EGYPTIAN MUSEUM, CAIRO.

Fig. 57. This painted detail appears on an outer face of the wooden coffin of Khuw. It shows, against a yellowish ground, a lively little group in red, white, and black. The deceased holds a stick with a hand on one end and leads his black and white dog on a leash. In faint blue hieroglyphs above the dog's back, the faithful companion is named: Menyupu, 'He is a Shepherd.' From the tomb of Khuw (no. 8) at Asyut. Twelfth Dynasty. THE EGYPTIAN MUSEUM, CAIRO.

house! It is it that saves me from them again and again, as often as I go out. It is ever with me as a leader upon the road. Then it barks, and I run to put the bolt on . . . .[14]

In the New Kingdom tale of *The Two Brothers*, the fate of the wicked wife was to be slain and cast to the dogs, probably a wild pack of feral canines. Another famous story, that of *Setne Khamwas and Naneferkaptah*, written during the Ptolemaic Period, tells how the hero Setne visited a lovely courtesan of Bubastis, who had Setne's children killed in front of him and thrown from a high window to be devoured by the feral dogs and cats of the street below.

The ancient Egyptian word for the domestic cat can be vocalized as the clearly onomatopoeic *miaw*. Zoologists basically agree—and most ardent cat-lovers already know—that the progenitor of the domestic cat (*Felis catus*) was in all probability the Wild Cat (*Felis sylvestris libyca*), the south-

ern race of *Felis sylvestris*. This ancestral species still occurs in Egypt today, frequenting the margins of the Nile Valley and Delta. According to the most recent scholarship, it is likely (even if firm proof is lacking) that the common cat was first domesticated by the ancient Egyptians. Throughout the long course of its history, Egypt has been first and foremost an agrarian society, with vast amounts of grain and other agricultural products stored in villages, towns, and temple precincts. No doubt the ancient Egyptians, from a remote age, recognized the value of the cat as a controller of pest and vermin, and encouraged, or at least tolerated, its presence in their communities. Over time, the relationship between cats and people became closer, and the cat's economic value more fully recognized, eventually leading to complete domestication. It was a mutually beneficial arrangement for both species. While mice and rats were destroyed, leading to

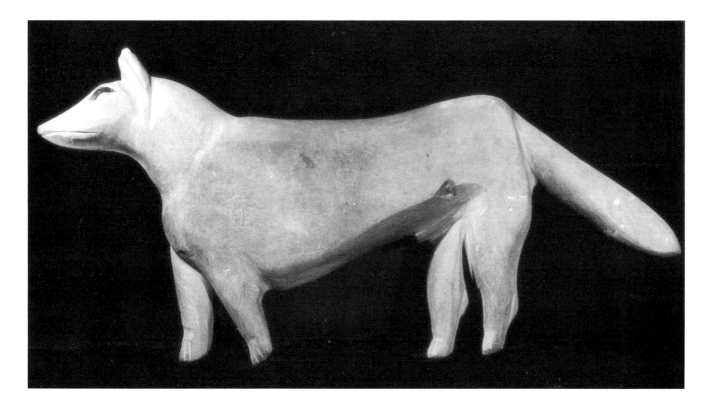

well-fed cats in happy homes, humans could enjoy the companionship and warmth of the inscrutable cat. The time of domestication, however, remains somewhat uncertain and awaits future clarification.

The oldest evidence of a relationship between cats and humans in Egypt extends back to the Badarian Period. Several early Predynastic human burials at al-Badari and al-Mustagidda were found to have small cats interred along with them, probably tamed wild animals, and the mandible of a cat was recovered during the course of the excavations of the Late Predynastic settlement site at Abydos. The identity of the cat species in these instances is unfortunately not known, and in any event their presence by no means indicates they were truly domesticated, as some have wishfully claimed. During the Old Kingdom, small to medium-sized felines are occasionally represented in hunting compositions on tomb-chapel and temple walls as inhabitants of the desert margin environment. Deserving our close scrutiny are a couple of adroitly rendered but now practically colorless animals on relief fragments illus-

trating desert fauna from the tomb-chapel of the Fifth Dynasty mastaba of the vizier and chief justice Pehenuka (D 70) at Saqqara (figs. 33, 39). The identification of these handsome felines cannot be made with certainty, although there are several possibilities. The Jungle Cat *(Felis chaus nilotica)* and the Wild Cat have been postulated, and Ludwig Keimer has suggested the Caracal *(Caracal caracal)* or Desert Lynx. In any case, these figures are certainly not the heavily-built big cats—Lions or Leopards—as some have mistakenly labeled them.

Significantly, the everyday household cat is absent from the scenes of daily life illustrated in tomb-chapels during the Old Kingdom. This suggests that the creature had not yet entered humankind's circle of domesticated animals. There is the singular reference to an otherwise unknown 'Cat Town,' mentioned on a fragment of wall relief found at al-Lisht and now in the Metropolitan Museum of Art, New York: if the dating of this piece to the Old Kingdom is correct, its cat hieroglyphs would be the oldest examples of the cat from ancient Egypt, but there is nothing to indicate if

Fig. 58. A Predynastic slate figure of what is probably a jackal, about forty centimeters in length, perhaps to be recognized as the funerary god Anubis. This object has been described by the Egyptologist William Stevenson Smith as one of the earliest images of an Egyptian deity in animal form. The eyes were originally inlaid. From al-Ahaiwa, in northern Upper Egypt. Gerzean Period (Naqada II). PHOEBE HEARST MUSEUM OF ANTHROPOLOGY, UNIVERSITY OF CALIFORNIA AT BERKELEY.

81

these were modeled after domestic or wild cats. And whether the several late Old Kingdom women bearing the charming nickname 'the Cat' were named after a wild or domesticated variety makes for interesting speculation.

The domestic cat played many different roles in ancient Egypt, although its value to humans as a hunter / mouser is a frequent motif. The first clear example of a domestic feline in Egyptian iconography is from the Eleventh Dynasty rock-cut tomb of the nomarch Baket III (no. 15) at Beni Hasan: a small painted vignette captures a cat face-to-face with a large Field Rat *(Arvicanthis niloticus)*. A humorous mathematical problem given in the Rhind mathematical papyrus from the Middle Kingdom refers to "seven houses, forty-nine cats, 343 mice," an obvious reference to the household cat as a mouse-catcher. A limestone ostracon from the Ramesside Period, found at the artisans' village of Deir al-Medina in the Theban necropolis, bears a drawing of a village tabby with a rodent dangling from its mouth. And there is, of course, the unforgettable tidbit of household advice offered in the Ebers medical papyrus from the New Kingdom: "To prevent mice from coming near things: put cat-grease on everything!"[15] The age-old conflict between cats and mice found its finest and most hilarious expression in ancient Egypt in an entire genre of comical or satirical drawings on figured ostraca and illustrated papyri from the Ramesside Period. These read like *Tom and Jerry* cartoon episodes and may reflect the existence of cat-and-mouse folk tales or fables in ancient Egypt (see chapter 9). A short passage on a New Kingdom papyrus, a reference book for the interpretation of dreams, states that: "If a man see himself in a dream: seeing a large cat—good: it means a large harvest will come (to him)."[16] Renowned for its ability to destroy not only rats but all kinds of noxious creatures, the cat also sometimes appears in the bestiary of apotropaic images and hieroglyphs carved on Middle Kingdom magic knives and rods, attacking and destroying menacing serpents.

Domestication of the household cat is clearly evident from the Middle Kingdom onward. It can first be recognized as a family pet sitting in a favored spot under the chair of a woman on a fragment of Twelfth Dynasty relief found at Koptos and now in the Petrie Museum of Egyptian Archaeology, University College London. At Abydos in Middle Egypt, the famed archaeologist Sir W. M. F. Petrie excavated a small Twelfth Dynasty tomb containing skeletons of seventeen cats, along with a row of small pots, which held what he speculated might have been milk offerings for the cats. Also from the Twelfth Dynasty come the earliest three-dimensional representations of the cat from ancient Egypt, the most noteworthy being a remarkable calcite vessel, probably a cosmetic container, which now graces the collections of the Metroplitan Museum of Art, New York. Theban tomb paintings and reliefs from the New Kingdom provide us with numerous representations of the now-elevated status of cats as beloved pets in the homes of the wealthy. Here, perky cats are shown beside or underneath the armchairs of their owners, nearly always women—napping, devouring fish, gnawing bones, or munching on fruit. In the Eighteenth Dynasty tomb-chapel of Anen (no. 120) at Thebes, the eminent Queen Tiye is portrayed seated upon her throne. Beneath it her frolicsome pets have gathered: a Green Monkey, a Pintail duck, and a cat. The painter has added a touch of humor to this already charming group by showing the cat with its leg wrapped around the back of the duck as though they were the closest of friends, while the monkey leaps over the pair. An especially fine example of a household cat appears on a block of crisply carved limestone relief that once decorated the late Eighteenth Dynasty tomb-chapel of the treasury official Merymery at Saqqara (fig. 60).

Since women seem to be the predominant cat-owners in these compositions, and because of its association with the goddess Mut, it has been postulated that the cat had some subtle erotic significance, or was perhaps even a symbol of female sexuality. However, women were by no means the only cat-lovers in ancient Egypt: men occasionally possessed pet cats as well. In the Nineteenth Dynasty tomb-chapel of Ipuy

Fig. 59. (opposite) This majestic image of a recumbent jackal represents the embalmer-god Anubis, carved from wood and coated with a black resin varnish and partly gilded, mounted upon a gilded wooden shrine. When it was discovered, a fine linen shawl was draped around the figure. From the tomb of Tutankhamun (no. 62) in the Valley of the Kings. Eighteenth Dynasty. THE EGYPTIAN MUSEUM, CAIRO.

(no. 217) at Thebes, a curious diminutive cat, probably a young kitten, is portrayed sitting on the tomb-owner's lap; what may be its mother, sporting a single golden earring and shown—unusually—face on, sits beneath the chair of Ipuy's wife. In the Eighteenth Dynasty, the crown prince Tuthmosis, son of Amenhotep III and older brother of Akhenaten, apparently cared so deeply for his pet she-cat that he had a magnificent limestone sarcophagus constructed and decorated with religious texts and images for her elaborate burial (fig. 61). The inscriptions and representations that adorn the object are quite reminiscent of those on funerary monuments belonging to people, so much so that this piece was at one time mistaken for a canopic chest belonging to a human and was even included in the Cairo Museum's official publication on canopic jars housed in the collection. Even though the cat is mentioned some eleven times in the incised texts covering the small stone sarcophagus, she is identified merely as "the female cat." There is only one known instance of a cat from ancient Egypt with a proper name. This New Kingdom tabby, represented in a wall painting in the Eighteenth Dynasty tomb-chapel of Puyemre (no. 39) at Thebes, was called 'the Pleasant One' by her loving mistress.

A skillfully painted cat, probably a wild species, amid the stems and umbels of a Papyrus *(Cyperus papyrus)* swamp in a scene in the Twelfth Dynasty rock-tomb of the nomarch Khnumhotep III (no. 3) at Beni Hasan, is one of the earliest examples of the standard theme of cats frequenting and hunting in the swamplands. During the New Kingdom, pet cats were sometimes pictured accompanying their well-heeled owners on pleasant, recreational fowling expeditions to the wetlands (pls. XXIII, XXIV). Here the sportive nobleman is characteristically exhibited poised with his throwsticks—a boo-

Fig. 60. (opposite) A finely carved limestone relief scene from the tomb-chapel of Merymery at Saqqara, portraying the tomb-owner sitting side by side on a Lion-legged chair of traditional form with his lovely wife, Merytptah, who fondly embraces him. Both have scented unguent cones on their heads. Beneath Merytptah's chair sits her attentive pet, a fine, large cat, with its right front paw upraised. Eighteenth Dynasty. RIJKSMUSEUM VAN OUDHEDEN, LEIDEN.

Fig. 61. The decorated limestone sarcophagus of crown prince Tuthmosis' beloved pet she-cat. This favored cat is pictured here wearing an elaborate collar and sitting before a loaded offering table. The inscriptions refer to her only as "the female cat." From Memphis. Eighteenth Dynasty. THE EGYPTIAN MUSEUM, CAIRO.

Fig. 62. Detail of a wall painting depicting a menacing-looking wild tom-cat with abnormally long ears, either an ally of the sun-god Ra or the deity himself, slaying the serpent Apophis, the sun's eternal enemy, under the sacred ished-tree of Heliopolis. From the burial chamber of the tomb of Inherkha (no. 359) at Thebes. Twentieth Dynasty.

merang-like sporting weapon—in hand, hurling them at throngs of water birds rising in flight from dense stands of flowering Papyrus stalks. Often, the family cats can be seen apparently enjoying themselves, busily stalking and catching birds independently. This motif is perhaps nowhere as admirably displayed as on a much celebrated fragment of Eighteenth Dynasty Theban wall painting featuring Nebamun's family outing at the swamplands (pl. XXIII). His frisky, cunning cat is remarkably depicted grasping three birds, one in its mouth, and one each in a front and hind paw. This cat may perhaps be viewed as assisting the sportsman by flushing up birds from the vegetation for him, but such a conclusion is highly speculative. It is even more doubtful whether cats

were ever trained in ancient Egypt to retrieve the birds the fowler may have brought down with his weapons, as some authorities have maintained.

The place of the cat in Egyptian mythology and religious thought is deeply complex and can only be highlighted here. The cat had associations with a number of deities in the Egyptian pantheon, and this results in a great variety of meanings from different cat images. During the New Kingdom, for example, the male cat was very closely connected with Ra, the sun-god, as a solar animal. In a vignette that accompanies Spell 17 of the *Book of the Dead*, a large, fierce tom-cat appears, brandishing a long knife and beheading the gigantic Apophis serpent, the rebel who daily fights against the

Fig. 63. Limestone stela dedicated by the royal craftsman Nebre, from the artisans' village at Deir al-Medina. The upper half of this votive stela shows a swallow perched on top of a shrine with a table of offering placed in front of it. The bird is called "the good swallow." The swallow evidently represented a minor deity who was closely connected with the region of the Theban necropolis. Below, Nebre's two sons kneel in front of a large cat, each holding a bouquet in one hand, the other hand raised in adoration before the cat, which is called "the good cat." Nineteenth Dynasty.
MUSEO EGIZIO, TURIN.

sun-god, coiled around the base of the sacred *ished*-tree of Heliopolis (fig. 62). At the same time, the female cat is associated with various goddesses known as the 'Daughter of Ra.' A Nineteenth Dynasty round-topped votive limestone stela, originating from the artisans' village at Deir al-Medina in the Theban necropolis and dedicated by the royal craftsman Nebre, for instance, depicts a cat and a swallow (Hirundinidae) being worshiped, and the accompanying inscription refers to "the good cat" (fig. 63). A

number of other votive stelae of this type featuring the cat are also known.

Today we generally associate the domestic cat in ancient Egypt with the goddess Bastet, because of this goddess's tremendous popularity and fame during the Late Dynastic and Greco–Roman periods. Nevertheless, Bastet is not specifically linked with the common cat until the Third Intermediate Period; before that, she always manifested herself in leonine form. Especially during the Late Dynastic Period, many thousands of bronze statuettes and figurines of cats of all shapes and sizes, some of superb quality and style (fig. 64), were fashioned for use as votive offerings to Bastet in her roles as patroness of joy and music, fecundity, and women in childbirth. Almost every museum housing Egyptian antiquities has at least an example or two of such works, and some of the great collections contain many dozens of them. It was during this late era that killing a cat, even unintentionally, was a crime punishable by death (see chapter 1). Meanwhile, millions of domestic cats were specially bred and raised in temple precincts associated with the cult of Bastet and other feline deities, only to be dispatched (usually by having their necks wrung) at a young age, mummified, and sold to faithful devotees as temple offerings. Some cat mummies were quite elaborately wrapped, using many yards of linen bandages, and then placed in highly decorated *cartonnage* coffins (fig. 6) or life-sized wooden statues. Most such cat mummies have been found to be ordinary tabbies, but a few have been identified as Jungle Cats. Cemeteries and subterranean catacombs for the interment of cat mummies have been discovered at a number of sites around the country: Abydos, Dendara, Koptos, Saqqara, Tanis, Tell Basta, and Thebes among others. One especially vast cat cemetery connected with the cult of the lioness goddess Pakhet at Speos Artemidos (known locally as Istabl Antar) in Middle Egypt, near Beni Hasan, produced at least 180,000 mummies, ap-

proximately nineteen tons of them. They were shipped to England late in the last century and ground up for use as fertilizer, though even today the burial ground is not entirely depleted. The ransacking of this sacred animal necropolis by the local peasants during the summer of 1888 was noted by Professor W. M. Conway, an English traveler of the day, who provides us with the following eyewitness account of the ghastly affair:

> The plundering of the cemetery was a sight to see, but one had to stand well to windward. All the village children came from day to day and provided themselves with the most attractive mummies they could find. These they took down to the river bank to sell for the smallest coin to passing travelers. Often they took to playing or fighting together with them on the way, and then the ancient fur began to fly as for three thousand years it had never been called upon to do. The path became strewn with mummy cloth and bits of cat skulls and bones and fur in horrid profusion, and the wind blew the fragments about and carried the stink afar. This was only the illicit part of the business. The bulk of the old totems went another way. Some contractor came along and offered so much a pound for their bones to make into something—soap or tooth-powder, I dare say, or even black paint. So men went systematically to work, peeled cat after cat of its wrappings, stripped off the brittle fur, and piled the bones in black heaps a yard or more high, looking from a distance like a kind of rotting haycocks scattered on the sandy plain. The rags and other refuse, it appears make excellent manure, and donkey loads of them were carried off to the fields to serve that useful, if unromantic, purpose.[17]

Nor was this an isolated instance. Sir Gaston Maspero reported in 1890 that just a few years previously an entire necropolis of mummified monkey remains was taken to Germany for the same purpose, to manure beet fields. The sacred cattle cemetery at Abusir was so extensive, Maspero tells us, that it took some ten years to completely exhaust. From it, thousands upon thousands of cattle mummies were transported

Fig. 64. (opposite) The renowned Gayer-Anderson bronze cat representing the living form of the goddess Bastet. Of the legions of votive bronze images of animals from ancient Egypt, this regal cat stands out for its beauty, grace, and charm. This hollow figure may have served as a coffin for a mummified cat. Bastet wears a protective silvered wadjet-amulet (the sacred eye of Horus) around her neck, a gold nose ring, and gold earrings. The eyes of the cat were originally inlaid. Late Dynastic Period. THE BRITISH MUSEUM, LONDON.

Fig. 65. This monumental votive or commemorative palette with relief decoration, the Battlefield Palette, depicts on this side the gruesome aftermath of a battle, the naked bodies of the slain enemy lying strewn on the ground in contorted positions, the dead being devoured by a flock of scavenging vultures and crows. The field is dominated by a great Lion, probably representing the triumphant Egyptian king, preying upon one of the fallen. Gray schist. Late Predynastic Period (Naqada III). THE BRITISH MUSEUM, LONDON.

to Europe to be converted into fertilizer. Already at the end of the last century some Egyptologists were voicing grave concern that Egyptian animal mummies should suffer such a fate and were saying they should be properly studied by specialists before they were all destroyed.

In a recent work, Dieter Kessler has again drawn attention to the apparent evidence from the Delta town of the goddess Bastet, Bubastis (Tell Basta), and perhaps from other sites too, indicating that during the Late Dynastic and Greco–Roman periods the ancient Egyptians may have cremated cats in addition to mummifying them. At least three separate archaeological missions to Tell Basta over the past hundred years or so have concluded as much. In addition, it has been suggested that there might be a hint of this curious practice in the writings of the historian Herodotus (II, 66), who observes that "when

a fire breaks out very strange things happen to the cats. The Egyptians stand around in a broken line, thinking more of the cats than quenching the burning; but the cats slip through or leap over the men and spring into the fire. When this happens, there is great mourning in Egypt." If cat cremations actually did occur this would seem to contradict our basic understanding of the ancient Egyptians' mortuary beliefs and practices, which were largely centered around the preservation of the body, needed for rebirth in the hereafter. The final word on this subject has surely yet to be written, but cremation should not be dismissed out of hand; such practices may have been the result of foreign influence. Further archaeological and zooarchaeological investigations will be required to resolve this interesting question.

As astonishing as it may seem today, the

Fig. 66. Drawing of a detail of limestone relief showing a Leopard (above) and a Lion, each imprisoned in a strong wooden cage drawn on sledges by a gang of hunters. From the tomb-chapel of the mastaba of Ptahhotep II (D 64) at Saqqara. Fifth Dynasty.

king of cats, the powerful Lion—that awesome symbol of royalty—was sometimes kept by ancient Egyptian monarchs as a tamed pet on palace grounds (see also chapter 8). We are probably justified in assuming that these 'house cats' had their dangerous fangs and claws removed. Originally, Lions must have been quite abundant in Egypt, and at one time they widely roamed the semi-desert landscape. They were evidently still rather plentiful in the country during the late New Kingdom and were regularly hunted by kings. They may still occasionally have been found in the wild during the Ptolemaic Period, if we are to believe the many magical stelae of Horus for cures from their bites (fig. 126). It is not known precisely when the Lion became locally extinct in Egypt. Writing near the close of the eighteenth century A.D., however, the French naturalist C. N. S. Sonnini de Manoncour observed that Lions approached the confines of Egypt but did not remain long in the land.

In tomb-chapel decoration during the Old and Middle kingdoms, single, free-roaming, savage Lions are frequently represented in the wild, pursuing various quarry along the desert margins, especially gazelles. Another lively motif depicts a Lion battling a huge Aurochs, the feline seizing the muzzle of its tormented victim (fig. 34). Already in the Late Predynastic Period (Naqada III), the Egyptian king was closely linked with the image of the mighty Lion. One side of the schist Battlefield Pal-

ette, a beautifully carved early ceremonial or votive object, is decorated with a vividly gruesome scene featuring a larger-than-life Lion, probably representing the victorious monarch, trampling upon and devouring his defeated and fallen enemies (fig. 65).

Recent findings from the royal funerary tomb complex of King Aha at Abydos, dating from the beginning of the First Dynasty, have identified the remains of seven Lion cubs associated with the burial, and it seems that tamed lions were already being kept as royal pets in Egypt during the Early Dynastic Period. Some stone statuettes and ivory Lion-shaped gaming pieces from the First Dynasty show lionesses wearing decorative collars, suggesting they were captive animals that might be held on leashes. A hieroglyph of a lioness sometimes used in the early Old Kingdom also sports such a collar. In the tomb-chapel of the Fifth Dynasty mastaba of Ptahhotep II (D 64) at Saqqara, a spirited vignette depicts the return home of a successful desert hunting expedition, with a captured Lion and a Leopard, each imprisoned in a strong wooden cage drawn on wooden sledges by a gang of retainers (fig. 66). Perhaps these cats were destined to become royal favorites. That the Leopard was also occasionally kept as a prestigious pet in the Old Kingdom is suggested by a unique detail on a fragment of limestone relief from the late Fifth or Sixth Dynasty tomb-chapel of Niankhnesut at Saqqara, now in the collec-

tion of E. and M. Kofler-Truniger, Lucerne. This slab portrays two achondroplastic dwarfs leading the tomb-owner's pets on leashes behind him: two hunting dogs, a Green Monkey, and a tame Leopard. During the New Kingdom, Cheetahs were also occasionally maintained by Egyptian sovereigns as pets and were probably housed with other rare animals in royal menageries (see chapter 8). While Leopards and Cheetahs were sometimes imported into Egypt from the African southern lands, Nubia and Punt, it must be remembered that both of these species were also indigenous to Egypt. Indeed, they may continue to exist in the wild today, but if so they are extremely uncommon.

Beyond a handful of examples, our knowledge of the Lion as a pet in ancient Egypt is very limited. In a scene on the small golden shrine from the Eighteenth Dynasty tomb of Tutankhamun (no. 62) in the Valley of the Kings, now in the Egyptian Museum, Cairo, the king is shown seated on a stool shooting arrows at waterfowl, while at his side sits a young tame lioness. During the Ramesside Period, the courageous Lion is occasionally shown in grand battle scenes trotting alongside the monarch's chariot, escorting him into battle or to war. Lions were sometimes rendered mauling foreign enemies as the king is about to smite the defeated foe with a mace. On a wall of the Nineteenth Dynasty rock-cut temple of Ramesses II at Beit al-Wali in Lower Nubia, the king's pet lioness is depicted near his side, lying next to the throne, and a caption names her: 'Slayer of his Enemies.' Also on this modest Nubian temple, Ramesses II is pictured receiving a triumphal procession of some rich, exotic products from the southern lands, including a live, tamed lioness on a leash. Lions were also occasionally imported from Syria. In the Eighteenth Dynasty tomb-chapel of Huy (no. 40) at Thebes, tribute bearers are pictured bringing goods from Syria, and present a gift of a fine, live Lion. A block of limestone relief recently recovered during the excavation of the late Eighteenth Dynasty tomb of the 'Great Commander of the Army'—later King—Horemhab at Saqqara, depicts on it several large captive felines held on leashes. At least one of these is certainly a Lion. Perhaps these cats were part of a booty from western Asia. Following a long tradition in Egyptian history, some of the Greek-speaking rulers of the

Fig. 67. (opposite) Statuette of a seated Lion, fashioned from clay and baked with a shiny red slip. Found in the temple enclosure at Hierakonpolis, in Upper Egypt, this piece was probably a votive object presented to the temple. Third Dynasty (?). ASHMOLEAN MUSEUM, OXFORD.

Fig. 68. Wall painting from the burial chamber of the foreman Inherkha (no. 359) at Thebes, portraying a vignette from Spell 17 of the Book of the Dead. The scene shows the tomb-owner, arms raised in an attitude of adoration, kneeling before the two aker-Lions, which sit back to back, supporting the sun disk on the horizon, from which hangs the sign of life ('ankh). These Lions are called 'yesterday' and 'today' and they symbolize eternity. Twentieth Dynasty.

Fig. 69. Brown quartzite statue of a squatting, shaggy-coated male baboon, a manifestation of the god Thoth. The sculptor has succeeded in conveying an aura of mystery in this image of a sacred baboon. The base of the piece is inscribed with the name of Amenhotep III. Eighteenth Dynasty. THE BRITISH MUSEUM, LONDON.

Ptolemaic Dynasty kept tame Lions as well. Berenike II, wife of Ptolemy III Euergetes I, is said to have loved to walk in the palace gardens accompanied by her tame lioness.

The Lion was associated with a multitude of leonine deities in the Egyptian pantheon (such as Aker, Mahes, Pakhet, Shu, Tefnut, Sekhmet, Bastet, Mut, Harmachis), and its image is steeped in deep mythological significance (figs. 67, 68, pl. xxix). Essentially, the Lion was seen as a powerful guard-

ian figure with apotropaic qualities and strong solar associations. As such, the creature was employed as an extremely popular motif in funerary decoration, as well as on an assortment of objects of daily use, such as furniture (figure on page vi). Surely the clearest visual link between the Lion and the monarch was the sphinx, that harmonious composite creation of animal and human, which served as the embodiment of royal power and strength (fig. 4). The best known example of course is the great, monumental Fourth Dynasty Sphinx at Giza, which was sculpted from a living outcrop of limestone and represented its builder, King Chephren, forever guarding over the vast Giza necropolis. This giant recumbent Lion with a human head, some sixty meters in length and twenty meters high, is the largest animal sculpture from ancient Egypt. During the New Kingdom, the colossal Sphinx was thought to embody Harmachis, 'Horus of the Horizon,' the sun-god rising in the east. From textual sources, there is evidence that during the Late Dynastic and Greco–Roman periods sacred Lions were housed in some temple precincts and could receive elaborate ritual burials upon their deaths. A fragment of a papyrus found at north Saqqara mentions a large catacomb of Lions there, but this has not yet been located. At Leontopolis (Tell al-Muqdam) in the Delta, there were also said to be tombs of sacred Lions. The Greek author Aelian (c. A.D. 170–235) in his *De Natura Animalium* (XII, 6–7) tells us that in this city "the Lions have temples and numerous spaces in which to roam; the flesh of oxen is supplied to them daily … and the Lions eat to the accompaniment of song in the Egyptian language." However, at neither Saqqara nor Leontopolis have Lion mummies or their sepulchers yet been discovered. Perhaps they await some future archaeologist's trowel.

Monkeys were favorite pets in ancient Egypt. During the Old and Middle kingdoms at least they were second in popularity only to dogs as beloved household animals. In no other creatures did the Egyptians take such obvious pure delight, and artisans were clearly not averse to outwardly expressing this feeling in their official and private undertakings. It is also in such depictions of monkeys that we see some of the clearest instances of humor and wit in ancient Egyptian iconography (see chapter 9).

Representations of two species of monkey are routinely met with in all historical periods: the Green Monkey and the Hamadryas Baboon. Modern examinations of mummified monkey remains have also indicated the presence of the Olive Baboon and the Barbary Monkey (*Macaca inua*), so it is possible that some portrayals may show these species. There is no evidence to suggest that the ancient Egyptians were acquainted with great apes. Monkeys do not occur in the wild in modern Egypt, nor is it entirely clear that they were ever indigenous, but the early Predynastic Egyptian environment would almost certainly have provided an adequate habitat for some species of monkeys, especially for baboon troops. A fascinating and unique vignette in a desert hunting scene in the Twelfth Dynasty rock-tomb of the nomarch Ukhhotep I (B.2) at Meir in Middle Egypt has a Green Monkey in the wild giving birth. This is one of the exceptional instances of monkeys depicted in Egyptian iconography in other than a purely domestic or religious setting, and it seems possible that these highly intelligent primates may have been known to the ancient Egyptians only from exotic imports from Nubia, Punt, and the African hinterlands. In any case, they amply figure as such on the walls of New Kingdom tomb-chapels and temples, delivered on leashes by delegations from these foreign southern lands (pl. XV).

Monkeys make their first appearance in Egyptian imagery even before the First Dynasty and continue to be an extremely important motif until the Ptolemaic and Roman periods. Skeletal remains of baboons have been discovered in connection with the royal cemetery of the Late Predynastic Period (Naqada III) at Hierakonpolis in Upper Egypt. They have also been found in association with the First Dynasty funerary tomb complex of King Aha at Abydos. It is uncertain whether every interment of a baboon in these locations was linked to religious practices or if some were related to pet-keeping. The name of King Narmer of the First Dynasty has been preserved on a

Fig. 70. This limestone pyramidion once capped a stone- or brick-built pyramid of a private tomb-chapel, and is inscribed for the scribe Mose. This side of the piece is decorated with a scene in sunk relief showing a male baboon standing on its hind legs with its forearms and paws upraised in a pose of adoration, worshiping the rising sun. From Thebes. Nineteenth Dynasty.
PELIZAEUS-MUSEUM,
HILDESHEIM.

Fig. 71. Fragment of limestone with colored paste inlay decoration. In the top register we see an abbreviated fowling scene, while below, a young boy plays with his pets, a Green Monkey, a baboon, and a Common Crane. A touch of humor is certainly evident in this group of characters: the baboon reaches out and clutches the boy's hand, while the Green Monkey seems to be pulling on the tail feathers of the crane. From the tomb-chapel of the mastaba of Nefermaat and Atet at Meidum. Early Fourth Dynasty.

NY CARLSBERG GLYPTOTEK, COPENHAGEN.

splendid large alabaster statue of a seated baboon, now in the Ägyptisches Museum, Berlin, which probably served as a royal votive offering for an early temple sanctuary. This baboon figure was very likely intended to be a representation of the god Hedjwer, 'the Great White,' who is also prominently displayed on reliefs below the Third Dynasty step pyramid of King Djoser at Saqqara. As a sacred animal, however, the thick, shaggy-coated baboon was most often viewed as a manifestation of the god Thoth, lord of the moon, inventor of the art of writing, and patron of the scribal profession (fig. 69). The Egyptians thought of the baboon as a special sun-greeting animal. It was said in religious literature to be a herald of the dawn and to proclaim the daily rebirth of the sun. A New Kingdom hymn to the sun describes the baboon's welcoming function in the following terms:

The baboons that announce Re when this great god is to be born again about the sixth hour in the netherworld. They appear for him after they have come into existence. They are at both sides of this god until he rises in the eastern horizon of the sky. They dance for him, they jump gaily for him, they sing for him, they sing praises for him, they shout out for him. When this great god appears before the eyes of [all humankind] then these hear the speech of jubilation of the *Wetenet*-country [= baboons?]. They are those who announce Re in heaven and on earth.[18]

The display described here, while obviously embellished, reflects direct knowledge of baboon behavior. Waking baboons have been observed in the wild to emit loud shrieks and howls and to jump about in the warmth of the early morning sun, an activity that could—with a little imagination—remind one of singing and dancing. The belief that baboons greet the rising sun gave rise to a profusion of representations during

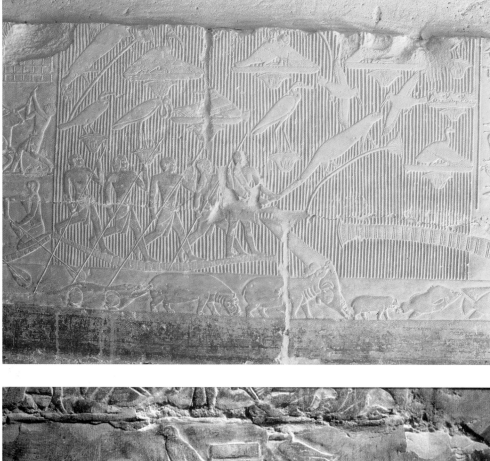

Pl. x. (above) This painted limestone relief scene shows five men in a punted Papyrus raft, completely surrounded by dense swampland vegetation teeming with animal life. Note that the man at the front of the craft is grasping the tail of a wild Egyptian Mongoose that is about to prey on a nest of young Pied Kingfishers, the parents attempting in vain to ward off the attacker. The other avian life roosting or nesting includes a splendid Gray Heron, Greater Flamingo, cormorant (Phalacrocorax sp.), Sacred Ibis, and Egyptian Goose. Beneath the water, a Hippopotamus is crushing a Nile Crocodile in defense of its young calf, and another crocodile appears to be devouring a newborn Hippopotamus as it emerges from its mother. From the tomb-chapel of the mastaba of the vizier Mereruka at Saqqara. Sixth Dynasty.

Pl. xi. (below) This detail of painted limestone relief from the tomb-chapel of the vizier Mereruka at Saqqara depicts a pair of farmhands force-feeding a Striped Hyena, lying on its back with its legs bound. This was not a domestic animal, but was captured from the wild and kept until needed. Once fattened up, the beast would have been slaughtered, providing Mereruka with food for eternity. Sixth Dynasty.

Pl. XII. This painted limestone relief, also from the tomb-chapel of Mereruka, shows a Nilotic fishing scene. A pair of fishermen are shown standing on a small Papyrus raft fishing with hand-held nets, which they dip into the water and fill with a bountiful catch. Drawn by the activities of the fishermen and the great congregation of fish, a cormorant and a pelican stand close by. The always voracious cormorant is pictured with a fish in its bill, about to swallow it whole. Sixth Dynasty.

Pl. XIII. Fragment of wall painting from the tomb of the high official Ita at Gebelein, in Upper Egypt. It shows an agricultural scene, consisting of the transport and storing of grain in giant granaries. A hard-working donkey with panniers is pictured delivering some of the crop, while fieldhands wearing short kilts carry the baskets up to the silos. Note the open, bloody wounds on the poor donkey's rump, the result of the punishing blows of the stern master who follows close behind, the stick held over his shoulder. In the middle register, three domestic goats can be seen eating fodder from mangers. First Intermediate Period.
MUSEO EGIZIO, TURIN.

Pl. XIV. This immediately appealing bright cerulean blue faience statuette of a standing Hippopotamus is decorated with a motif of the swampy vegetation characteristic of its haunt, with a shorebird roosting on a bending stem. During the Middle Kingdom, charming Hippopotamus figurines such as this one, in various poses, were routinely included in human burials, almost certainly as apostrophic devices to protect the dead from evil. From Thebes (?). Twelfth Dynasty. THE EGYPTIAN MUSEUM, CAIRO.

Pl. xv. (opposite) Wall painting from the celebrated tomb-chapel of the vizier Rekhmire (no. 100) at Thebes, showing a portion of a scene illustrating the arrival of foreign tribute, including live animals. In the top register, Nubians are shown bringing a Giraffe, which is restrained by two men using ropes tied to its forelegs. Note the perky little Green Monkey that is humorously climbing up the Giraffe's long, spotted neck. Then there follows a herd of long-horned cattle and, above

them, a pack of hunting hounds wearing collars. In the lower register, Syrians deliver some prize products and fauna from their distant country. They bring a team of spirited horses, followed by a Syrian Bear, wearing a collar and held on a leash. The man with the bear also carries a great elephant's tusk. Bringing up the rear is a rather diminutive Syrian Elephant, also collared and leashed, but with a fine pair of ivory tusks of its own. Eighteenth Dynasty.

Pl. xvi. (above) Detail of wall painting from the tomb-chapel of the vizier Rekhmire (no. 100) at Thebes, showing a procession of foreign tribute delivered to the tomb-owner. This splendid picture of a spotted Leopard originates from the same composition as pl. xv, where it is part of the live, exotic fauna brought by the Nubian delegation. The tame beast is depicted wearing a collar and walking on a leash. This valued gift from the deep southern lands may have been destined for the royal menagerie. Though damaged today, this is a deftly executed portrait of a Leopard. Eighteenth Dynasty.

Pl. XVII. (opposite) Userhet, 'Royal Scribe and Child of the Nursery,' is represented in this detail of wall painting from his tomb-chapel (no. 56) at Thebes, charging headlong in his horse-drawn chariot after a multitude of game animals along the desert margin. The tomb-owner is shown with the reins of the galloping steeds placed around his lower waist, thus freeing his hands and allowing him to fire a hail of arrows with his bow at the desperately fleeing beasts, slaying many of them. Some of these wild animals can be seen beneath the horses, including a leaping Cape Hare and a dying Striped Hyena. See also pls. XVIII and XXI. Eighteenth Dynasty.

Pl. XVIII. (above) Amid the mêlée of desert animals being chased by Userhet (see pl. XVII) are a number of bounding gazelles, including the three juveniles illustrated here. In their panic to escape, two of the gazelles have fled in the wrong direction and are rushing directly into the path of the oncoming hunter, whose arrow has already found its mark on one of them. Eighteenth Dynasty.

the Dynastic period where the beast is poised in an attitude of adoration, with arms upraised, facing the new sun, as though offering prayers and salutation to the first rays of the dawn (fig. 70, pl. XXVI). At Hermopolis (al-Ashmunein) in Middle Egypt, King Amenhotep III of the Eighteenth Dynasty set up perhaps four colossal quartzite statues of squatting baboons in honor of Thoth, two of which still stand in situ today (pl. XXX).

From at least the beginning of the Fourth Dynasty, both the Green Monkey and the Hamadryas Baboon appear in the tomb-chapels of the elite as everyday domestic pets. They are illustrated in a considerable variety of settings and situations. Monkeys were particularly appreciated for their comic appeal, especially in imitating human occupations. During the Old and Middle kingdoms, vivacious monkeys customarily occur collared and leashed under the care of a retainer, who was sometimes an achondroplastic dwarf or a hunchback (pl. VI). Sometimes they even ride perched on top of the heads of their diminutive guardians, nibbling on a piece of fruit. In other tomb scenes a monkey can be seen riding on the back of a dog, participating in ship-building wielding a baton of author-

ity, grasping the tail feathers of a crane (fig. 71), helping with the pressing of the must-sack during wine making, dressing in women's clothes, carrying a yoke on its shoulders bearing a heavy load, piloting the steering oar of a boat, and, quite often, scampering up the mast and rigging of Nile traveling ships. In the Eighteenth Dynasty tomb-chapel of the vizier Rekhmire at Thebes, one little Green Monkey is painted in a procession of foreign tribute humorously catching a ride on the long neck of a Giraffe (pl. XV). These same pampered household monkeys are sometimes pictured wearing decorative jewelry, such as golden bracelets, anklets, and earrings.

An especially interesting vignette on a block of limestone relief from the tomb-chapel of the Fifth Dynasty mastaba of Tepemankh (D 11) at Saqqara depicts an open-air market scene, with a man brandishing a short stick or truncheon terminating in an open hand and holding two pet baboons on leashes, walking them through the marketplace (fig. 72). The female monkey is realistically shown with her small baby clinging beneath her underside, while the male has firmly seized the leg of a young boy, probably a thief, who

Fig. 73. Glossy, deep-blue faience figurine of a Green Monkey with a ball or perhaps a sack of fruit between its legs. The monkey's head is turned and directly faces the viewer. The perforations in its ears indicate that the monkey was once adorned with gold earrings, which they are sometimes shown wearing in Theban tomb paintings. Eighteenth Dynasty (the Amarna Period?). THE BROOKLYN MUSEUM.

has approached a large basket of produce and is about to pilfer some. The startled thief turns his head and cries out to the baboon-keeper: "Hey! Help! Strike to restrain this baboon!"[19] This humorous episode is directly paralleled in at least two other examples of market scenes in Old Kingdom mastabas, and appears on the late Fifth Dynasty causeway of Wenis at Saqqara. In one of the mastaba scenes, in the well preserved tomb-chapel of the Fifth Dynasty mastaba of two senior officials, the brothers Niankhkhnum and Khnumhotep, at Saqqara, the baboon actually sinks his long and very pointed teeth into the culprit's leg! These baboon-handlers were almost certainly not policemen, the monkeys their trained assistants, as some writers have asserted. Rather, they may have been official market attendants exercising their pet baboons, their apprehension of a criminal merely a touch of levity in an otherwise formal composition. Baboons (even tamed ones) can be quite aggressive, and this was well known in antiquity—so much so that the ancient

Egyptians used the image of a baboon as a determinative in writing 'to be furious.'

Besides being highly prized as family pets in ancient Egypt, monkeys were also valued as performers. During the Old Kingdom, and possibly even earlier, these primates were apparently trained to dance, sing, and play wooden flutes, and their 'aping' of human concerts must have been viewed as enormously amusing (in a Ramesside Period text that offers advice to a youthful scribe, the student learning to write is reminded that even "monkeys are taught to dance"). Some painted limestone figurines of musical monkeys are known from the Middle Kingdom, but their appreciation expands tremendously during the late New Kingdom, when their images are featured in a range of media, and the monkeys are frequently joined by other animals playing musical instruments. Together they form ensembles: a Lion plays a lyre, a crocodile a lute, a hyena a double oboe, a goat a drum, a donkey a harp, and so on. With these illustrations, however, Egyptian artisans have crossed over into

Fig. 74. Detail of a painted limestone relief illustrating a pet Dorcas Gazelle standing directly beneath the animal-legged chair of a deceased Theban notable. The favored gazelle holds a long-stemmed lotus blossom in its mouth. From the tomb-chapel of Pabasa (no. 279) at Thebes. Twenty-sixth Dynasty.

the realm of make-believe, into what are probably comic or satirical animal stories, a phenomenon not previously encountered in Egyptian art (see chapter 9).

The same comic approach to the monkey is observed on a delightful Eighteenth Dynasty toy found at al-Amarna of a monkey driving a horse-drawn chariot, now in the Petrie Museum of Egyptian Archaeology, University College London, and in an amusing New Kingdom blue and black faience statuette now in the Royal Museum of Scotland, Edinburgh: this unusual figurine, certainly with a degree of humorous intent, shows a Nubian woman suckling a monkey she holds to her breast, nursing the animal as though it were a human child. The appeal of monkeys playing music was very long-lasting. A large baboon strumming a lute is prominently displayed on a column of the temple of Hathor at Philae, from the late Ptolemaic Period. There is also Aelian's pronouncement (*De Natura Animalium* VI, 10) that "under the Ptolemies, the Egyptians taught baboons their letters, how to dance, how to play the flute and the harp." Well into this century, performing monkeys could still routinely be seen busking on busy Cairo streets, dancing to the sounds of loud drums and other musical instruments, a link to an ancient tradition.

Especially on Ramesside Period figured ostraca, baboons regularly appear climbing the trunks of Doum Palms (*Hyphaene thebaica*) that are heavy with ripe nuts, and occasionally these bright, agile creatures are shown on leashes or wearing girdles tied to their waists and under the charge of keepers who sometimes wield a short stick to drive them forward (fig. 145). They are also often sketched on limestone ostraca pilfering doum-nuts from great harvested sacks of them. These small compositions recall a much earlier Twelfth Dynasty painted vignette of some hungry baboons in the branches of a large Sycamore Fig (*Ficus sycomorus*) in the rock-tomb of the nomarch Khnumhotep III (no. 3) at Beni Hasan, helping themselves to the appetizing ripe fruit. The vexing question before us is whether these tame baboons should be thought of as assisting or, conversely, hindering the work of the fig-gatherers. Such scenes, and others, have traditionally been interpreted in the Egyptological literature as proof that trained monkeys were employed as workers in ancient Egypt to harvest fruit from trees. This explanation, however, remains somewhat doubtful and is not corroborated by other evidence. These charming details should rather be viewed for their undeniable humorous appeal (see chapter 9). On the other hand, it is at least plausible that in a few instances where baboons are depicted climbing to the tops of tall Date Palms (*Phoenix dactylifera*), which can grow to around twenty meters in height, the monkeys may have been taught to shake the branches of the tree and cause the ripe dates to fall so that they could be collected.

In the wall decoration of the Middle Kingdom rock-tombs at Beni Hasan, Deir al-Bersha, Meir, and elsewhere, domestic monkeys are occasionally seen in views of daily life. A few family pet baboons with names are known on a monument from this period now in the Musée du Louvre, Paris. The names sound strange to us: 'His Father Awaits Him,' for instance, and 'When the Foreign Country is Pacified, the Land is Happy.'

With the coming of the New Kingdom, monkeys continued to be tremendously popular as pets and are often pictured in tomb-chapels sitting under their masters' chairs or scampering about nearby. The monkey in these contexts is thought to have had subtle, erotic connotations, perhaps as a symbol of female sexuality (fig. 73). Some pet monkeys were so dearly regarded that their owners had them embalmed and buried close to their own graves. Three Eighteenth Dynasty pit tombs (nos. 50–52) in the Valley of the Kings, dated to the reign of Amenhotep II or perhaps Horemhab, contained favored royal pets: six monkeys (consisting of at least two different species of baboons), a dog, a Sacred Ibis, and three ducks (probably Egyptian Geese). King Tuthmosis III had his beloved pet baboon buried with him in his tomb in the Valley of the Kings (no. 34), and that most famous courtier, Senenmut, during the reign of Queen Hatshepsut

(Eighteenth Dynasty), buried his pet monkey in a large wooden coffin with a dish of grapes or raisins close by his Theban tomb-chapel (no. 71). Probably the best known burial of a pet baboon from ancient Egypt is the one interred with the God's Wife of Amun, Maatkare Mutemhet, of the Twenty-first Dynasty, discovered in the Deir al-Bahari cache of royal mummies (DB 320) in 1881. Egyptologists had long presumed that the small mummy found with the priestess in her sarcophagus was her child, but upon X-ray examination, it proved to be a female Hamadryas Baboon.

During the Late Dynastic and Greco-Roman periods, monkeys were mummified not because they were pets, but because the baboon was regarded as a sacred animal. Baboon cemeteries are known from several sites, but especially Wadi Gubbanet al-Girud at Thebes, Tuna al-Gebel, and north Saqqara. At Saqqara, approximately four hundred baboons were buried during the Ptolemaic Period, all of them exotic imports, in a large catacomb on two levels. In life, the holy baboons lived in the temple of 'Ptah under his Moringa Tree' at Memphis, as incarnations of the god Thoth, and upon their deaths they were mummified and entombed, thus becoming 'Osiris the Baboon.' A recent examination of the poorly preserved remains of about thirty-five baboons interred at Tuna al-Gebel concluded that they were all Olive Baboons. Some of these animals appear to have been plagued by poor health in life, suffering from caries, rickets, and arthritis. One unfortunate baboon even had a very pronounced facial deformity. At north Saqqara, zooarchaeological evidence indicates that other smaller species of monkeys, Green and Barbary monkeys for example, were sometimes also laid to rest there. This finding has been used to suggest that baboons may have been in short supply, and that substitutes for them were occasionally enlisted when the need arose.

Only a couple of species of wild gazelle are clearly attested in Egyptian imagery, but

none more so than the attractive Dorcas Gazelle. Swift-footed gazelles are abundantly featured in scenes of the chase of desert game from Predynastic times onward (see chapter 3). The species also appears in the file of animal offerings presented to the deceased on tomb-chapel walls. During the New Kingdom, gazelles

Fig. 76. *This striking detail of carved, painted tomb relief pictures the tomb-owner's young daughter, naked, and holding a pet Lapwing by its wings in her left hand. Her right hand holds the flower of a White Lotus Waterlily (Nymphaea lotus) to her nose and she is enjoying its pleasant fragrance. The bejeweled girl wears her hair neatly braided into a long lock (a symbol of childhood) that falls past her shoulder. From the rock-cut tomb of Nefer at Saqqara. Fifth Dynasty.*

Fig. 77. *(opposite) In a wall painting illustrating the tomb-owner fowling in the Papyrus swamplands, his wife appears alongside him on the sporting vessel. She is sumptuously dressed and wears a long wig—not the sort of attire appropriate for the occasion—and holds in her right hand, near her breast, a gosling or duckling. It has been suggested that in these instances the bird may have subtle erotic meaning. From the tomb-chapel of Nakht (no. 52) at Thebes. Eighteenth Dynasty.*

also commonly appear as a decorative element on wooden toilet spoons, on scarabs, on women's festive diadems, on wooden chests, and on the interior of faience drinking bowls. And the graceful and nimble gazelle was also occasionally kept by the elite as a tamed household pet, a practice occasionally recorded in the country in more recent times as well. In the Twenty-sixth Dynasty tomb-chapel of the high official Pabasa (no. 279) at Thebes, under the tomb-owner's chair stands his tame pet gazelle (fig. 74). During the Twenty-third Dynasty or later, a Theban woman named Ankhshepnupet felt so close to her pet gazelle that she had it interred along with

her in a small pit tomb, curled up near her feet. Also, a small pet (?) gazelle, buried in a wooden coffin in the shape of its own body, was found in the famous Deir al-Bahari cache of royal mummies (DB 320) in 1881, and is now on display in the Egyptian Museum, Cairo. This obvious affection for the gazelle may go a long way in explaining

111

an exquisite and thoroughly charming rendering of a wide-eyed gazelle, fashioned of tinted ivory, from a grand Theban tomb of the Eighteenth Dynasty, standing on a wooden base painted with flowering plants (fig. 75). Although the statuette is today slightly damaged, its S-shaped horns and long ears now vanished, it ranks as a masterpiece of the *art animalier*.

A handful of birds were kept for pleasure in ancient Egypt. Several well-appointed tombs dating from the Early Dynastic Period at Helwan in Lower Egypt contained burials of birds (at least one of which was evidently a falcon) in wooden and pottery coffins. Three similar birds were apparently discovered associated with the First Dynasty mastaba of the chancellor Hemaka (S 3035) at Saqqara. The Egyptian excavator of the Helwan cemetery, Zaki Y. Saad, interpreted these interments as the tomb-owners' favored pets. If correct, this would be the oldest indication of the practice of keeping pet birds in Egypt.

During the Old Kingdom, children of both sexes regularly appear on tomb-chapel walls standing naked close at their parents' side. More often than not, they clutch a small bird by its wings, typically a colorful, pert Hoopoe, more rarely a Lapwing (*Vanellus vanellus*) (fig. 76), a Turtle Dove (*Streptopelia turtur*), or a duck of some kind. Later, during the New Kingdom, elaborately dressed women are seen carrying fledglings, often holding them to their breasts (fig. 77), but here, rather than being pets, the birds appear to have subtle erotic associations or perhaps are symbolic of regeneration.

Also during the New Kingdom the Egyptian Goose, despite its infamous aggressive behavior, was valued as a pet by Theban notables and popularly featured in their decorated tomb-chapels at Thebes. This goose-like duck is often portrayed under the chairs of the tomb-owners and joining them on pleasurable family outings into the swamplands (pl. XXIII). The motivation for keeping the Egyptian Goose as a pet during the New Kingdom, and later in the Twenty-fifth Dynasty, was that it was sacred to the great Amun, chief god of the city of Thebes. Because of its strong relationship with this powerful deity, a flock of revered Egyptian Geese was maintained on the waters of the sacred lake of Amun's magnificent state temple of Karnak. Today's visitor to the temple can still inspect the covered stone runway that led from their fowlyard down to the lake. Notwithstanding its privileged position, the Egyptian Goose had an unflattering, pugnacious reputation in ancient Egypt. A short didactic text dating from the Ramesside Period, intended to assist in the preparation of young men for the scribal profession, compares the worth of an idle scribe to that of a useless animal: "You are worse than the Egyptian Goose of the riverbank, that abounds in mischief. It spends the summer in destroying the dates, and the winter in destroying the emmer. It spends its free time of the year pursuing the cultivators, and allows not the seed to be thrown to the ground before it has got wind of it. It cannot be caught by snaring, nor is it offered up at the temple, that evil bird of piercing sight that does no work."[20]

There is little proof that other bird species were kept as household pets by the ancient Egyptians. Ludwig Keimer has suggested there could be textual evidence from the New Kingdom for the practice of falconry, but while some sacred falcons were unquestionably kept in captivity during antiquity, perhaps as far back as Predynastic times, conclusive documentation for the sport of falconry is absent. Finally, an especially noteworthy fragment of limestone wall relief from the Thirtieth Dynasty tomb of Hapiu depicts the tomb-owner sitting for a musical performance, with his pet rooster in a privileged position at his feet (fig. 142). The chicken was apparently still considered an exotic curiosity at this time in Egypt, making the bird worthy of special attention.

Chapter Five

The Waters of the Nile

*H*erodotus, following his predecessor Hecataeus, aptly observed that Egypt is "the gift of the Nile" (II, 5). This classic and often repeated epithet encapsulates how the entire ancient Egyptian civilization centered around the great River Nile. The world's longest river at 6,671 kilometers, the Nile's Egyptian section descends on a course of over thirteen hundred kilometers from the Sudanese border in the south to the Mediterranean coast in the north. The life-giving waters of the Nile flow gently through the very driest of sun-parched

deserts, nourishing a rich, ribbon-like, green oasis along its banks, in an otherwise inhospitable and virtually barren landscape. The vital importance of the Nile in the lives of the ancient Egyptian people is obvious. The very heartbeat of the country, then as today, the river supported life both within the depths of its waters and along its fertile banks; it was a hub of activity and the principle artery of communication.

The daily routines of ancient farmers, fishermen, herders, fowlers, water carriers, clothes washers, and bathers brought them down to the riverside or to the canals stemming from it, where they had to be ever vigilant for surprise attacks from that scourge of the waters, the ferocious Nile Crocodile *(Crocodylus niloticus)*. This very real danger was a part of everyday life in ancient Egypt. Even today, on the African continent crocodiles are responsible for more human deaths than any other animal (the massive Hippopotamus is reported to be a close second). Although the Nile Crocodile was on the brink of extinction in modern Egypt, it is currently experiencing a rebound and is said now to proliferate in the vast, newly created Lake Nasser in Lower Nubia. In January 1989, a Nile Crocodile roughly two and a half meters long was reportedly caught in the lake with fishing nets not far from the Aswan High Dam, and between December 1988 and March 1989, the Egyptian Wildlife Service confiscated fifty to sixty juvenile crocodiles (thirty centimeters long or less) from pet shops and street vendors in Cairo and Aswan. It is plausible, therefore, that this species may one day again inhabit Nile waters north of the dam, through introduction by humans.

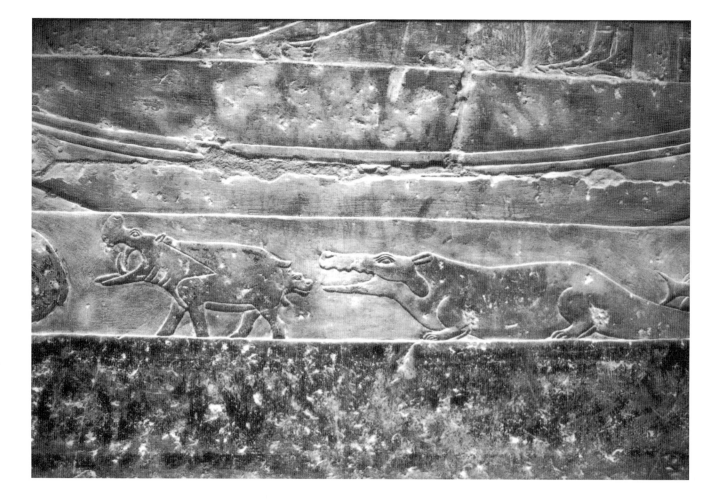

Fig. 78. This chilling episode of river life, carved in limestone relief, shows a female Hippopotamus giving birth to her baby calf, which emerges from its mother head first. Waiting for a chance to strike, a stealthy Nile Crocodile, jaws open, is ready to prey upon the young Hippopotamus. From the tomb-chapel of the mastaba of the princess Idut at Saqqara. Sixth Dynasty.

Justly credited for its strength, voracious appetite, and fierceness, the armor-plated Nile Crocodile can reach a length of six meters and weigh up to nine hundred kilograms. Lurking in the shallows along the riverbank, the crocodile supplements its basic diet of fish by aggressively hunting domestic and game animals, birds, and sometimes an unwary human being. It usually seizes its prey directly with its powerful jaws, then plunges underwater to dispatch it by drowning. It is evident from the pictorial and textual records that the ancient Egyptians greatly feared this wily, giant reptile—and with good reason!

The Nile Crocodile first appears in the faunal repertoire as a white, painted decoration against a dark ground on pottery vessels from the Amratian Period (Naqada I). There is some suggestion on these wares that the creature was hunted during this period. The crocodile is very frequently

met with as a common inhabitant of the Nile waters on tomb-chapel walls from all periods, but particularly the Old Kingdom. Here, Egyptian artisans demonstrate more than just a passing familiarity with this cunning beast. A standard scene features herders driving cattle to pasture by fording a canal. Often one of the cowherds is pictured at the head of the group, carrying a young calf on his shoulders, to protect it from hidden dangers or drowning and to encourage the other animals to cross the stream (frontispiece, pl. VIII). Off to the side, an enormous crocodile or two, submerged in the murky water, waits motionless for an opportunity to strike. The drovers were not entirely helpless and took preventive measures against just such an attack. A frequent inscription accompanying these vignettes takes the form of a magical spell to stave off the troublesome crocodile. Such an episode is labeled in the tomb-chapel of

Fig. 79. This small vignette of painted relief illustrates a dramatic Nilotic scene. The Nile Crocodile locked in the powerful jaws of the Hippopotamus on the left may or may not have hunted Hippopotamus calves, as in fig. 78, but it will certainly never do so again, as it is about to have its back broken and be crushed to death. The baying Hippopotamus on the right is the target of hunters' harpoons, its large body riddled with barbs attached to their ropes. From the tomb-chapel of the mastaba of Ti (no. 60) at Saqqara. Fifth Dynasty.

the Sixth Dynasty mastaba of the vizier Ankhmahor at Saqqara: "Crossing the canal by the cattle. Warding off death. Warding off the crocodile by the herdsman." One of the drovers is depicted in this composition pointing to the water with his index finger in a protective gesture and reciting the 'water spell': "Oh herdsman there! Let your face be watchful for this marsh-inhabitant who is on the water, to prevent these here [i.e., the cattle] falling a victim to this marsh-inhabitant. May he come as a sightless one. Let your face be very watchful for him!"[21] The charm seems to have worked, too, because the malignant hunter is never shown going after the vulnerable herd and seems content with other prey. The stealthy predator is sometimes rendered in art feeding on fish or other animals. In the tomb-chapel of the Sixth Dynasty mastaba of the princess Idut at Saqqara, for example, a detail in a swampland scene illustrates a roaring female Hippopotamus *(Hippopotamus amphibius)* giving birth; a huge, hungry crocodile is opportunistically ready to devour the newborn baby as it emerges from its mother (fig. 78). This is surely the result of direct

observation along the Nile. In nature, enraged Hippopotamuses have been known to kill crocodiles in defense of their young by biting them in two. One-to-one confrontations between the two species appear in tomb decoration (fig. 79, pl. x), and, as in life, the Hippopotamus is the winner of the battle, always shown with its mighty jaws locked around the crocodile, utterly crushing its body. Such vignettes are among the more dramatic episodes in the birth and death cycle of wildlife depicted on the walls of Old Kingdom monuments.

A curious cameo scene set against a swampy backdrop in the offering-chapel of the Sixth Dynasty mastaba of the vizier Kagemni (LS 10) at Saqqara shows two large Nile Crocodiles mating in the water, in a belly-to-belly fashion (fig. 131), while in the tomb-chapel of the Sixth Dynasty mastaba of Kairer at the same site, a representation in carved relief shows a crocodile laying its clutch of eggs in a canal. Both of these incidents, while interesting, are completely fanciful, because the species does not copulate belly-to-belly, nor does it lay its eggs underwater. The Egyptian artisans who decorated these tomb-chapels were

115

Fig. 80. Sculpted black granite figure of a Nile Crocodile, a votive offering to the crocodile-headed god Sobek. The beast appears at repose on top of a shrine-shaped pedestal, part of a damaged statue depicting Mayi, an official of the ancient town of Sumenu, on his knees petitioning Sobek. From al-Mahamid al-Qibli (Sumenu) in Upper Egypt. Late Eighteenth or early Nineteenth Dynasty. THE LUXOR MUSEUM OF ANCIENT EGYPTIAN ART.

Fig. 81. Upper portion of a fragmentary round-topped limestone votive stela with crocodiles, honoring the god Sobek. The uppermost crocodile wears a plumed headdress with a sun disk and is mounted on a shrine, with offerings heaped before it. Ramesside Period. Probably from al-Mahamid al-Qibli (Sumenu). THE BROOKLYN MUSEUM.

primarily concerned with expressing the behavioral characteristics of these reptiles in general terms within the strict conventions that governed their work, rather than feeling any need to satisfy the ardent naturalist with complete precision. Similar anomalies are routinely encountered in Egyptian iconography in most periods, but these should not necessarily be construed as reflecting ignorance of the ways or morphology of the particular species involved. Indeed, Egyptian artisans were astute observers of the animal world and our admi-

ration of their work should not be diminished by occasional lapses.

There are numerous references to crocodiles in Egyptian literature and a whole host of spells to prevent being eaten by one. In the well-known *Dispute Between a Man and His Ba*, a peasant relates a grim story of losing his wife and children in a lake that was infested with hungry crocodiles, while one of the tales in *King Cheops and the Magicians* tells how a magician, the chief lector priest Webaoner, wishing to punish his unfaithful wife and her lover, fashioned a crocodile in beeswax: when thrown into the water, the beast magically grew to seven cubits (over three and a half meters) and seized the adulterer when he came to the lake to bathe. There were other ways in which the awesome abilities of this rapacious beast could be harnessed for the service of humans, albeit through the power of magic (pl. xxxv). During the Middle Kingdom, the crocodile routinely appears amid the procession of apotropaic animal images, some real and many others fabulous, on so-called magic knives and rods (fig. 125). Engraved figures on curved strips of Hippopotamus ivory, when used in conjunction with certain spells, served to keep pregnant women and infants safe from the clutches of evil, especially from the venomous bites of snakes, scorpions, and other harmful creatures. On several examples of these, crocodiles are poised with their jaws gaping open, ready to destroy. On others, a crocodile's body is fused to the back of an upright Hippopotamus (the goddess Taweret) forming a composite beast, sometimes wielding a knife. Similarly, in later times, a popular type of healing statue, known today as the *cippi*, or magical stelae, of 'Horus on the crocodiles,' typically features the youthful god Horus standing on top of a pair or more of menacing crocodiles, as though divinely keeping the creatures at a distance (or perhaps trampling them), while grasping in his hands various other noxious animals (fig. 126). In the scene of final judgment, pictured in a vignette that accompanies Spell 125 of the *Book of the Dead*, the damned were destroyed by the 'Devourer of the Dead,' a hungry hybrid crocodile-headed monster.

As a sacred animal, the Nile Crocodile was most closely associated with the god Sobek, whose major cult centers were in the Faiyum and at Kom Ombo. Sobek was a water and fertility god, later a primordial deity and creator-god. Evidence of keeping and breeding sacred crocodiles in temple precincts extends back to at least

Fig. 82. The salient features of a frog have been successfully captured in this small stone vessel with tubular handles. The eyes are inlaid with white stone beads and the markings on the body are indicated by means of tiny chips of lapis lazuli. From Naga al-Deir, in Upper Egypt. Gerzean Period (Naqada II). PHOEBE HEARST MUSEUM OF ANTHROPOLOGY, UNIVERSITY OF CALIFORNIA AT BERKELEY.

Fig. 83. *This detail from a fragment of limestone relief depicts, against a field of dense Papyrus stems, an Egyptian Mongoose about to carry out a raid on the nest of three young Pied Kingfishers, imaginatively placed on a bending stem of Papyrus (this species actually nests in holes in cliffs or river banks; nor could any real bird's nest balance on such a thin stem). From the tomb-chapel of the mastaba of Khnumhotep (D 49) at Saqqara. Fifth Dynasty.* ÄGYPTISCHES MUSEUM, BERLIN.

the New Kingdom. In recent years, an elaborate installation or sanctuary for this purpose has been uncovered at the modern village of al-Mahamid al-Qibli (Sumenu), near al-Rizeiqat in Upper Egypt, dating from the reign of Amenhotep III in the Eighteenth Dynasty. Also unearthed here was a colossal calcite statue, over two and a half meters in height, of a crocodile-headed manifestation of Sobek, presenting Amenhotep III with the sign of life, the *'ankh*. This exquisite statue is now beautifully displayed in the Luxor Museum of Ancient Egyptian Art. Other finds from the site include a number of decorated votive or commemorative monuments and stelae to Sobek dating from the Ramesside Period (figs. 80, 81). Numerous sources conclusively indicate that live crocodiles were kept in large numbers during the Late Dynastic and Greco–Roman periods, but the discovery at al-Mahamid al-Qibli is quite extraordinary, and indicates a much earlier date for this activity than was previously thought. Prior to the Eighteenth Dynasty, only one selected representative of a particular species was kept at a temple (see chapter 1).

Herodotus relates (II, 69) that the people who lived during his day on the shores of Lake Moeris (the modern Birket Qarun in the Faiyum) adored crocodiles to such a point that "they put ornaments of glass and gold on [their] ears and bracelets on [their] forefeet, provide for [them] special food and offerings, and give the creatures the best of treatment while they live; after death the crocodiles are embalmed and buried in sacred coffins." The Classical historian and geographer Strabo, who visited Egypt around 30 B.C., included in his book *Geographica* (XVII, 1) a fascinating and detailed account of his visit to see the tame, holy crocodile shown to tourists in the Faiyum:

> Sailing along shore for a distance of one hundred stadia, one comes to the city of Arsinoê, which in earlier times was called Crocodeilonpolis; for the people in this Nome hold in very great honor the crocodile, and there is a sacred one there which is kept and fed by itself in a lake, and is tame to the priests. It is called Suchus; and is fed on grain and pieces of meat and on wine, which are always being fed to it by the foreigners who go to see it. At any rate, our host, one of the officials, who was introducing us into the mysteries there, went with us to the lake, carrying from the dinner a small cake and some roasted meat and a pitcher of wine mixed with honey. We found the animal lying on the edge of the lake; and when the priests went up to it, some of them opened its mouth and another put in the cake, and again the meat, and then poured down the honey mixture. The animal then leaped into the lake and rushed across to the far side; but when another foreigner arrived, likewise carrying an offering of first-fruits, the priests took it, went around the lake in a run, took hold of the animal, and in the same manner fed it what had been brought.

Crocodile cemeteries, some containing many thousands of mummies and eggs, dating from this later period of Egyptian history, are known from a number of sites in the country, including Tebtunis, Hawara, al-Lahun, Thebes, and Medinet Nahas. At Kom Ombo, modern tourists can view crocodile mummies, still in their clay coffins, housed in a small chapel at the Greco–Roman temple, and visitors to the Graeco–Roman Museum in Alexandria can inspect some of the objects from the Ptolemaic temple of the crocodile-god Pnepheros from Batn Ihrit (Theadelphia) in the Faiyum, including a portable shrine on which the living god was borne during processional feasts: a grisly crocodile mummy is now displayed on the wooden stretcher.

Unlike the Nile Crocodile, the Hippopotamus is today thoroughly extinct from Egyptian waters, and has not been documented in the country since 1816 or 1818 (although at least one authority puts the date of its final disappearance from Upper Egypt as late as 1850). Nevertheless, this ponderous species continues to live still in innumerable images that have been preserved from

Fig. 84. Detail of carved relief from the great swampland scene in the tomb-chapel of the mastaba of Ti (no. 60) at Saqqara. A preying Common Genet is about to attack a nest filled with ducklings, while the mother bird—probably an Egyptian Goose—attempts to drive the ravaging predator away. Fifth Dynasty.

ancient Egypt. From its oldest representations during the Amratian Period (Naqada I), the ferocious and highly aggressive Hippopotamus appears as a hunted beast, and this becomes a recurring subject in Egyptian iconography. There is ample zooarchaeological evidence that this corpulent herbivore served as food in Predynastic settlement sites along the Nile. It is already attested as such at the Neolithic

site of Merimda Beni Salama in the Nile Delta, which had an initial occupation in the early part of the fifth millennium B.C. It is very possible that some Egyptians continued to enjoy eating Hippopotamus flesh into the pharaonic age.

Writing in the mid-first century B.C., the well-informed Classical author Diodorus Siculus had it right when he made the following observation regarding this species in Egypt (I, 35): "Being a river and land animal, it spends the day in the streams exercising in the deep water, while, at night, it forages about the country-side on the grain and hay, so that, if this animal were prolific and reproduced each year, it would entirely destroy the farms of Egypt." He further states that the Hippopotamus was recognized as a nuisance and continued to be hunted even in his day, and he provides an excellent description of the method employed in taking the animal. It is true that a single adult Hippopotamus can consume as much as sixty kilograms of grass in one evening; several of them foraging in an agricultural area could have a devastating impact in a very short while. Egyptian texts also speak of the lumbering beast's ravenous appetite and destruction of valuable field crops. Excessive hunting of the Hippopotamus in Egypt, and probably habitat destruction as well, already took their toll on numbers during antiquity. The Roman historian Ammianus Marcellinus of the late fourth century A.D. sadly mentions (XXII, 15, 19) the depletion of this species from the Nile Delta by his time: "But now they are nowhere to be found, since, as the inhabitants of those regions conjecture, they became tired of the multitude that hunted them and were forced to take refuge in the land of the Blemmyes [i.e., in Lower Nubia]."

The male Hippopotamus came to represent for the ancient Egyptians an embodiment of evil, and was held sacred to the evil god Seth; as such, it became a mythical enemy of the ruling king. The elimination of this species from the waters of the Nile is a frequent theme in the decorative program of temples and tomb-chapels, particularly in the Old Kingdom (figs. 79, 94, pl. IX). First attested during the First Dynasty, the motif of the harpooning of the demonic Hippopotamus can be traced unbroken to its appearance on temple wall reliefs during the Greco–Roman Period. Amid the lush stalks and umbels of dense Papyrus swamps, roaring wounded Hippopotamuses are depicted, bellowing out in pain and fury. Gangs of hunters in large Papyrus rafts plunge barbed harpoons into their bodies, while the tomb-owner calmly looks on. After a number of barbs have entered the animal's body and it has become sufficiently weak, the beast is hauled by ropes to the bank and finally dispatched. It seems likely that the animal would then have been butchered and consumed. While such scenes likely correspond to some degree with actual events during the Old and Middle kingdoms, it is quite possible that they also have a ritualistic significance. Just as the monarch is sometimes conventionally shown single-handedly killing this river monster, magically destroying the harmful forces of chaos and securing order in the world, noblemen during the New Kingdom do the same, performing a religious rite, triumphantly harpooning this Sethian creature.

Certainly some of the most delightful and estimable animal images that have come down to us from ancient Egypt are the brilliant blue or green faience figurines of Hippopotamuses from the Middle Kingdom (pl. XIV). With the characteristic fauna and flora of their swampy haunts painted on their rotund bodies, these statuettes were probably placed in tombs to serve as apotropaic devices, intended to ward off evil. The female Hippopotamus had a more benevolent nature than the male in mythology and was closely associated with the goddess Taweret, 'the Great One,' patroness of women in pregnancy, of childbirth, and of fertility (pl. XXXIV). This deity is frequently shown in the form of a pregnant or very fat Hippopotamus with sagging breasts standing upright and leaning on a *sa*-amulet, the symbol of protection, often with a crocodile on her back. She is often encountered as one of the protective beings on magic knives from the Middle Kingdom, which were fashioned from Hippopotamus tusks and used to safeguard the home (fig. 125).

Both the frog (*Rana* sp.) and the toad (*Bufo* sp.) are represented in Egyptian art. As might be expected, in many instances Egyptian artisans did not always clearly distinguish between the two forms. Because of this, and the absence of preserved diagnostic features in other pictures, it becomes rather hazardous to attempt to identify these illustrations to the species level. For our purposes, therefore, we use the general term 'frog' without being confined to zoological exactness.

The frog was, as it remains today, an abundant dweller in Nile waters. So common was it, in fact, that the hieroglyphic sign for 'one hundred thousand' was a tadpole. The reproductive process of the frog, which results in huge numbers of offspring, was a mystery to the ancient Egyptians. It is probably on account of this, and its highly visible fecundity, that the frog became a powerful symbol of self-propagation and regeneration of life. The Egyptians were, of course, aware of the frog's incessant croaking, and beginning in the Twentieth Dynasty used the onomatopoeic *kerer* to name it. As a sacred animal, the frog was associated with Heket, a goddess of childbirth. Terra-cotta figures and stone vessels in the shape of frogs were used as early as the Gerzean Period (Naqada II) and were included in some burials (fig. 82), and *ex voto* figurines have been discovered in temple sanctuaries at several sites from the Early Dynastic Period. The Cleveland Museum of Art houses an unusually large alabaster sculpture of a fine frog that dates from the First Dynasty: it probably represents the frog-goddess Heket, and may be a royal votive offering to her temple. In swamp scenes featured in tomb-chapels, especially during the Old and Middle kingdoms, frogs are occasionally included as an element of the teeming wildlife of the Papyrus thicket (pl. IX). In the tomb-chapel of the Sixth Dynasty mastaba of the vizier Kagemni (LS 10) at Saqqara, for instance, one sits on a stem of flowering Pondweed (*Potamo-*

geton lucens), just about to snap up some insects (fig. 131). In the Middle Kingdom, frog images, intended to be apotropaic, occur routinely on magic knives and rods (fig. 125), giving protection to mothers and the nursery. Particularly common at all times were frog amuletic objects in faience or stone, charms that could be used by both the living and the dead (figure on page ix).

Living most of its life in the dimly lit world beneath the waters of the Nile, the shy and reclusive African Softshell Turtle (*Trionyx triunguis*) was well known to the ancient Egyptians. This freshwater species, which is seldom met with today in Egyptian waterways, is first attested in art during the Amratian Period (Naqada I). Representations appear in the Predynastic era in the form of numerous small stone and clay figurines and vessels. Especially plentiful are turtle-shaped palettes of dark schist, dating from the Gerzean Period (Naqada II), which were used for grinding malachite and galena eyeliner. Although these are rather summarily carved, the species' diagnostic pointed snout is readily apparent.

From Predynastic times onward, there is a considerable amount of zooarchaeological evidence that the Egyptian diet was occasionally enriched by turtle meat. Turtles, however, are not mentioned in the extensive offering-list menus of the tomb-chapels of the privileged classes of society, nor do they ever appear among the victuals heaped before the deceased in scenes on tomb walls. Their absence here may have been the result of a religious taboo, at least for the Egyptian elite, that restricted their consumption. Probably on account of its dark, mysterious underwater haunt, the turtle came to be viewed as an enemy of the sun-god Ra and, like the male Hippopotamus, regarded as a symbol of evil as early as the Old Kingdom. Later, in the Nineteenth Dynasty tomb-chapel of Nebwenenef (no. 157) at Thebes,

Fig. 85. *The red animals painted on the sides of this buff-colored pottery vase cannot be identified with complete certainty, but are likely to be Egyptian Mongooses. It is tempting to see the wavy lines on the lower part of the vessel as snakes, particularly given the mongoose's well-earned reputation for destroying serpents. Reportedly from Awlad Yahya, near Naga al-Deir. Gerzean Period (Naqada II).* THE BROOKLYN MUSEUM.

the tomb-owner is portrayed harpooning a diminutive turtle from a raft in the Papyrus swamplands, thereby achieving victory over forces of evil and chaos. Inscriptions on New Kingdom coffins state in no uncertain terms: "The turtle is dead, long live Ra!" Turtles are also represented being ritually destroyed on the walls of temples during the Late Dynastic and Greco–Roman periods.

The image of the turtle also occasionally appears on magic knives and rods during the Middle Kingdom. Apparently, the species' reputation as a vicious biter, suddenly grabbing its prey when it comes within reach, could be harnessed to keep evil at bay. Two fine examples of the African Softshell Turtle appear amid the famous exotic fauna and flora of the tropical land of Punt, displayed in the Eighteenth Dynasty mortuary temple of Queen Hatshepsut at Deir al-Bahari (see chapter 8). The ancient Egyptians valued from the earliest times the shell, or carapace, of the indigenous Egyptian Tortoise *(Testudo kleinmanni)*, and probably that of the Green Turtle *(Chelonia mydas)* and the Hawksbill Sea Turtle *(Eretmochelys imbricata)* of the Red Sea as well, for various utilitarian and ornamental purposes: knife handles, bracelets, toilet articles, bowls, and sound-boxes for long-necked lutes.

Egyptian Nilotic swampland scenes, rich with a variety of animal life, commonly appear in the decoration of tomb-chapels beginning early in the Fourth Dynasty, through the New Kingdom and beyond. Frequently included in these compositions, practically as a stock element, especially during the Old Kingdom, is the Egyptian Mongoose *(Herpestes ichneumon)*, sometimes better known as the Ichneumon. It is customarily portrayed stealthily creeping up on a bird's nest, usually filled with a clutch of eggs or frantic fledglings (figs. 83, 95, pl. x); the panicked parents often swoop down in a vain attempt to drive off the marauding beast, and sometimes the young are pictured being violently yanked out of the nest and quickly devoured. This is entirely consistent with the predatory behavior of this agile waterside-dweller, as mongooses regularly consume birds and their eggs. On the other hand, the creature is often fancifully rendered climbing up thin, fragile

Fig. 86. (opposite), Two bronze statuettes of Egyptian Mongooses mounted on shrine-shaped pedestals. The sacred beasts are standing upright with their forelegs and paws raised in an attitude of adoration. The one on the left wears a uraeus (cobra) on its forehead. The small amulet in the foreground represents a shrew: such a charm was worn as a sign of devotion to the god Horus-Mekhentienirty of Letopolis. Late Dynastic Period. MEDELHAVSMUSEET, STOCKHOLM.

Fig. 87. This painted limestone relief scene of life on the Nile shows the pursuit of fishermen. To the right, several men are struggling to pull ashore a seine teeming with various fish. Among the haul a mullet, an Egyptian Eel, an upside-down catfish, and a Nile Perch can be recognized. On the left, men are transporting the bountiful catch, and below, fish are split open to dry. From the tomb-chapel of the mastaba of Akhethotep at Saqqara. Fifth Dynasty. MUSÉE DU LOUVRE, PARIS.

Fig. 88. Drawing of a now nearly destroyed detail from a wall painting in the tomb-chapel of the royal scribe Horemhab (no. 78) at Thebes, showing a Nile boat with gutted fish hung up to dry in the sun and breeze, and a bold Black Kite perched on the mast-head of the vessel, waiting for an opportunity to seize an easy meal. Eighteenth Dynasty.

Papyrus stalks that merely bend under its weight: this is purely artistic convention, as Papyrus stems could not support the weight of a mongoose under any circumstances. The animal is regularly joined in the thicket by the sly Common Genet (*Genetta genetta*), which is likewise frequently depicted raiding bird's nests while balanced on thin Papyrus stems (figs. 84, 95, pl. XXIV). In more recent times in Egypt, tamed Egyptian Mongooses have been known to be kept as much valued household rat-catchers and destroyers of snakes (fig. 85), but despite some persistent claims to the contrary, there is no firm evidence for this practice in the pharaonic age.

A somewhat surprising relief episode, set against a swamp backdrop in the many-chambered Sixth Dynasty tomb-chapel of the vizier of Mereruka at Saqqara, portrays a man in a Papyrus raft grasping the tail of a preying Egyptian Mongoose as it climbs a Papyrus stem (pl. X). The precise interpretation of this scene, however, remains quite elusive, and it cannot be used to demonstrate that mongooses were somehow trained. Another intriguing vignette in Mereruka's mastaba shows a small mammal in a waterside haunt devouring a fish. This figure has usually been described in

the Egyptological literature as an otter (*Lutra* sp.), but this identification is not without some doubt, and it could be an Egyptian Mongoose lunching on one of its favorite foods. Classical writers such as Diodorus Siculus (I, 87) recount the mongoose's worth in Egypt for its supposed ability to kill dozing crocodiles and their hatchlings, as well as its habit of killing snakes and consuming their eggs.

It is not until the Late Dynastic and Ptolemaic periods that the Egyptian Mongoose comes into prominence as a sacred animal. From this time, there are many bronze figures of the animal, some finely crafted, others crude and mass produced, which were offered as votive presentations by pious visitors at temples or sanctuaries where the Egyptian Mongoose was revered (fig. 86). These figures are usually hollow and quite often contain bits and pieces of bone remains, indicating that they were originally also used as coffins for the animal itself, which was sealed up inside. A great deal of confusion surrounds the identification of mongoose statuettes and those of another minor worshiped beast, the shrew (*Crocidura* sp.). It is sometimes difficult to distinguish between representations

Fig. 89. A balding angler sitting in a portable seat of reed matting on a small Papyrus raft is shown in this detail of relief bringing in a catch, a large catfish. His right hand is poised ready to dispatch the feisty fish with a wooden mallet. Below, the waters of the Nile are thick with schools of fish. From the tomb-chapel of the mastaba of Ti (no. 60) at Saqqara. Fifth Dynasty.

of the two because their forms were often treated by Egyptian artisans in an overly simplified manner, and Egyptologists have not always been quick to notice their differences (further confounding this mix-up, some mongoose figurines have mistakenly been identified as otters). According to Emma Brunner-Traut, the mongoose and the shrew jointly had mythological associations with Horus-Mekhentienirty, "the blind and seeing god," in the Lower Egyptian town of Letopolis (Awsim). The Egyptian Mongoose also had connections with the god Atum of Heliopolis, as well as with the goddess Wadjet of Buto, and is regularly shown wearing the sun-disc with a uraeus on its head. According to one ancient tradition, the sun-god Ra appeared in the form of a mongoose to defeat Apophis, the dreaded serpent of the underworld. At the Delta town of Tell Basta (Bubastis) mongoose remains and bronze images of them have been discovered in tremendous numbers, interred along with those of the domestic household cat, in an extensive mixed animal cemetery. Shrews were likewise subject to ritual mummification. Two species have been described

from their extensive remains: the Giant Musk Shrew (*Crocidura flavescens*) and the Dwarf Shrew (*Crocidura nana*).

Egyptian swampland compositions occasionally reveal some rather surprising inhabitants. A fragment of painted limestone relief, part of a large wetlands scene, now in the British Museum, London, and almost certainly from the Twenty-fifth or Twenty-sixth Dynasty Theban tomb-chapel of Montuemhat (no. 34), features on it a unique detail in Egyptian art: a small lizard, very probably a European Chameleon (*Chamaeleo chamaeleon*), slowly climbs up a bending stem of Papyrus, looking like it is scouting for a meal.

By any measure, one of the most beneficial gifts the Nile bestowed on the ancient Egyptians was the wealth of fish that abounded in the depths of its waters. Diodorus Siculus' statement (I, 36) concerning the fish life of the country was appropriate: "The Nile is home to many species of scaly fish in unbelievable numbers, providing the natives with all the freshly caught fish they can eat and yielding an inexhaustible supply for salting

as well. And in truth, the Nile surpasses all other rivers of the known world in its usefulness to man." Fish and fishing were integral to the Egyptians' secular and religious spheres of life and essential to the country's economy, providing an easily obtained, relatively inexpensive, delicious, and highly nutritious source of protein for the tables of the aristocracy and humble folk alike. From the earliest Predynastic settlement sites in the Nile Valley, zooarchaeological evidence clearly indicates that Nile fish was a readily exploited food staple. Various hooks of bone, ivory, and shell, as well as harpoons fashioned from bone and the net-sinkers used for catching them have been discovered on these sites too. At the extensive Neolithic site of Merimda Beni Salama on the western Delta margins, for example, tremendous quantities of fish bones have been recovered during the course of excavation, belonging to some fourteen families of Nile fish, consisting of at least twenty-one species.

One of the principal functions of the ancient Egyptian tomb was to provide a suitable environment for rebirth and maintenance in the hereafter. As a means of magically ensuring a bountiful supply of victuals the deceased owner could draw upon throughout eternity in the netherworld, affluent Egyptians decorated the walls of their tomb-chapels with a wide repertory of scenes that recorded aspects of daily life, with a particular emphasis on the procurement and preparation of food. Within this decorative program, some space was almost always devoted to fishing scenes: fishermen hauling in heavy seines teeming with fish (fig. 87), gutting and drying them (figs. 87, 88), extracting roe for the preparation of botargo, angling with hook and line (fig. 89, pl. VII), catching fish using small hand-held nets or wickerwork basket-traps (pls. VII, XII), and fishmongers plying their trade at open-air markets. Noblemen are traditionally pictured in their elaborate tomb-chapels standing on light Papyrus rafts engaged in spearing fish or, occasionally in the New Kingdom, quietly angling with a rod in a pond under the cool shade of Sycamore Fig trees, a loved one sitting nearby. Fishing was clearly a pleasurable sporting activity that some ancient Egyptians hoped to enjoy throughout eternity.

When Egyptian artisans turned their powers of keen observation to the tremendous variety of fish life around them, the result was quite successful; so much so that we can readily identify approximately twenty-six different species of Nile fish in Egyptian art and hieroglyphs—and this tally does not include a selection of wonderful exotic species of fish that can also be distinguished. In the magnificent tomb-chapel of the Fifth Dynasty mastaba of Ti (no. 60) at Saqqara, fifteen species or genera, some varieties represented more than once, can be discerned among the spoils swimming in an enormous seine that is being hauled ashore: upside-down catfish (*Synodontis schall* and *S. batensoda*), mullets (*Mugil* sp.), mormyrids (*Mormyrus caschive, M. kannume, Petrocephalus bovei,* and *Gnathonemus cyprinoides*), *Tilapia* sp. (best known now by its Arabic name, *bulti*), Puffer Fish (*Tetrodon fahaka*), a carp (*Labeo* sp.), an Egyptian Eel (*Anguilla vulgaris*), clarid catfish (*Clarias anguillaris* or *C. lazera*), a moonfish (*Citharinus* sp.), a schilbeid catfish (*Schilbe* sp.), and an Electric Catfish (*Malapterurus electricus*). These fish must have been among the most popular and sought-after table fare in ancient Egypt (many of them are recognized even today as excellent eating), as they are commonly figured in the catch on other funerary monuments as well. Once this vast haul was dragged ashore, the fresh fish were cleaned, gutted, dressed, and cooked by roasting or boiling or simply split open with a broad flint knife and allowed to dry in the sun and breeze (perhaps salted as well) to be preserved for future use (figs. 87, 88). Some of these same species of fish are routinely encountered in modern Egyptian fish markets in Cairo, Luxor, Aswan, and elsewhere.

While compositions featuring various fishing-related activities are standard in Old

Fig. 90. (opposite), Painted detail of limestone relief of an offering-bearer, wearing a short kilt and curled wig, bringing a generous supply of freshly caught Nile fish. These include a mullet, two kinds of catfish, and a massive Tilapia. From the tomb-chapel of the vizier Kagemni (LS 10) at Saqqara. Sixth Dynasty.

Fig. 91. This deep cerulean blue faience drinking bowl is decorated on its interior face with a swirling design of four swimming Tilapia fish and some closed lotus blossoms. This motif refers to the theme of rebirth. Bowls such as this one were used at banquets. Eighteenth Dynasty. THE MUSEUM OF FINE ARTS, BOSTON.

Kingdom tomb-chapel decoration, and bearers are even sporadically depicted proffering them to the deceased owner, fish are always omitted from the extensive funerary offering-list menus in tombs, and they do not appear among the victuals on tables of the orthodox dead. Their absence certainly seems to indicate that fish were viewed, at least by some members of the wealthy classes, as ritually impure or otherwise unacceptable as food in the beyond. A degree of fear of fish is also evidenced by the omission of fish-hieroglyphs in inscriptions near the deceased in the burial chamber. Concern for ritual cleanliness from fish is exhibited in the New Kindom *Book of the Dead*. Spell 64 contains the instructions that for effectiveness it should be recited only if one is pure, "without going near women, without eating goats, without consuming fish." Even if this may have been the case in funerary circumstances, it does not necessarily mean that well-to-do ancient Egyptians did not enjoy fish dishes during life, although priests may always have been prevented by strict regulations on purity from consuming certain foods such as fish or pig. The funerary restriction on fish may have been because of the dark, mysterious, underwater world they inhabit, which, to the Egyptian mind, was outside the normal order of the universe. On the other hand, it has also been suggested that the peculiar odor of fish may have been offensive to the departed. In any case it is apparent that fish were deemed inappropriate for offering lists and tables in the Old Kingdom, and some prohibition against them was in effect.

As far as the living were concerned, there does not seem to be any convincing evidence for a taboo against fish consumption until at least the Twenty-fifth Dynasty. The first mention comes from a curious, brief passage on the triumphal granite stela of the Nubian king Piye from Gebel Barkal, now in the Egyptian Museum, Cairo. The inscription states that this victorious monarch refused to have any dealings with three defeated Egyptian kings because they were uncircumcised and "fish-eaters": they were therefore impure and could not be brought before him. The entry also seems to indicate that some very highly placed ancient Egyptians were not averse to eating fish. The Classical authors during the Late Dynastic and Greco–Roman periods refer to an assortment of taboos against fish consumption then current in the country (see below), but the direct relevance of these late records to earlier periods in Egyptian history remains a matter of conjecture.

During the Middle and New kingdoms, Nile fishing episodes continued as prominent themes on tomb-chapel walls. In scenes of everyday life during the New Kingdom, a number of affluent tomb-owners appear not to shun fish. In the Eighteenth Dynasty tomb-chapel of Menna (no. 69) at Thebes, for example, a wall painting illustrates Menna receiving the various produce of his estate, including two handsome fish placed before him. Other compositions show some Theban notables lunching on fish. Fish also occasionally appear as victual gifts to the departed. A particularly noteworthy detail appears in the Eighteenth Dynasty rock-cut tomb of Meryre I (no. 4) at al-Amarna, where, in a scene displaying royal storehouses, a large magazine is shown well stocked with dried fish stacked row upon row, awaiting distribution. And this is probably a realistic view, because we know from textual sources that enormous numbers of dried fish were kept in temple stores. The great Harris papyrus of the Twentieth Dynasty records that during his thirty-one year reign, Ramesses III delivered some 474,200 fish of various sorts and 440 jars of pickled fish to Theban temples alone.

To what degree fish was a part of the day-to-day diet of the average ancient Egyptian citizen is, in the present state of our knowledge, not altogether certain. Fish are represented in Old Kingdom market scenes and seem to be sold cheaply. Proof of fish consumption during the Eighteenth Dynasty also comes from zooarchaeological findings from the workers' village at al-Amarna, where quantities of fish bone remains have been uncovered. Evidence gleaned from

Fig. 92. This handsome gold fish pendant, shown greatly enlarged, represents a Synodontis catfish. The fish was part of a set of five found around the neck of a child in a burial and may have been a magical charm against drowning. From Haraga, near al-Lahun. Twelfth Dynasty. ROYAL MUSEUM OF SCOTLAND, EDINBURGH.

Fig. 93. Wall painting from the burial chamber of the tomb of Khabekhnet (no. 2) at Thebes, portraying the jackal-headed god Anubis tending an enormous mummified fish on a Lion-legged couch, between small figures of the godesses Isis and Nephthys and the four Sons of Horus. The precise meaning of the fish mummy is not certain, but it probably represents the deceased, who associates himself with the god Osiris. Nineteenth Dynasty.

documents listing fish deliveries to the Ramesside Period artisans' village at Deir al-Medina in the Theban necropolis, whose standard of living was certainly well above the majority of the population, indicates that each worker received a ration from the state of approximately eleven kilograms of fish per month. Other written sources from the Ramesside Period also suggest fish was an affordably priced foodstuff: Ludwig Keimer once referred to fish as the 'meat' of the poor in ancient Egypt.

One hazard of eating fish is that an undetected bone may become lodged in the diner's throat, which can be life-threatening. The ancient Egyptians knew this problem only too well, and a late New Kingdom magical charm entitled 'A Spell for Getting Right a Fish Bone' was employed when the emergency arose: "The Unique One belongs to me, (as) my servant! The Unique One belongs to me! (My) bread is in the town, (my) portion of meals is in the field—bone, get right! A man will say this spell (over) a cake. To be swallowed by a man in whose throat a fish bone is (stuck)."[22]

A unique collection of remarkable fish portrayals, about forty of them, along with other marine animals, dwellers in the Red Sea and the Indian Ocean, is displayed in wall reliefs at Queen Hatshepsut's Punt colonnade in her Eighteenth Dynasty mortuary temple at Deir al-Bahari. These captivating scenes commemorate the famous sea-borne trading expedition to the southern, tropical land of Punt during the queen's reign (see chapter 8). Among the variety of exotic aquatic marvels, a fierce looking scorpionfish (Scorpaenidae) can be distinguished (fig. 134), as well as a deftly executed Swordfish *(Xiphias gladius)*, with its extended sword-like upper jaw (fig. 135). Many of the representations of fish are so precise that one is tempted to speculate that the queen had an interest in ichthyology! Fish were also regularly employed by artisans in ancient Egypt as ornamental motifs on a range of objects, including jewelry, palace floor paintings, cosmetic dishes and spoons, glass perfume bottles (pl. xxv), and ceramic tiles, or simply gracefully swimming as a stock element of most aquatic compositions.

Living so close to the natural world along the river, the Egyptians were familiar with the mouth-breeding habits of some members of the genus *Tilapia*. After the eggs are laid and then fertilized, either the male or female *Tilapia* (depending on the species) picks them up and holds them in its mouth until they hatch, then releases them. Even after they are born, the fry swim back into the parent's mouth for protection at the first sign of danger, leaving again when it has passed. The ancient Egyptians interpreted the fish's behavior as self-propagation, and because of this the *Tilapia* developed into a powerful symbol of renewed life and of fertility. In combination with lotus *(Nymphaea)* flowers, another image of regeneration, the *Tilapia* fish is a favorite decorative device during the New Kingdom, especially pleasing when painted on the interiors of bright faience bowls (fig. 91). In Theban tomb-chapels, the deceased owner is sometimes shown spearing a pair of *Tilapia* with his harpoon in the swamplands, or catching them in a pond with a rod, which probably alludes to the rebirth of the dead, perhaps having subtle erotic associations as well.

The Egyptians were also well acquainted with the curious habit of the upside-down catfish *(Synodontis batensoda)* doing precisely what its name implies, swimming upside-down, and it is repeatedly depicted that way in art. During the Middle Kingdom, amuletic pendants in the form of a *Synodontis* catfish were fairly popular and may refer to this species. Some of the loveliest examples, fashioned in pure gold (fig. 92), were worn perhaps as magical protection against drowning or as a fertility charm.

As with many animals, a range of Nile fish in ancient Egypt were viewed as sacred in some way or other, particularly during the Late Dynastic and Greco–Roman periods. One such fish was the Nile Perch *(Lates niloticus)*, which was linked with the goddess Neith. Another, the most revered of all fish, was the famous Oxyrhynchus-fish, unquestionably a *Mormyrus*, with its very distinctive long, down-curving snout. According to an an-

cient legend, it was thought to have been one of the varieties of fish that swallowed the phallus of the god Osiris, and was thus forbidden for consumption by a late taboo in some areas of the country. Its diagnostic appearance is known from a score of outstanding bronze statuettes used as votive objects during the Late Dynastic Period. The Greek traveler and prolific writer Plutarch (c.A.D. 46-120) records in his *De Iside et Osiride* (380B=72) the hostilities that arose between the neighboring towns of Kynonpolis and Oxyrhynchus because of their respective sacred animals: "Since the inhabitants of the 'Town of the Dogs' eat oxyrhynchus-fish, the inhabitants of the 'Town of the Oxyrhynchus-fish' seized in our time a dog, slaughtered it and devoured it as a piglet. As a result, they went to war and treated each other maliciously; and they were punished and separated later by the Romans." Such was the intensity of the devotion to sacred animals during this later age of Egyptian history!

As early as the New Kingdom, certain species of Nile fish were subject to mass mummification for religious reasons, and were interred in sacred animal necropolises. A most unusual scene in a wall painting on the burial chamber of the Nineteenth Dynasty tomb of Khabekhnet (no. 2) at Thebes shows the jackal-headed god Anubis embalming or resuscitating a gigantic holy *abdu*-fish, which rests on a funerary bier, just as a human mummy would (fig. 93). This unique detail appears to represent the deceased tomb-owner under the guise of a sacred fish and may be connected with the symbolical significance of the fish in the hoped-for regeneration in the beyond. At Esna (Latopolis), scores of thousands of *Lates* fish of all sizes, from fry to giants over two meters in length, were interred in a vast cemetery west of the town during the Greco–Roman Period. Fish cemeteries have also been discovered at Kom Medinet Ghurab, where the burials apparently date from the Nineteenth Dynasty reign of the Ramesses II, and at al-Bahnasa (Oxyrhynchus).

Chapter Six

 # A Bevy of Birds

*T*hou art the sole one, who made [all] that is, [the] solitary sole [one], who made what exists, from whose eyes mankind came forth, and upon whose mouth the gods came into being. He who made herbage [for] the cattle, and the fruit tree for mankind, who made that (on which) the fish in the river may live, and the birds soaring in the sky. He who gives breath to that which is in the egg . . . and gives life to flying things in every tree. Hail to thee, who did all this! Solitary sole one, with many hands . . . .[23]

Thus reads a beautiful passage from a hymn to the god Amun on an Eighteenth Dynasty papyrus roll, now in the Egyptian Museum, Cairo, which proclaims that it is the mighty creator-god who sustains all life and provides for humankind, and at the same time sees to the needs of every other member of the animal kingdom, even the birds on the wing.

Modern Egypt has a rich and diverse bird life in a variety of habitats. Fifty centuries ago, at the beginning of the pharaonic age, this mosaic of avifauna was even richer. A number of bird species that are routinely portrayed in ancient Egyptian art and hieroglyphs, including some that have been identified from extensive mummified remains, are now locally extinct or are extremely rare visitors. One would have to journey up the Nile many hundreds of kilometers to southern Sudan to find some of these varieties today.

This loss of bird life from the Egyptian landscape is principally associated with the ever-increasing disappearance of prime swamp habitat, largely the result of human expansion into these areas. However, the decline is also very closely related to over-exploitation and disturbance of the local bird populations (see chapter 3). It is the extensive wetland areas that historically have provided abundant food, breeding grounds, and needed protection for both indigenous species and migrating visitors. Owing to its geographical setting in the northeast corner of Africa, a bridge between two continents, Egypt lies on a major migratory flyway for birds of passage from the Palearctic region. Twice each year, during the spring and autumn, since time

Fig. 94. The great Papyrus swampland scene in the tomb-chapel of the mastaba of the high official Ti (no. 60) at Saqqara, showing a Hippopotamus hunt, with a variety of bird life roosting in the field of vegetation above. The deceased is indicated in the composition by his prominent size. He does not participate in the chase, but calmly observes the action from his own Papyrus raft while holding a tall staff. Fifth Dynasty.

immemorial, astonishing numbers of migrant birds—thousands of millions—pass through on their journey from Europe and western Asia to central and southern Africa and back again. Egyptian wetland areas, especially the northern Nile Delta lakes, are also extremely important for wintering water bird populations from nearly the entire Palearctic area. Birds of all kinds—

breeding residents, overwintering and passage migrants, waterfowl, songbirds, soaring raptors—served significant functions in both secular and religious spheres of ancient Egyptian life.

From the earliest Predynastic times through the Greek and Roman periods, a dazzling array of bird life abounds in Egyptian art, featured in a wide range of media.

Fig. 95. Fragment of wall painting illustrating the stems and umbels of the Papyrus thicket, with some of the characteristic species of this watery habitat. Waterfowl and butterflies are winging overhead, while a nesting Barn Owl defends its clutch of eggs from a preying Egyptian Mongoose. On the left, a Common Genet is creeping up on a pair of unguarded nestlings. From the tomb-chapel of Neferhotep (A. 5) at Thebes. Eighteenth Dynasty. MUSÉE DU LOUVRE, PARIS.

Always accomplished *animaliers*, when turning their keen powers of observation to the abundant denizens of the sky the highly-skilled Egyptian artisans achieved remarkable results. Many of the birds illustrated display a close fidelity to nature in form, coloring, and mode of behavior. So far, about seventy-two different wild and domestic bird species can be distinguished in Egyptian iconography. Images of birds are also a salient feature of the formal, ornamental hieroglyphic script. It is impossible to make a rigid distinction between ancient Egyptian art and hieroglyphs, as the hieroglyphic signs are really a miniature form of art in their own right and serve as a complementary part of an overall artistic composition. This is readily apparent in the gamut of bird-signs, often first-rate bird portraits that can stand alone, possessing their own individuality and charm, and in detail these can often favorably compare with that of any large-scale representation (figs. 111, 116, 121, pl. XX). In Sir Alan Gardiner's classic *Egyptian Grammar* sign-list, sixty-two standard hieroglyphs are enumerated that depict birds or parts of birds.

The ancient Egyptians clearly delighted in the intrinsic beauty of birds and cel-

ebrated their pleasure in both picture and word. A rich concourse of colorful avifauna was traditionally pictured inhabiting the dense fields of stems and umbels of the Papyrus swamp environment, as displayed on the walls of tomb-chapels and temples from the Old Kingdom onward (figs. 94, 95, pl. XXIII). First and foremost, however, the avian world was most valued as providing a readily available, inexpensive, highly nutritional, and delicious source of food, appreciated on the tables of the humble and elite alike, although we can be reasonably certain that the choicest plump, specially hand-fed birds carved on tomb-chapel walls were always reserved for the most affluent Egyptian citizens, who could afford such luxurious fare. No doubt kings also dined on splendidly prepared bird dishes, as indicated by the stores of victuals recovered from their tombs. Some species of birds were also important for sacrificial offerings, and were thus pleasing to the palates of the gods (fig. 96). Today's most characteristic farmyard bird worldwide, the familiar chicken or Red Junglefowl *(Gallus gallus)*, was apparently unknown to the ancient Egyptians until the Ramesside Period, and then only as a rare

exotic marvel imported from western Asia. The chicken did not become commonplace along the banks of the Nile until at least the Ptolemaic Period (see chapter 8).

The Egyptians relied upon an assortment of other birds for eating, but to a marked degree were particularly fond of migratory waterfowl, especially geese and ducks, and trapped immense flocks of these traveling birds during their yearly migrations (fig. 97). Inscriptions in the so-called 'chamber of the seasons' in the Fifth Dynasty sun temple of King Niuserre at Abu Ghurab disclose that as early as the Old Kingdom, the ancient Egyptians were evidently well aware of the annual movements of some birds and fishes, and they were readily able to distinguish between resident and migrant birds (fig. 19). This should really come as no surprise since, living so close to the natural world, the ancient Egyptians depended on an intimate knowledge of the yearly cycles of the local fauna and flora for their livelihoods. Observing migratory birds even allowed them to mark the passage of time with figures of speech. In

the well-known late New Kingdom literary work *The Report of Wenamun*, Wenamun, complaining about his long stay at far-off Byblos on the Phoenician coast and wishing to return home to Egypt, observes: "Do you not see the migrant birds going down to Egypt a second time?" And in a Ramesside Period text, an Egyptian official grumbles about the hardships of his post abroad and laments: "I spend the whole day watching the birds."

Zooarchaeological findings from some of the oldest Predynastic settlement sites in the Nile Valley indicate that tremendous numbers of wild birds, predominantly waterfowl, were eagerly exploited by the first Egyptians. Just how plentiful and comparatively easy water birds are to obtain in Egypt is demonstrated by the fact that from 1979 to 1986, by a conservative estimate between 260,000 and 374,000 of them were taken annually in the Nile Delta alone, using essentially the same technology, aside from firearms, as in the days of the pharaohs.

Within the extensive repertory of motifs on tomb walls, geese, ducks, cranes,

Fig. 96. This limestone block of sunk relief is carved with a unique scene showing King Akhenaten making an offering of a Pintail to the Aten, god of the sun disk, whose rays, terminating in small hands, stream down upon him. One of the hands holds the hieroglyphic sign for 'life' ('ankh) to Akhenaten's nostrils. The king is pictured wearing the khat-headdress, his arms extended before him, as he ritually wrings the neck of the sacrificial Pintail. Originally from an edifice of Akhenaten at al-Amarna, found at Hermopolis (al-Ashmunein) in Middle Egypt. Eighteenth Dynasty. THE METROPOLITAN MUSEUM OF ART, NEW YORK.

Fig. 97. Tempera copy of a detail from a wall painting depicting a mixed flock of water birds being trapped with clap-nets in the wetlands. In the clap-net above, three European Teal can be counted among the rich spoils of the hunt. Below, a fowler is removing some captured Pintails, one of which has escaped and flies into the sky on the right. From the rock-cut tomb of the nomarch Khnumhotep III (no. 3) at Beni Hasan. Twelfth Dynasty.

and doves of various species figure prominently, and were no doubt regarded as quite desirable for table dishes. The decoration sometimes takes the form of compositions showing teams of professional fowlers working with large, rectangular-shaped clap-nets in the Papyrus swamplands (figs. 97, 109, pl. IV), enabling the capture of dozens of water birds at one fell swoop. In many of these instances, the men of the wetlands were aided in their trapping by tame decoy birds (customarily the long-legged Gray Heron, *Ardea cinerea*; pl. X), used to attract clouds of waterfowl to their nets. This toilsome occupation of the lowly was disparagingly described in the Middle Kingdom work *The Satire on the Trades*: "The bird-catcher, he is very miserable, when he looks at the denizens of the sky. If marsh-fowl pass by in the heavens, then he says: 'Would that (I had) a net!', (but) god does not let (it) happen to him, being neglectful of his affairs."[24] Other common themes related to birds as a food source for the departed include rearing domestic birds in huge aviaries and fowlyards, where attendants fattened them by forcing food

down their gullets (fig. 98); men tending mixed flocks, wielding long sticks, with captions listing the birds' names and numbers; plucking, eviscerating, and cooking a catch of birds; and, almost always, many offering-bearers bringing generous numbers of birds, wringing their necks, and heaping them before the deceased (fig. 99). Various waterfowl are also ubiquitous in the extensive offering-list menus inscribed in tomb-chapels during most periods.

One of the most enduring scenes encountered in funerary monuments from the Old Kingdom to the close of pharaonic times and beyond was the tomb-owner engaged in an idyllic sporting excursion to the Papyrus swamps, hunting throngs of water birds with his boomerangs or throwsticks while standing in a light raft made of Papyrus stalks (pl. XXIII), often in the company of friends or family. This popular rural pastime of the well-to-do was extolled in a Middle Kingdom literary work entitled *The Pleasures of Fishing and Fowling*: "A happy day when we go down to the marsh, that we may snare birds."[25] Without necessarily excluding the recre-

ational aspects of these hunting compositions, at least by the time of the New Kingdom such scenes had in addition acquired
symbolical significance, and they very likely
allude to the deceased magically overcom-
ing adverse forces that may threaten their
welfare in the beyond. The Egyptian monarch is also occasionally pictured on gigantic temple wall reliefs trapping teeming
numbers of waterfowl with a clap-net, as
Ramesses II of the Nineteenth Dynasty does
in a scene in the great hypostyle hall at the
temple of Karnak helped by the gods Horus,
Khnum, Thoth, and Seshat-Neith. Here,
the confusion of wild birds appears to represent malignant powers or demons that
might threaten Egypt, and with the aid of
the gods the king is able to triumph over
them and secure order in the universe.

Considering the abundance of water
birds in Egyptian art and hieroglyphs, it is
quite rare to be able to identify the precise
species of goose, duck, or other waterfowl, due to the absence of preserved de-

tails and their overall summary treatment.
Generally speaking, no more can be said
of most geese than that they are members
of the genus *Anser* or *Branta*. Nevertheless, a White-fronted Goose (*Anser
albifrons*) or a Lesser White-fronted Goose
(*Anser erythropus*) can occasionally be
sighted in tomb-wall scenes, and this bird
also appears as a hieroglyphic sign. Several species of duck can be identified, especially the ubiquitous Pintail (*Anas acuta*),
which is by far the most frequently depicted fowl (figs. 96, 97, pl. XXIV). The very
colorful plumages of the European Teal
(*Anas crecca*) and the European Widgeon
(*Anas penelope*) can be distinguished amid
the painted decoration in the splendid
Middle Kingdom rock-tombs of the
nomarchs at Beni Hasan (fig. 97).

The pictorial record of which birds were
seemingly the most esteemed for the table
is confirmed by finds of victuals deposited
in tombs as offerings for the dead to par-
take of in the netherworld. The pair of

*Fig. 98. This block of finely
carved limestone relief
displays the inside of a busy
aviary. An attendant is
depicted on the right
standing between two lotus
bud columns, wearing a short
kilt and curled wig, force-
feeding a tall Common
Crane. To the left, various
kinds of poultry are roosting,
and a man is shown force-
feeding a duck or a goose.
These fat birds would have
enriched the diet of the
deceased throughout eternity.
This old photograph of the
piece shows it before it was
severely damaged during
World War II. From the
tomb-chapel of the mastaba of
Sopduhotep (D 15) at
Saqqara. Fifth Dynasty.*
ÄGYPTISCHES MUSEUM, BERLIN.

Fig. 99. This detail of painted limestone tomb-relief illustrates an offering-bearer bringing a generous number of ducks, geese, and a crane to the deceased. With his left hand the retainer firmly holds the wings of the birds, while with his right he wrings the neck of one of them. From the tomb-chapel of the mastaba of the vizier Mehu at Saqqara. Sixth Dynasty.

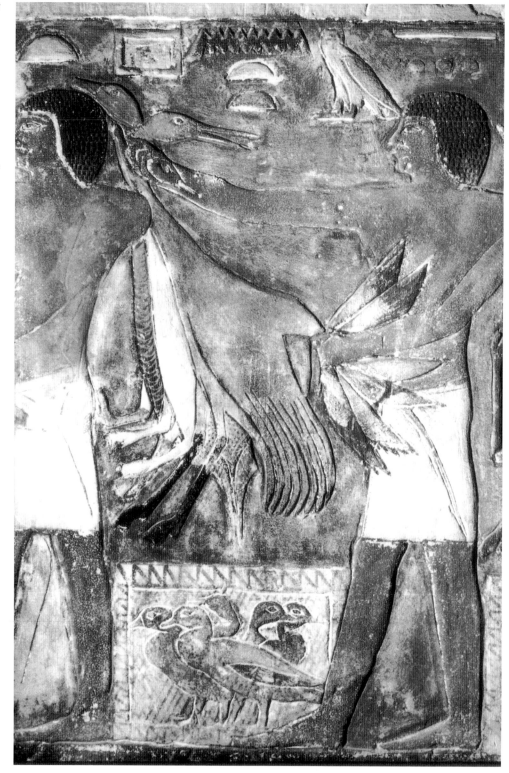

queens' burial chambers discovered in the Twelfth Dynasty pyramid of Amenemhat III at Dahshur contained a sumptuous funerary repast comprising fourteen White-fronted and Graylag geese *(Anser anser)*, seven Pintails, two Garganey *(Anas querquedula)*, three European Teal, and four Turtle Doves *(Streptopelia turtur)*. Similarly prepared birds have been found buried in other tombs, such as that of King

Fig. 100. (above) Tempera facsimile of a famous fragment of wall painting from the tomb-chapel of the mastaba of Nefermaat and his wife Atet at Meidum, known nowadays as the 'Geese of Meidum.' These birds are among the finest achievements of Egyptian painting. The panel exhibits three species—White-fronted Geese, Bean Geese, Red-breasted Geese—along a sparsely covered mud flat in the wetlands. It originally formed a sub-scene in a larger composition showing men trapping fowl with a clap-net. See detail, pl. III. Early Fourth Dynasty. THE EGYPTIAN MUSEUM, CAIRO.

Fig. 101. (above left) This attractive detail of wall painting portrays a Turtle Dove roosting on a branch of a small flowering Nile Acacia tree near a pond of water, where it is joined by a group of other perching birds. From the rock-cut tomb of the nomarch Khnumhotep III (no. 3) at Beni Hasan. Twelfth Dynasty.

Tutankhamun of the Eighteenth Dynasty, who was originally interred with provisions of waterfowl consisting of one Brent Goose *(Branta bernicla)*, one White-fronted Goose, two Bean Geese *(Anser fabalis)*, four European Teals, two Shovelers *(Anas clypeata)*, one Gadwall *(Anas strepera)*, and two other ducks that were not identified.

An indisputable masterwork of ancient Egyptian painting is the frieze known as the 'Geese of Meidum' (fig. 100). This famous work, a fragment of wall painting nearly two meters long and about twenty-three centimeters high, is from the tomb-chapel of the early Fourth Dynasty mastaba of Nefermaat and his wife Atet at Meidum, where it formed a small cameo scene in a much larger composition illustrating their sons trapping birds with a clap-net. Exceptionally well preserved and frequently re-produced, this is without doubt among the best known and most widely appreciated pictures from all of ancient Egypt and has been referred to as the earliest ornithological record in history. The panel exhibits a magnificent frieze of six large geese of three species: two White-fronted Geese, two Bean Geese, and two Red-breasted Geese *(Branta ruficollis)*. These vividly colored portrayals are the result of careful observation of the living birds, and the level of accuracy achieved by the artisan or painter here is seldom encountered elsewhere. The beautiful and pristine Red-breasted Geese in particular (pl. III), with their bold, arresting, painted plumage, successfully capture this handsome ornamental species of waterfowl from top to bottom. These are the only extant examples in Egyptian iconography of the Red-breasted Goose, a species which

Fig. 102. This almost life-size wooden statue of a Mute Swan was found in the tomb of the princess Itiwert at Dahshur. The precise function of this figure is uncertain, but evidently the swan had some symbolical significance for the ancient Egyptians that led to it being deposited in the tomb. Similar wooden swans were discovered in the tombs of two other Twelfth Dynasty princesses at Dahshur. During the New Kingdom, statues of swans were included in the funerary equipment of several monarchs buried in the Valley of the Kings. Twelfth Dynasty. THE EGYPTIAN MUSEUM, CAIRO.

has not been documented in Egypt since 1882. In recent years, however, bone remains of the Red-breasted Goose have been identified from the early First Dynasty funerary tomb complex of King Aha at Abydos, perhaps suggesting that the ancient Egyptians knew the goose better than was previously supposed.

Equally deserving of our admiration and notice is the justly celebrated painted scene executed in the Twelfth Dynasty rock-tomb of the nomarch Khnumhotep III (no. 3) at Beni Hasan. This illustrates the tomb-owner and his son, under the cover of a blind, engaged in trapping a flock of bright and varied ducks on a pool using a clap-net. The pond is flanked by two small flowering Nile Acacia trees *(Acacia nilotica)*, on whose branches are roosting a bevy of nine passerines, some of the most extraordinary and charming birds in all of ancient art (fig. 101).

The ancient Egyptians were well acquainted with the graceful and elegant Mute Swan *(Cygnus olor)* (fig. 102), the troublesome Egyptian Goose (see chapter 4), the strikingly colored and highly gre-

garious Greater Flamingo (fig. 42), and an assortment of other kinds of water birds. During the Old Kingdom, sacred pelicans *(Pelecanus* sp.) were housed within precinct walls at the Fifth Dynasty sun temple of Niuserre at Abu Ghurab, as evidenced by a fragment of limestone relief now in the Ägyptisches Museum, Berlin, depicting three of these large, ungainly, tame birds, slowly walking under the charge of their priest-keepers. The pelican had mythological associations with both the rising and the setting sun, and this no doubt was the reason the animals were kept at the solar temple. In the Eighteenth Dynasty tomb-chapel of Horemhab (no. 78) at Thebes, a small flock of charmingly expressed shaggy pelicans (almost certainly Dalmatian Pelicans, *Pelecanus crispus)* and their eggs are painted among the spoils of fowlers; they were evidently captured along the periphery of the swamplands (fig. 103). This vignette seems to suggest that pelicans may also have been table fare in ancient Egypt. Sad to report, this lovely tomb-chapel has re-

Fig. 103. (above) This detail of wall painting is from the tomb-chapel of the royal scribe Horemhab (no. 78) at Thebes. It shows a small flock of five captured Dalmatian Pelicans, which seem to be engaged in some social interaction. On the left, their eggs are depicted neatly arranged in a pottery vessel and covered with layers of straw to protect them during transport. Eighteenth Dynasty.

Fig. 104. (left) A lovely ivory unguent or eye-paint container in the form of a swimming duck. The engraved wings of this small piece pivot outward to expose a cavity where the cosmetic substance was stored. Eighteenth Dynasty.
THE WALTERS ART GALLERY, BALTIMORE.

cently been vandalized by thieves, and this delightful little group was severely damaged in the process.

During the New Kingdom, vibrant patterns of flocks of wild ducks winging in flight were occasionally employed in Egyptian art as a decorative theme, sometimes boldly painted on palace floors or the ceilings of tombs. In certain contexts, the image of a comely duckling or gosling could also have subtle erotic connotations (figs. 77, 104, 105); it has even been sug- gested that these elements might allude specifically to female sexuality. Some- times, a representation of one or more hatchlings in a nest, with bills open and wings outstretched, was incorporated into vase decoration. A thoroughly delightful example of such a fledgling, surrounded by eggs in a nest, served as a lid to an alabaster jar discovered in the Eighteenth Dynasty tomb of Tutankhamun (no. 62), in the Valley of the Kings, now in the Egyptian Museum, Cairo. This figure may

Fig. 105. Decorative wooden cosmetic spoon with openwork carving showing a naked young woman strumming a lute which has a duck's head on the end of its long neck. She is depicted in a swampland environment, and is precariously poised standing on a small Papyrus raft, whose prow and stern also terminate in the shape of duck heads. A motif of ducks could have subtle erotic associations. From Sidmant, near the Faiyum. Eighteenth Dynasty. THE PETRIE MUSEUM OF EGYPTIAN ARCHAEOLOGY, UNIVERSITY COLLEGE LONDON.

refer to the miracle of regeneration the deceased king hoped for in the beyond. The wild goose was also evoked in love poetry during the New Kingdom: "The wild goose soars and swoops, it alights on the net; many birds swarm about, I have work to do. I am held fast by my love, alone, my heart meets your heart, from your beauty I'll not part!"[26]

Certainly by the Eighteenth Dynasty, if not considerably earlier, Egyptian aviculturalists were actively breeding domestic ducks and geese on agricultural estates to supplement those taken from the wild. The great Harris papyrus of the Twentieth Dynasty records that during his thirty-one-year reign, Ramesses III donated enormous quantities of waterfowl, in excess of 426,395 individuals, to various temples in the land, a number that probably comprised both wild and domestic varieties. In order to meet this ever-increasing demand for table birds, clever Egyptian poulterers, sometime during the Late Dynastic or Ptolemaic periods, devised a method of artificially incubating fowl eggs on a massive scale in specially constucted ovens. Writing in the mid-first century B.C., Diodorus Siculus remarks on the practice (I, 74): "The men who have charge of poultry and geese, in addition to producing them in the natural way known to all mankind, raise them by their own hands, by virtue of a skill peculiar to them, in numbers beyond telling; for they do not use the birds for hatching the eggs, but in effecting this themselves artificially by their own wit and skill in astounding manner, they are not surpassed by the operations of nature." If they were similar in size to such installations known from more recent times in modern Egypt, these amazing hatcheries were presumably capable of handling many hundreds of birds' eggs at a time. It is also quite probable that ibis and falcon eggs, and perhaps eggs of other species too, were incubated in these ovens in the Late Dynastic and Greco–Roman periods, supplying the popular and burgeoning animal cult industry with birds (see below).

In the magnificent temple of Hathor at Dendara, a curious wall relief, which dates from the reign of Ptolemy XV Caesarion and his mother Cleopatra VII Philopator at the very end of the Ptolemaic Period, displays an instance of the well-known ceremony of releasing birds to the four cardinal points, which took place at festivals during the coronation of the king. These birds were identified with the four Sons of Horus and were given instructions to fly to

Pl. xx. From the temple of Tuthmosis III at Deir al-Bahari, this well preserved ornamental hieroglyph of a Barn Owl (the letter m) is sculpted in limestone relief and realistically painted. The morphological features and coloring of a living Barn Owl have been admirably achieved in this portrait. However, there is one spurious feature: note that the owl is depicted with 'ears' on its forehead, similar to those of the Eagle Owl (Bubo bubo) or the Long-eared Owl (Asio otus), but not characteristic of a Barn Owl. The reason for this zoomorphic anomaly is probably that the owl hieroglyph was originally modeled after a species of 'eared' owl, and for reasons of tradition this feature was carried over onto the Barn Owl. In ancient Egyptian drawing and painting, the human or animal head is as a rule shown in profile only. One of the handful of exceptions to this is the owl sign. As our illustration shows, the head is turned toward the observer and is viewed full face. This distinguishes it from all other bird hieroglyphs. Although the Barn Owl was a standard hieroglyphic sign, the species is extremely rare in art. See fig. 95 for one such uncommon occurrence. Eighteenth Dynasty.

Pl. XXI. This illustration of a dying Red Fox seeking refuge behind a bush is a detail from a wall painting in the tomb-chapel of Userhet (no. 56) at Thebes, which exhibits a lively scene of the desert hunt (see pls. XVII, XVIII). Death is very close at hand for this beast, which has been mortally wounded by Userhet's arrows, and blood is flowing freely from its mouth and left eye. Eighteenth Dynasty.

Pl. XXII. This handsome detail is from a large fragment of wall painting from the unlocated Theban tomb-chapel of the scribe Nebamun. In the pastoral scene, cowherds deliver their long-horned cattle for the annual count and inspection. The group of five overlapping beasts is wonderfully shown, using a range of color and patterning on their hides. The scribe carrying out the recording can be seen sitting on the left holding a papyrus roll, as one of the herders offers him a respectful greeting. Eighteenth Dynasty. THE BRITISH MUSEUM, LONDON.

Pl. XXIII. The classic scene of the tomb-owner fowling in the Papyrus swamplands teeming with wildlife. The scribe Nebamun is shown on the Papyrus raft in the company of his sumptuously dressed wife and his daughter, who wears the sidelock of youth, hunting birds with a throwstick. In his right hand he holds three live decoy herons. His pet cat energetically attacks three birds on its own. The woman's elaborate costume, wig, and sistrum may have subtle erotic associations, as may the Egyptian Goose (a family pet or a decoy) poised on the prow of the vessel. From the unlocated tomb-chapel of Nebamun at Thebes. Eighteenth Dynasty. THE BRITISH MUSEUM, LONDON.

Pl. XXIV. Detail of a wall painting from the Theban tomb-chapel of Menna (no. 69), part of a swampland composition, where the deceased hunts birds for pleasure. We view a portion of a dense stand of Papyrus with a flock of Pintails and two butterflies winging high above the umbels. Menna's unerring throwsticks find their marks, knocking the ducks right out of the sky. A cat and a Common Genet are ready to prey upon the ducks' nests, which are filled with appetizing eggs. Eighteenth Dynasty.

Pl. XXV. This striking fish-shaped polychrome glass vessel may have once served as a perfume or unguent container for a no doubt well-heeled resident of Akhetaten, the royal city built by Akhenaten at al-Amarna in Middle Egypt. It is fashioned in the form of a Tilapia, a variety of fish known in Egypt nowadays by its Arabic name bulti. This common Nile species was frequently incorporated into decorative designs in ancient Egypt and was regarded as a symbol of rebirth. Eighteenth Dynasty. THE BRITISH MUSEUM, LONDON.

Pl. XXVI. (opposite) This splendid openwork pectoral fashioned from gold, inlaid with semiprecious stones, lapis lazuli, turquoise, and carnelian, was discovered in the tomb of Tutankhamun (no. 62) in the Valley of the Kings. The young monarch may have worn this necklace during his lifetime. The central motif contains a solar bark with a Dung or Sacred Scarab Beetle holding the sun disk, flanked by two baboons, each wearing a crescent and full moon on its head and crouching on top of a shrine with its arms upraised in an attitude of adoration, greeting the morning sun. On either side of the monkeys is the hieroglyphic sign for 'dominion' (was). Eighteenth Dynasty. THE EGYPTIAN MUSEUM, CAIRO.

Pl. xxvii. An exquisite painted ivory cosmetic container in the shape of a large-eyed grasshopper, which looks as though it is about to take off. When the wings of this small toilet box are removed, a cavity for holding costly eye-makeup is revealed. The insect originally had antennae springing from the head and was completed by a stand of some sort. From Thebes. Eighteenth Dynasty. Reign of Akhenaten. THE BROOKLYN MUSEUM.

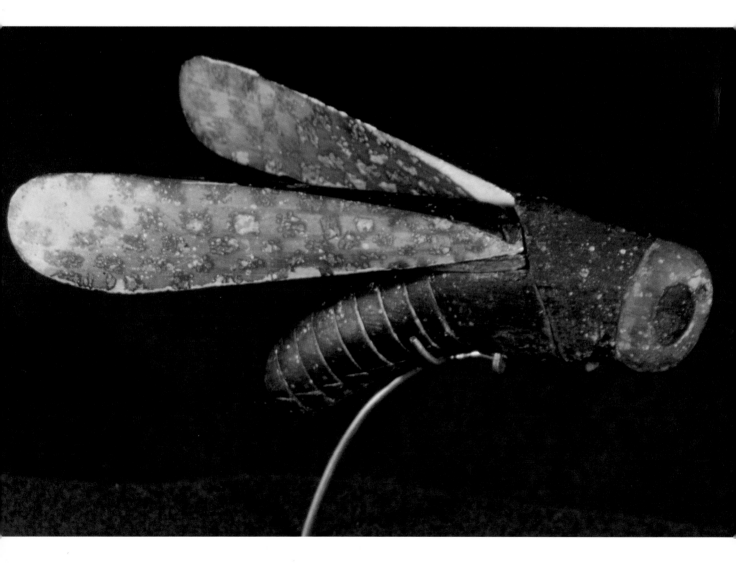

Fig. 106. Fragment of painted limestone relief showing an unknown spoonbill-headed god, wearing a long wig or pleated headdress. This is the only representation of a deity in the form of a European Spoonbill (Platalea leucorodia) presently known in Egyptian iconography. Late Dynastic Period. MUSÉES ROYAUX D'ART ET D'HISTOIRE, BRUSSELS.

the corners of the earth and announce to the gods that a new monarch had come to the throne. In much older versions of the rite, during the New Kingdom, the four birds are Pintail ducks and, on at least one occasion, doves or Rollers *(Coracias garrulus)*. But the birds at the temple of Dendara have been interpreted by several authorities as the earliest instance of carrier Pigeons *(Columba livia)* in recorded history (fig. 108). Indeed, the four diminutive birds clearly do have what seem to be tiny tablets attached to their necks by means of a string, and these could be letters or messages of some kind. On the other hand, the specific identification of these interesting figures as Pigeons remains somewhat problematical, and the birds might just as well be doves. Whether communication by carrier Pigeon was in operation during the days of the pharaohs, as some have maintained, can only be speculated upon, since conclusive evidence does not exist. The colossal pi-

geon cotes that are so typical of the Upper Egyptian landscape today, and from which nitrogen-rich guano is harvested for use as a valuable fertilizer in the cultivation of certain vegetables, are only first attested in the country during the Greco–Roman Period.

Representations of the ostentatious peacock *(Pavo* sp.) do not appear in ancient Egyptian iconography. This ornamental, exotic bird probably became known in the Nile Valley only in the Greco–Roman Period and was imported from India. During the Ptolemaic Period, it developed close ties with the Greek god Dionysos. Considerably later in Egyptian history, the strutting peacock became a standard decorative and symbolic motif in Coptic art.

A very popular dish served at great tables of the elite in ancient Egypt, from the First Dynasty at least through the New Kingdom, was the crane—either the Com-

Fig. 107. Inlaid decorative faience tile with symbolical design of Lapwings. As a standard hieroglyphic sign, the Lapwing represents rhyt, 'the common people.' The birds are shown sitting— with wings twisted around one another, human arms and hands upraised in an attitude of worship added to their breasts—on top of baskets (nb, 'all') and with a five-pointed star (dwa, 'adore') in front of them. Together this group can be read as the phrase "all the people in adoration" before the king. This tile is from the palace of the mortuary temple of Ramesses III at Medinet Habu, Thebes, and was probably part of a long frieze used to decorate the jamb of a doorway or window. Twentieth Dynasty. THE EGYPTIAN MUSEUM, CAIRO.

Fig. 108. (right) Drawing of a detail from a wall relief composition on the temple of Hathor at Dendara, showing four birds on the wing with little tablets attached to their neck. These are probably letters or some other sort of written communication. The small birds appear to represent carrier Pigeons. From Dendara, in Upper Egypt. End of the Ptolemaic Period.

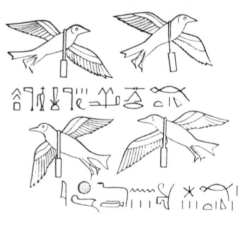

mon Crane (*Grus grus*) or the Demoiselle Crane (*Anthropoides virgo*). There are two extant scenes of trapping cranes, both from Saqqara: a small, black steatite gaming disk with inlays (fig. 109) from the First Dynasty tomb of the chancellor Hemaka (S 3035) and a more detailed vignette in the well preserved tomb-chapel of the Sixth Dynasty mastaba of the vizier Mehu both illustrate the capture of these migratory, long-legged birds with clap-nets in the swamplands. Once brought into captivity and tamed, large mixed troops of both species, probably with their wings pinioned, were managed by attendants brandishing long sticks. These fairly large birds sometimes appear in aviaries being fed and are occasionally depicted being fattened up by force-feeding (fig. 98). Cranes are also routinely glimpsed on temple and tomb-chapel walls being carried by offering-bearers as gifts for the meal of the gods or the deceased. Sometimes they are also depicted with their long bills tied to the lower portion of their necks with a cord (fig. 37), which prevented the cranes from lashing out with their pointed bills and injuring their handlers and hindered the birds' ability to take to the wing.

Also highly thought of on the menus of prosperous ancient Egyptians from the very earliest times was the Common Quail

(*Coturnix coturnix*). It is routinely represented in art, and a fledgling quail occurs as a standard hieroglyph from earliest times (pl. XXIX). Migrant flocks of these comparatively tiny game birds were annually trapped during the spring in harvested grain fields, as illustrated in the tomb-chapel of the Sixth Dynasty mastaba of the vizier Mereruka at Saqqara, and again on a fragment of wall painting from a Theban tomb-chapel from the Eighteenth Dynasty (fig. 110), using a technique still employed in rural Egypt today. After being netted, the small quails were often tied to sheaves and then presented as offerings to the deceased tomb-owner, particularly during the New Kingdom. There is no direct evidence from ancient Egypt for the well-known modern method of quail capture in Egypt along the Mediterranean coast

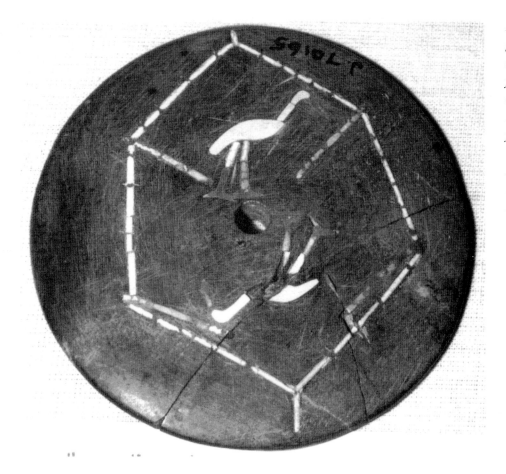

Fig. 109. Black steatite gaming disk with calcite inlay decoration depicting a fowler's clap-net with two cranes trapped in it. Discovered with some forty-four other disks (see pl. II) in the tomb of the chancellor Hemaka (S 3035) at Saqqara. First Dynasty. THE EGYPTIAN MUSEUM, CAIRO.

during the autumn, when great waves of migratory birds arrive after their long flights of passage from Europe and are easily taken as they alight, but one would assume that it took place in some form. The first reference to this kind trapping is from Diodorus Siculus (I, 60), who reports the practice along the northern coast of Sinai.

Now long extinct from its former range in Egypt, the Helmeted Guineafowl *(Numida meleagris)* is portrayed in Predynastic Egyptian art, but in the historical period it is confined to its appearance as a hieroglyph (fig. 111). When this unmistakable species disappeared from Egypt is not known, but it was apparently considered sufficiently rare during the Ptolemaic Period to be carried in cages during Ptolemy II Philadelphus's extraordinary pageant in Alexandria during the early 270s B.C.

Egyptian farmers, then as now, were quite keen on trapping flocks of marauding birds to prevent them from pilfering valuable crops in orchards of fruit-bearing trees at the time of the harvest (fig. 112). During the Old and Middle kingdoms, tomb and temple scenes occasionally illustrate the netting of Rollers and Golden Orioles *(Oriolus oriolus)*, the two principle crop pests, in orchards of Sycamore Fig trees. Once caught, the birds were probably prepared and consumed as a welcome meal. From the New Kingdom, there are a number of bird-scaring episodes pictured on tomb-chapel walls, where women and children are portrayed making a noise and waving long strips of cloth in order to frighten and drive away flocks of hungry birds from trees and vines that are heavy with tasty, ripe fruit. Also at this time, crafty, large, black crows *(Corvus* sp.) are regularly encountered in ancient Egyptian art, especially on figured ostraca, pilfering fruit, usually nuts from Doum Palms. In pharaonic Egypt, as today, the predacious

Fig. 111. (opposite)

Fig. 110. This fragment of Theban wall painting, probably from the unlocated tomb-chapel of the scribe Nebamun, features a rarely represented activity of country life, a group of farmers trapping a flock of Common Quails in a grain field. It is the time of the harvest and all that remains of the field is the tall stubble, over which a fine-meshed net has been stretched. The feeding birds have been flushed from the cover of the stubble and have flown directly up into the net. This is the moment that has been captured in the painting, and we view two of the peasants running swiftly to retrieve some of the quails entangled in the net. Eighteenth Dynasty. ÄGYPTISCHES MUSEUM, BERLIN.

Fig. 111. (opposite) An ornamental hieroglyph of a Helmeted Guineafowl in sculpted limestone relief, illustrated on the sed-festival shrine of King Sesostris I at Karnak. The sign stands for the two letters nḥ. The unmistakable features of the species are readily apparent in this crisply fashioned portrait. Twelfth Dynasty.

Black Kite *(Milvus migrans)* had a reputation as a bold opportunist. This aerial pirate was always ready to snatch a fish from the catch of an unwary fisherman (fig. 88). Farmers, too, were plagued by the highly aggressive Black Kite and occasionally turned to magical charms to keep fields safe from this cunning species. A papyrus roll from the Eighteenth Dynasty contains such a spell, entitled "For Preventing a Kite from Plundering," to be recited when setting up a scarecrow to watch over important agricultural crops. In Egyptian mythology the Black Kite had close associations with the sister goddesses Isis and Nephthys.

One of our most fascinating and insightful sources of information on the ancient Egyptian bird world comes from the Eleventh Dynasty rock-tomb of the nomarch Baket III (no. 15) at Beni Hasan. Among the wealth of scenes of everyday life pictured on the walls of this tomb-chapel is a painting featuring a collection of twenty-nine different bird forms (there may have been more originally), almost all of which are named in a brief hieroglyphic caption inscribed above each of them. Also present are three bats (order Chiroptera) of

two kinds—large and small—drawn with deft certainty. The ancient Egyptians seem to have classified this winged mammal as a type of bird, as numerous other cultures in the past have done, a 'bird of the night,' as it were (fig. 113). The entire group of bats and birds is presented, neatly arranged, in a series of long registers on the wall, and is not associated with any particular setting or environment. The artisan has grouped the land birds to the left and the water birds to the right, and thus the whole resembles a natural history museum display. This rare collection has unfortunately suffered considerably with the passage of time, especially at the hands of anchorites, who have left their mark in the form of Coptic graffiti. Many of the figures can still be confidently identified, however, and some of them are not only exceedingly accurate but unique to their appearance in this tomb. We are able to recognize among others the Purple Gallinule *(Porphyrio porphyrio)*, Common Crane, Pied Kingfisher *(Ceryle rudis)*, European Coot *(Fulica atra)*, Spur-winged Plover *(Vanellus spinosus)*, Black Stork *(Ciconia nigra)*, Night Heron *(Nycticorax nycticorax)*, sandpiper *(Tringa* sp.), Painted

Snipe *(Rostratula benghalensis)*, Bittern *(Botaurus stellaris)*, Avocet *(Recurvirostra avosetta)*, Ringed Plover or Little Ringed Plover *(Charadrius hiaticula, C. dubius)*, Golden Oriole, Masked Shrike *(Lanius nubicus)*, Roller, and Pin-tailed Sandgrouse *(Pterocles alchata)*. Probably the most re-markable aspect of the composition is that it was included in the tomb not so much to magically serve as food in the next world but, apparently, as a small ornithological compilation of the local bird life. The scene

Fig. 112. This painted limestone relief illustrates the trapping of birds in a Sycamore Fig orchard. A flock of Golden Orioles, along with a sprinkling of Hoopoes, has invaded a tree that is heavy with fruit, in order to pilfer the ripe morsels. A large triangular mist-net stretches from the crown of the tree down to the ground. Two men (one of them an achondroplastic dwarf) are shown on the left shouting and running toward the tree, frightening the feeding birds, which in their panic take to the wing, only to fly into the net and become entangled in its meshes. Some of the captured birds are shown on the right being placed in crates for transport. From the tomb-chapel of the mastaba of Akhethotep at Saqqara. Fifth Dynasty. MUSÉE DU LOUVRE, PARIS.

suggests that Baket may have been an ardent bird-fancier and wished to continue to enjoy the earthly pleasure of these winged creatures in the afterlife. Another intriguing collection of birds, albeit foreign ones from western Asia, was proudly displayed as a show of exotic wonders on the walls of the so-called 'botanical garden' of the Eighteenth Dynasty king Tuthmosis III at the temple of Karnak (see chapter 8).

The ancient Egyptians were familiar with three species of ibis and clearly distinguished them in art and hieroglyphs: the Glossy Ibis (*Plegadis falcinellus*), the Hermit Ibis or Waldrapp (*Geronticus eremita*) (fig. 114), and the Sacred Ibis (*Threskiornis aethiopicus*). This final species has earned tremendous notoriety, its fame reflected in its vernacular name, but the modern traveler on the Egyptian Nile will no longer find it: this beautiful wetlands-dwelling bird has not been documented in Egypt since November 1891, when one was recorded in the Sinai peninsula, although it is possible that the new wetlands areas created behind the Aswan High Dam may one day lure the Sacred Ibis back to Egypt from its nesting grounds in Sudan. Nevertheless, memory of the Sacred Ibis continues to live in its many portrayals in art and as a hieroglyphic sign in ancient Egypt, and

from literally millions of ibis mummies, preserved for eternity. Almost every major museum with a collection of Egyptian antiquities contains a specimen of this bird: bronze or wooden statuettes (fig. 115), faience amulets, handsome near-life-size statues that may have served as ibis coffins, and of course mummified remains.

As a divine animal, the Sacred Ibis was regarded as a manifestation of Thoth, the god of wisdom and learning, patron of the scribal profession, and lord of the moon. This graceful waterside bird can be recognized during the Fourth Dynasty, and thereafter routinely appears in Egyptian iconography, usually roosting and nesting amid the stems and umbels of the Papyrus swamp thickets (pls. V, X). (Some Predynastic representations of ibis may refer to this species, but the absence of color precludes their precise identification.) There is evidence that at least small numbers of Sacred Ibis were already being kept in captivity in Egypt during the New Kingdom. This is borne out by a scene carved on a block of relief from a tomb or temple dating from the late Eighteenth or early Nineteenth Dynasty and now in the Museo Archeologico, Florence, which shows an attendant feeding several ibises in an open-air poultry yard. It is doubtful that these birds were being kept for table use. Rather, it is quite possible they were sacred birds; if so, they would probably have been mummified and buried upon their deaths. Ludwig Keimer has dated some Sacred Ibis mummies, on stylistic grounds, to the Ramesside Period. Much later, by the time of the Late Dynastic and Greco–Roman periods, the Sacred Ibis had been elevated to such a lofty status that killing one, even unwittingly, was, according Herodotus (II, 65) and others, a crime punishable by death. By this time the birds were bred and reared on an enormous scale in large sanctuaries connected with the temples of Thoth's cult, situated all over Egypt: Abydos, Tuna al-Gebel, Kom Ombo, Saqqara, al-Baqliya, and elsewhere. Worshipers at these sacred sites purchased the mummified birds (sometimes very well wrapped in many yards of linen bandages and often stylishly decorated with appliqué) and offered them to the god in anticipation of his answering their pleas or in thanks for petitions already realized. The wealthier pilgrim might, in addition, dedicate a fine bronze or wooden figure of a Sacred Ibis as a votive gift (fig. 115). The ibis mummies were usually placed in ceramic pots after their offering at the temple and then interred by the priests *en masse* in cemeteries or catacombs situated nearby. The numbers of Sacred Ibis and their eggs buried during this late period of Egyptian history is nothing short of astounding. The number of ibis mummies in the sacred animal necropolis at north Saqqara alone, at a conservative estimate, is thought to be well over one and a half million birds, and textual evidence indicates that more than four million were probably interred there during antiquity. Perhaps an equal number were deposited in the catacombs at Tuna al-Gebel in Middle Egypt, the cemetery for Thoth's main cult center at Hermopolis (al-Ashmunein). The tourist visiting this interesting site today can inspect a fine selection of ibis mummies, bronze statuettes of sacred animals, and other related artifacts from there at the nearby Mallawi Antiquities Museum. Not all the birds interred at these sites were Sacred Ibises, it should be noted: a small number of the mummies have been identified as Glossy Ibis.

Several eminent researchers over the years have maintained that the veneration

Fig. 113. A figured limestone ostracon, about the size of a human hand, with a black ink drawing of a bat. This rarely portrayed beast is sketched with its wings outstretched as if in flight. The head of the bat is turned to the right and the mouth is gaping open. The ancient Egyptians thought of the bat as a kind of bird, much as they classified the turtle and crocodile along with fish. From Deir al-Medina. Ramesside Period. THE EGYPTIAN MUSEUM, CAIRO.

Fig. 114. Gold funerary (?) diadem from the burial of a princess at Giza (tomb of shaft 294), decorated with a motif featuring Hermit Ibises. The piece is ornamented with three roundels of gold with carnelian inlay. The central disk has a chased design and is flanked by two others composed of two opposed Papyrus umbels with a Hermit Ibis perched on top of each. This species of ibis may have been fairly abundant in Egypt during antiquity, but today it is extremely rare: it has not been recorded in the country since March 1962. Late Fifth or early Sixth Dynasty. THE EGYPTIAN MUSEUM, CAIRO.

accorded to the Sacred Ibis in antiquity eventually resulted in the species' extermination in Egypt. While quite interesting, this theory has yet to be convincingly proven, and it seems more likely that the disappearance of the Sacred Ibis is directly related to the loss of its prime swamp habitat in the Nile Delta than to its treatment more than two thousand years ago. What these authorities have failed to note is that the Sacred Ibis was still fairly common in Egypt up until about 1800, even being occasionally sold for food in bird markets in the Delta. In addition, the majority of birds that were mummified in pharaonic Egypt were domestically bred in captivity, not taken from the wild, and so the impact on the wild population may have been minimal.

When examining the raptorial species, we find, once again, that the skilled ancient Egyptian artisans were acute observers of nature. Little ornithological expertise is required to confidently distinguish in art and hieroglyphs the Black Kite (fig. 88), Egyptian Vulture *(Neophron percnopterus)* (fig. 116), Griffon Vulture *(Gyps fulvus)* (fig. 123), Lappet-faced Vulture *(Aegypius tracheliotus)* (figs. 117, 121), Long-legged Buzzard *(Buteo rufinus)*, Lesser Kestrel or Kestrel *(Falco naumanni, F. tinnunculus)* (pl. XXIX), and Barn Owl *(Tyto alba)* (pl. XX). These and many other varieties of birds of prey are also known from truly vast numbers of mummified

specimens entombed in sacred animal necropolises, most from the Late Dynastic and Greco–Roman periods.

Probably the single most frequently represented bird throughout the long course of Egyptian history, especially as a hieroglyph, is the falcon of Horus (pl. XXXIII), that potent emblem of the god of the sky, son of Osiris, and symbol of the monarchy. The Egyptian king was viewed as the representative of Horus on earth, the living Horus (fig. 118). Other deities such as Ra-Harakhty or Montu could appear under the guise of the same falcon form, but it is with Horus (whose name, 'the Lofty One,' is well suited to this bird of prey) that this famous falcon is most closely associated. The Horus falcon was the nearest thing the ancient Egyptians had to a national bird, but the precise identification of the falcon used to depict Horus is impossible, since the image was surely influenced by several species of falcon, of more or less similar appearance, that are indigenous to Egypt. Nevertheless, one cannot help thinking that the large, high-flying, power-diving Peregrine Falcon *(Falco peregrinus)* in particular may have served as something of a model. The Horus falcon was employed as a tremendously popular decorative motif in Egyptian art, its form used to adorn anything from temple walls to ornate royal jewelry.

Falcons can first be recognized in art from the Late Predynastic Period (Naqada

160

III), mounted on top of standards, depicted on ornamental, dark schist votive palettes, and on a macehead. However, it is not until the very beginning of the First Dynasty that we can first see the highly distinctive and prominent mustachial streak or eye marking that, later, was always prominently indicated on carefully executed depictions of the Horus falcon (fig. 119). There is some zooarchaeological evidence that already during the Early Dynastic Period the ancient Egyptians kept captive falcons and buried them in cemeteries close by the tombs of their owners. Some of these birds have been interpreted as pets (see chapter 4).

As sacred birds, falcons, like the Sacred Ibis, were mummified and interred in mass burials during the Late Dynastic and Greco–Roman periods. Falcon eggs were probably artificially incubated in ovens and the hatchlings raised by hand then dispatched at a young age to provide pilgrims with birds they could purchase as votive presentations when visiting sites where Horus or other falcon gods were worshiped. Various species were mummified in tremendous numbers, perhaps millions, and interred in animal cemeteries and subterranean galleries around the country. The Kestrel, the most abundant falcon in present-day Egypt, also seems to have been the most frequently mummified species in antiquity, but this may have more to do with its associations with the sister goddesses Isis and Nephthys (pl. XXIX) than with Horus, whose falcon the Kestrel does not closely resemble; on the other hand, perhaps other species of falcon were in short supply and Kestrels were used in their stead. The birds were often intricately wrapped in linen bandaging with

Fig. 115. Gilded wood and bronze statue of a Sacred Ibis sitting upon a shrine, a manifestation of the god Thoth. Before the bird is a squatting bronze statuette of Maat, goddess of truth and order, who is shown as usual with an Ostrich plume on her head. This fine piece was probably dedicated to Thoth by a well-to-do pious pilgrim when visiting his cult temple. From Tuna al-Gebel. Late Dynastic Period.
KESTNER MUSEUM, HANNOVER.

Fig. 116. (opposite) Ornamental hieroglyph of an Egyptian Vulture on a fragment of wall painting from the tomb-chapel of the mastaba of Nefermaat and his wife Atet at Meidum. The sign represents aleph, the glottal stop. Anyone who has had the opportunity to observe an Egyptian Vulture at close quarters will agree that a keen likeness of this distinctive-looking species has been captured in this portrait. Early Fourth Dynasty. THE EGYPTIAN MUSEUM, CAIRO.

Fig. 117. (left) This gilded wood anthropoid coffin is decorated with a great figure of a Lappet-faced Vulture crafted in semi-precious stones and glass, representing the sky-goddess Nut. With her long wings spread across the abdominal region, she served the deceased by giving magical protection. The image of a Lappet-faced Vulture was well chosen for the goddess, since this species is certainly the largest and most powerful vulture on the African continent. The bird grasps in its talons the hieroglyphic sign for 'infinity' (shen). This coffin once held the mortal remains of Yuia, father of the illustrious Queen Tiye. From the tomb of Yuia and his wife Thuya (no. 46), Valley of the Kings. Eighteenth Dynasty. THE EGYPTIAN MUSEUM, CAIRO.

Fig. 118. (opposite) This unsurpassed masterpiece of ancient Egyptian sculpture represents King Chephren, builder of the second pyramid at Giza. He is shown seated, wearing the ceremonial royal beard and nemes-headdress. His high-backed throne supports the falcon of the god Horus, with outstretched wings embracing the head of the aloof god-king, signifying that Chephren is the living Horus. Diorite. From Giza. Fourth Dynasty. THE EGYPTIAN MUSEUM, CAIRO.

Fig. 119. (left) Detail of the round-topped limestone royal stela of King Djet (Uadji). The majestic falcon-god Horus is pictured in relief, standing above the king's name, represented by a hieroglyph of a snake with an upraised head within a serekh, the elaborate niched façade and rectangular enclosure wall of his palace. From Abydos. First Dynasty. MUSÉE DU LOUVRE, PARIS.

geometrical patterns, and were sometimes even given painted cartonnage masks or placed in decorated coffins (fig. 6). The more ardent or well-heeled devotees might have also dedicated a finely cast bronze effigy of a falcon. The falcon catacomb at Saqqara is filled with mummies of these birds buried in neatly stacked, plain pottery jars in their hundreds of thousands.

We close our overview of the ancient Egyptian avian world with that giant flightless

Fig. 120. This tempera facsimile reproduces a now damaged vignette from a wall painting in the chapel of the tomb of User (no. 21) at Thebes. An adult Ostrich captured alive in the desert hunt is delivered by an attendant in a nonchalant manner to the deceased as a trophy of the chase. That a wild, fully grown Ostrich (which could easily strike out with its powerful legs and inflict serious if not fatal wounds) is shown being handled by a single man only underlines the caveat that Egyptian tomb-scenes should not always be interpreted as a record of reality, but more as an expression of an ideal.

creature, prized for its beautiful and useful plumes, valuable eggs, and as swift-footed quarry for the desert chase—the Ostrich (*Struthio camelus*). Long thought to have disappeared from its former distribution in Egypt, the Ostrich is currently experiencing something of a comeback, especially in the Gebel Elba region in the extreme southeastern corner of the country. The age-old tradition in Egypt of utilizing this highly distinctive African species probably continues to this day: Rashaida tribesmen living in the Gebel Elba area are thought to consume Ostrich meat and perhaps eggs as well. The Ostrich's diagnostic silhouette can be recognized from the oldest series of rock drawings carved by hunters on cliffs along the edge of the Nile Valley and in the deserts of Upper Egypt, probably during the Amratian Period (Naqada I) (fig. 30).

From its earliest appearance in the Predynastic record, and continuing at least through the Ramesside Period, the Ostrich customarily occurs in Egyptian art as a favorite desert game animal for pharaohs, nobles, and intrepid hunters, who let fly their arrows at flocks of these fleeing birds. By the Eighteenth Dynasty, however, the object of the chase was sometimes to capture adult Ostriches alive (fig. 120), and they are pictured in Theban tomb-chapels under the charge of attendants who present them as trophies to the deceased. Ostriches are also portrayed in scenes on tomb and temple walls delivered as tribute, booty, or spoils of warfare from the southern Nubian lands. It is possible that some of these Ostriches may have been tame or domestic birds. There is some textual documentation from the Ramesside Period for the import of live, perhaps tamed, Ostriches from Nubia (see chapter 8). The purpose of such birds remains largely unknown. They may have been intended for consumption, or to serve as breeding stock for captive propagation, or merely to replenish royal hunting parks or reserves with fresh game.

It was clearly for its plumes and eggs that the Ostrich was most valued in pharaonic Egypt. The Ostrich feather was a standard hieroglyph and was also the symbol of Maat, the goddess of truth, right, and orderly conduct. Maat was always portrayed wearing a large, prominent Ostrich plume on top of her bewigged head (fig. 115). Ostrich eggs have been found in some human burials from the Predynastic Period, perhaps as victuals offered to the deceased. The eggs make delicious eating, and, emptied of their contents, the huge shells were sometimes used in antiquity as containers. The demand for Ostrich plumes and eggs was such that by the New Kingdom, additional supplies of these luxury goods were often imported or brought as tribute. They figure among the products carried by bearers from Libya, Punt, Syria, and especially from Nubia. In a passage of a text from the New Kingdom, the Ostrich is said to greet the dawn each day by 'dancing' in the desert wadis in honor of the rising sun, and there are at least three instances in art illustrating the 'dance of the Ostrich.' And indeed, Ostriches have been observed in the wild at sunrise running around, spinning, and flapping their diminutive wings, an activity that could be seen (with a little spirited imagination) as a kind of dance.

Chapter Seven

Serpents, Scorpions, and Scarabs

*T*he crocodile be against him in the water, the snake be against him on land—(against) him who may do a thing to this (tomb). I never did a thing to him. It is the god who will judge (him).[27]

So states a threat directed by the deceased at potential tomb-robbers in an inscription in the tomb-chapel of the Sixth Dynasty mastaba of Meni at Giza, now in the Staatliche Sammlung Ägyptischer Kunst, Munich. The image of a menacing snake is clear warning.

From their ordinary daily activities in the fields, along the riverside, on the desert margins, and in their homes and villages, the ancient Egyptians were exceedingly aware of the harmful—sometimes lethal—capabilities of the venomous snakes that inhabited their environment, especially the large and often aggressive Egyptian Cobra *(Naja haje haje)*, reaching more than two meters in length, and the equally dangerous, although significantly smaller in size (no more than one meter long), horned viper *(Cerastes* sp.). While attacks from poisonous snakes in Egypt are seldom fatal to healthy adults, deaths do sometimes occur, particularly among the weak, young, and aged. As an example, the number of deaths reported annually from snakebites in Egypt between 1944 and 1948 ranged from twenty-six to forty-six, although the true figures may well have been higher.

Most victims of the bites of the Egyptian Cobra or the horned viper experience intense pain and discomfort, but paralysis and even profound unconsciousness have been reported as well. Pity the unwary herder or humble farmer in antiquity who chanced upon and angered either of these two or the large and now extremely rare Black-necked Spitting Cobra *(Naja mossambica pallida)*, which can aim its spray of toxic venom up to three meters into the eyes of an aggressor and can leave an adversary permanently blinded. It is little wonder, then, that the ancient Egyptians seem to have been utterly terrified of snakes and went to considerable lengths to protect themselves, albeit through the power of magic, from these noxious creatures.

A tremendous wealth of textual evidence exists from all periods of history in the form of charms and spells used for protection against serpents. Even the *Pyramid Texts*, a corpus of powerful magical texts and utterances inscribed in the burial chambers of pyramids during the Fifth to Eighth Dynasties to safeguard the deceased king's well-being in the hereafter, included a host of spells to prevent snakebites and

Fig. 121. A detail of a group of ornamental hieroglyphs sculpted in limestone relief and inscribed on a pillar of the sed-festival shrine of King Sesostris I at Karnak. These crisply carved animal-signs represent an aggressive long-horned bull (the letters ka), a Lappet-faced Vulture (mut), and the deadly horned viper (f): Kamutef—'bull of his mother' (i.e., self-begotten, an epithet of the gods Min and Amun). Twelfth Dynasty.

Fig. 122. This gilded wood figure of a cobra with a dilated hood and upraised head, mounted on a wooden base coated with a black resin varnish, represents the serpent deity Netjerankh, the 'living god.' It was discovered housed in a wooden shrine chest in the tomb of Tutankhamun (no. 62) in the Valley of the Kings. Not much is known about this minor divinity, but we may be certain that this benevolent cobra would have aided the young king on his dangerous journey through the underworld. Eighteenth Dynasty. THE EGYPTIAN MUSEUM, CAIRO.

other dangers. During the New Kingdom, the compendium of religious texts of the so-called *Book of the Dead* likewise contain spells to prevent the dead from being injured by dreaded snakes in the beyond. In Spell 33, for instance, in order to drive off a serpent, the deceased owner of the papyrus is advised to recite the following: "Oh snake, take yourself off, for Geb protects me; get up, for you have eaten a mouse, which Ra detests, and you have chewed the bones of a putrid cat."[28] Valuable farmyard animals also occasionally fell prey to the assaults of poisonous snakes, and they too needed to be defended from them. For this reason, the Egyptian monarch is occasion-ally rendered in scenes on temple wall reliefs, from the Old Kingdom onward, performing a ceremonial rite at the harvest called 'driving the four calves,' which was intended, at least in part, to magically protect all the cattle in the land from serpent bites. On the other hand, not all snakes in ancient Egypt were viewed with disdain and fear, or as creatures of evil. Egyptian mythology features a considerable number of deities in the guise of a cobra, who were seen as beneficial and protective in nature and function, such as the serpent-goddesses Renenutet and Merseger. All of this results in a plurality of meanings in the pervasive snake imagery in Egyptian ico-

Fig. 123. Block of limestone relief with carefully executed hieroglyphic signs used in rendering two titles of the royal titulary of King Djoser. 'He of the Sedge and Bee' (that is, King of Upper and Lower Egypt) is written using the sedge-like plant and the bee. The large, thick-billed vulture, probably a Griffon Vulture, associated with the goddess Nekhbet, and the rearing cobra (uraeus), linked with the goddess Wadjet, are used in the title 'He of the Two Ladies.' This piece may have served as a sculptor's model for monumental inscriptions. From Hurbeit, in the eastern Delta. Third Dynasty. THE METROPOLITAN MUSEUM OF ART, NEW YORK.

nography. The deadly horned viper does not normally appear in Egyptian art following the Late Predynastic Period (Naqada III), where it was employed as a decorative motif. In pharaonic Egypt, however, the horned viper was retained for use as a standard hieroglyphic sign (fig. 121).

The first Egyptians living in the Predynastic Period appear to have been familiar with the gigantic African Rock Python (*Python sebae*), although the spe-

cies' present-day distribution is limited to tropical Africa. Serpent representations carved as decorative elements on several Late Predynastic Period (Naqada III) ivory knife handles, combs, and a gold mace handle from Sayala in Lower Nubia have generally been identified as African Rock Pythons. On these early objects, single and intertwined pairs of extremely long snakes with upraised heads are pictured, often being trampled by African Elephants (fig.

31). Their identification as African Rock Pythons is strengthened by their legendary reputation, according to the Classical writers of Greece and Rome, as mortal enemies of the African Elephant. Long, coiled snakes also appear on some Predynastic schist palettes, and as the playing board of the popular game 'serpent,' first attested around the beginning of the First Dynasty. Some authorities believe the rock python vanished from the Egyptian faunal community some time during the Early Dynastic Period, but there is some textual indication that a few pythons were imported into Egypt during the Ptolemaic Period for display as exotic wonders from the mysterious southern lands (see chapter 8).

The most characteristic and widely celebrated occurrence of a serpent in Egyptian art and hieroglyphs is the powerful and chilling image of an enraged cobra, referred to by Egyptologists as the uraeus, poised in an erect position, hood expanded, ready to strike in an instant. 'Uraeus' is a Latinized Greek rendering of the Egyptian word for a coiled, rearing cobra. The royal uraeus seems to have been modeled after

the Egyptian Cobra or the Black-necked Spitting Cobra, but probably mainly the latter, since written sources sometimes refer to the beast as flame-spitting and fire-breathing, and numerous pictures on the walls of New Kingdom royal tombs in the Valley of the Kings vividly illustrate uraeuses doing just that. The funerary composition known as the *Book of Amduat*, for example, features twelve apotropaic uraeuses who illuminate the darkness of the netherworld with blasts of their fiery breaths and light the way for the deceased, while in an underworld scene from the ninth hour of the *Book of Gates* figured in the late Nineteenth Dynasty tomb of Queen Tausert (no. 14) in the Valley of the Kings, a giant, nightmarish serpent spews venom or fire directly into the faces of bound sinners, men dammed for eternity.

While a sizable number of deities in the Egyptian pantheon had associations with the cobra (fig. 122), the creature is certainly best known as the sacred animal of the goddess of Lower Egypt, Wadjet. She and the Upper Egyptian tutelary goddess Nekhbet, whose emblem was a large, thick-

Fig. 124. (opposite) This haunting image is the golden face of King Tutankhamun, as portrayed on the outermost anthropoid coffin discovered in his tomb (no. 62) in the Valley of the Kings. From his forehead protrude the 'Two Ladies,' Wadjet and Nekhbet, shown as a rearing cobra (uraeus) with dilated hood and the head of a Lappet-faced Vulture, who protect the king. A small wreath of Olive (Olea europaea) and Cornflower (Centaurea depressa) leaves has been tied around the pair of goddesses. Eighteenth Dynasty. THE EGYPTIAN MUSEUM, CAIRO.

Fig. 125. (left) A large apotropaic wand or 'magic knife' fashioned from a curved Hippopotamus tusk, featuring a great bestiary of protective demons, real and imaginary animals, and symbols engraved on its surface. These could be summoned by the owner with spells to prevent evil — especially in the form of serpents and scorpions — from entering the nursery and harming mothers and their newborn children. An inscription carved on a similar piece of the same date now in the Metropolitan Museum of Art, New York, reads: "Words spoken by the multitude of amuletic figures: 'We have come in order to protect the lady, Merisenb.'" From Thebes. Late Middle Kingdom. THE BRITISH MUSEUM, LONDON.

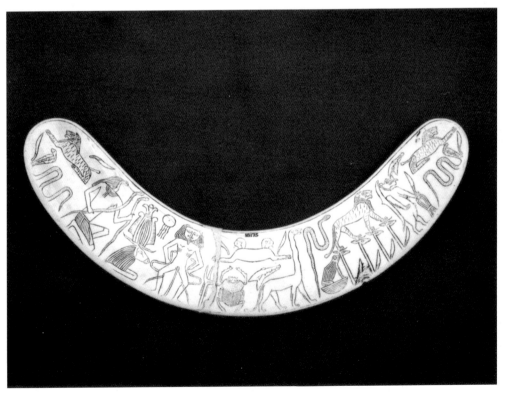

Fig. 126. Round-topped black steatite cippus, or magical stela, of 'Horus on the crocodiles.' The young Horus is shown naked, triumphing over various harmful creatures: serpents, scorpions, Lions, Scimitar-horned Oryx, and two Nile Crocodiles, with a prominent image of the god Bes above his head. Statues such as this one were thought to provide magical protection from, and miraculous cures for, the bites and stings of all sorts of noxious beasts, particularly the ones pictured on it, by drinking or washing in the libation of wine or water poured over it. Ptolemaic Period. THE WALTERS ART GALLERY, BALTIMORE.

billed vulture (either the Griffon Vulture or the Lappet-faced Vulture), formed a mighty alliance (fig. 123). Together, the 'Two Ladies' symbolized the union of the two mythical ancient Egyptian kingdoms, Upper and Lower Egypt, and defended the divine king and kingship in general. Their emblems, cobra and vulture, were routinely depicted flanking each other in a protective role, typically protruding from the front of the monarch's crown or headdress (fig. 124). According to one ancient

Fig. 127. Bronze votive (?) figure of a scorpion with its tail upraised. Late Dynastic Period. RIJKSMUSEUM VAN OUDHEDEN, LEIDEN.

legend, the cobra's lidless eyes never close, and thus this snake was fittingly always ready to guard and accompany the pharaoh. Apart from its appearance in this capacity, the uraeus was also popularly used as a decorative device in long friezes on royal monuments, and often figured in vignettes on funerary papyri, as well as being a standard hieroglyphic sign.

To the ancient Egyptians, the underworld was replete with monsters of all kinds, and was infested with swarms of snakes with multiple heads and wings. The most notorious was the serpent-demon Apophis, the embodiment of evil and the eternal enemy of Ra, the sun-god. In the vignette that accompanies Spell 17 of the *Book of the Dead*, a fierce tom-cat, probably

representing Ra, is portrayed slaying this hostile beast with a knife under the sacred Persea tree of Heliopolis (fig. 62). Serpents are also a recurring theme amid the bestiary of real and fabulous apotropaic animals, hieroglyphs, and other benevolent demons engraved on magic knives from the Middle Kingdom, which were fashioned from long curved strips of Hippopotamus ivory. When used in conjunction with certain spells, these objects magically helped to ensure the safety of the nursery or a pregnant woman's bedroom from harmful forces, especially the venomous bites of cobras and vipers, and the poisonous stings of scorpions, which could easily carry off a youngster or expectant mother (fig. 125). When placed in tombs, these devices ap-

Fig. 128. Fragment of a rectangular-shaped ceremonial or votive palette with relief decoration, showing a pair of click beetles, and to the left another pair incorporated into the central emblem of the fetish of the goddess Neith, which is supported on a staff and crossed by arrows. Gray schist. From Abydos (?). Late Predynastic Period (Naqada III). MUSÉES ROYAUX D'ART ET D'HISTOIRE, BRUSSELS.

Pl. XXVIII. (opposite) This detail of colorful wall painting from the beautiful tomb of Queen Nefertari (no. 66) in the Valley of the Queens depicts the union of the gods Ra and Osiris in the guise of a ram-headed mummy, which wears the sun's disk between its horizontal, corkscrew horns, characteristic of a breed of sheep that had been extinct in Egypt since the Middle Kingdom. The mummy is gently supported by the two sister goddesses Isis, on the right, and Nephthys, on the left. Nineteenth Dynasty.

parently offered similar protection to their deceased owners. Dangerous snakes are shown on these ivory wands being destroyed, devoured, or cut into pieces, while cobras, sometimes winged, seem beneficent and are able to act as helpers to the dead by warding off evil spirits.

Professional ancient Egyptian magicians had to learn (and possibly compose) a vast repertoire of incantations and rituals to stave off rapacious snake attacks: entire papyri are devoted to the subject. The Brooklyn Museum houses a unique papyrus roll from the Late Dynastic Period that has been described as a veritable manual of an Egyptian snake charmer. The document contains a comprehensive list of all the harmful serpents that inhabited the country at that time, their colors and lengths,

their names, and the particular deities with which they were associated. Then follows a treatise on cures for snakebites that explains, case by case, the treatment of the wound, the dressing of it, drugs to be prescribed, and the chances for the patient's recovery! In a world where no more than approximately one or two percent of the population could read and write, the skilled ancient Egyptian magician was part of the small literate and educated elite of society, and also served as an important medical practitioner.

A common type of powerful healing statue, known as the *cippus*, or magical stela, of 'Horus on the crocodiles,' was particularly popular in the Ptolemaic Period; it was designed to bring miraculous therapeutic cures for all kinds of severe

Pl. XXIX. (opposite) A well preserved detail of wall painting from the tomb of Queen Nefertari (no. 66) in the Valley of the Queens. It shows three mythological characters regularly featured in a vignette that accompanies Spell 17 of the Book of the Dead. On the right, the goddess Nephthys is pictured in the form of a kestrel, her name in hieroglyphs on top of the bird's head. The long-legged benu-bird was modeled after the Gray Heron, and is better known in the Classical world as the phoenix. It was identified with Ra, the sun-god, at the rising sun, and with Osiris, god of the underworld, at sunset. On the left, we see one of the two aker-Lions, which supported the sun on the horizon. Note the owl and quail chick hieroglyphs in the inscription below. Nineteenth Dynasty.

Pl. XXX. One of the brooding colossal baboon statues erected by Amenhotep III, and still in situ, at Hermopolis (al-Ashmunein) in Middle Egypt, site of the god Thoth's main cult center. This impressive squatting quartzite figure of a baboon, approximately four and a half meters in height excluding its base and weighing around thirty-five tons, has been carved with a considerable degree of skill. With the great Sphinx at Giza, these enormous figures are among the largest extant animal sculptures from ancient Egypt. Eighteenth Dynasty.

Pl. XXXI. This detail comes from the tomb of the prince Khaemweset (no. 44), the eldest son of Ramesses III, in the Valley of the Queens. It shows the scorpion-goddess, Selket, one of the four 'protector' goddesses, who guarded coffins and canopic jars. She is portrayed as a woman with a large scorpion resting on top of her head, its dangerous tail upraised; she is further identified in the accompanying inscription. The goddess's green skin tone recalls the color of new vegetation and may reflect a role in the rejuvenation of the dead. Twentieth Dynasty.

Pl. XXXII. *Carved in sunk relief and painted, this detail comes from the tomb-chapel of Pabasa (no. 279) at Thebes. It shows the deceased, sitting on a Lion-legged chair. He wears a wig that falls to the shoulder, a broad collar, and a short pleated kilt and he holds a handkerchief in his left hand. Beneath the chair sits his attentive pet saluki, which wears a collar. The dog is named in the caption before him: Hekenu ('Exultation'). Twenty-sixth Dynasty.*

Pl. XXXIII. (opposite) Colossal gray granite statue of a falcon wearing the double crown of Upper and Lower Egypt, representing the sky-god Horus, standing three meters in height in situ at the entrance to the great hypostyle hall of his temple at Edfu, in Upper Egypt. Ptolemaic Period.

Pl. XXXIV. (previous page) Vignettes from a papyrus copy of the Book of the Dead prepared for Userhetmos. The deceased owner is shown elaborately dressed, with his hands raised in a gesture of adoration, standing before the Hippopotamus-goddess Taweret, a beneficent fertility deity, who was the patron of women in childbirth. She holds a was-scepter in her right hand and leans on a sa-amulet with her left. The long appendage that extends from her headdress down her back is actually the stylized body of a crocodile. Behind her is the sacred cow of Hathor, the goddess of western Thebes, emerging from the mountain of the desert necropolis, surrounded by a clump of Papyrus. Between her long, lyre-shaped horns she wears the sun disk and a pair of Ostrich plumes. Around the goddess's neck is a large ceremonial menyet-necklace. From Thebes. Nineteenth Dynasty. THE EGYPTIAN MUSEUM, CAIRO.

Pl. XXXV. (above) Two highly lustrous, cerulean blue faience amulets, one in the form of a falcon-headed crocodile supporting a large sun disk on its head, representing some composite deity, the other in the shape of a Nile Crocodile, perhaps the god Sobek. Both are pierced with holes for suspension. Early Ptolemaic Period. THE METROPOLITAN MUSEUM OF ART, NEW YORK.

animal bites and stings, but particularly those of snakes and scorpions. By pouring a libation of wine or water over one of these monuments, which were covered with potent magical texts and illustrations, and then by drinking or washing with the powerfully charged liquid, the owner of the statue or other petitioner might receive relief through divine assistance (fig. 126). From the Late Dynastic Period also come a mass of bronze boxes with images of one or more serpents mounted on top. These served as votive offerings, and some might have been used as coffins for sacred snakes as well.

Scorpions, arachnids of the order Scorpionida, are usually quite small in size, generally no more than eight centimeters from head to tip of tail, but unmistakable in appearance. They have lobster-like pincers and narrow segmented tails arched over their elongated bodies, with a venomous stinger at the tip of the tail. This they use to inflict a poisonous stab into their prey or the hapless human victim who accidentally treads on one, pokes a hand under a rock, or reaches into a damp, dark crevice without adequate caution. The potency of the venom varies from species to species and with the size of the scorpion—for instance, the Palestine Yellow Scorpion (*Leiurus quinquestriatus*), which is found in Egypt, is the most venomous species in the world, but because of its small size (it delivers only 0.255mg of poison) it rarely kills adult humans. However, the endemic Egyptian populations have been known to inflict severely painful stings, sometimes leading to death, and should therefore be considered dangerous. The fatality of a scorpion attack may depend on the size of the victim and the person's overall fitness; not surprisingly, infants and children have a significantly higher death rate from their bites than adults. Scorpions are still fairly abundant in Egypt, as many field archaeologists can attest, but judging from the extant body of magical texts and images for

protection against and recovery from their harmful stings from all periods of Egyptian history, they must have been far more numerous and troublesome four thousand years ago. The picture one gains from this material is that the tiny scorpion was a bane of everyday life along the Nile, regardless of station in society. Not even divinities were entirely immune from the noxious scorpion: a spell on the grand Thirtieth Dynasty Metternich stela, now in the Metropolitan Museum of Art, New York, informs us that a scorpion dared to sting a cat, probably the goddess Bastet, and the poison was exorcised by the great god Ra:

> Oh Ra, come to your daughter, whom the scorpion has stung on a lonely road. Her cries reach heaven; harken on your way. The poison which has entered into her limbs flows through her flesh. She has used her mouth against it but lo! the poison is in her limbs. Come then with your might, with your frightfulness, with your magnificence. Behold, it hides from you.[29]

Scorpions first appear as a painted motif on Amratian (Naqada I) pottery, and there is probable evidence of an early scorpion cult in Egypt in the many votive figurines of them discovered in temple sanctuaries dating from the Late Predynastic and Early Dynastic periods. The scorpion is also one of the oldest known hieroglyphs: it was used to write the name of the Late Predynastic Period (Naqada III) ruler, King 'Scorpion.' In the ornamental hieroglyphic script, the scorpion sign was usually rendered, for magical reasons, with its tail and venomous stinger eliminated or modified in some way. Besides the magic knives discussed above, scorpion amulets were particularly plentiful throughout the long course of pharaonic history and were worn by both the living and the deceased, with potent apotropaic powers to keep scorpions at a distance.

As a sacred animal, scorpions were closely connected with the goddess Selket (at times Isis-Selket) (fig. 127). During the Old Kingdom, this scorpion-goddess was

known by the more complete name Selket-hetu, 'She who Causes (the Throat) to Breathe.' This would seem to be a straight-forward reference to the critical respiratory problems that may result from a scorpion attack, which her magic could relieve. Selket was famed for her powers in magically treating and healing the nasty bites of both snakes and scorpions. She was usually represented in human form with a large scorpion resting on top of her head, tail raised and ready to deliver a deadly sting (pl. xxxi). For this reason she was one of the 'protector' goddesses who watched over the deceased. Her priests were often skilled physicians and professional magicians. Some ancient Egyptian magicians were trained to specialize in the field of curing scorpion stings and snakebites, and were sometimes attached to desert expeditions to take care of these maladies on the long journey.

During the Ramesside Period, the detailed attendance registers from the artisans' village at Deir al-Medina—situated in the desert environment of the Theban necropolis—indicate that workmen were occasionally off the job after being stung by scorpions! In the Nineteenth Dynasty, during the reign of King Siptah, there must have been a severe outbreak of such scorpion attacks in the village, and records show that many men missed work as a result of painful stings. Little wonder then, that a man named Amenmosi, owner of a Theban tomb (no. 9), bore the magical title 'Charmer of Scorpions' and plied his curious profession as an active member of the artisans' community, caring for their wounds, reciting the correct magical spells, and getting the men back to work. A papyrus roll with a useful compilation of magical texts against scorpions has also been recovered from the site. A contemporary Ramesside Period magical charm to drive off a scorpion went as follows:

> Hey you scorpion who came forth from under the tree with its sting erect, the one who has stung the herdsman in the night

when (he) was lying down! Was no reciting done for him? Reciting was done for him over *hdb*-drink and beer, as (for) any strong fighter. The seven children of Pre stood lamenting; they made seven knots in their seven bands and they hit the one who was bitten (with them). May he stand up, healed for his mother, like Horus stood up, healed for his mother Isis in the night when he was bitten. The protection is a protection of Horus![30]

The ancient Egyptians were very familiar with the invertebrate world around them, portraying a wide range of insect life within the vast faunal repertoire that appeared in art and hieroglyphs; some of these creatures also held an esteemed place in religious thought. What follows, then, can only be an overview of some of the most habitually encountered and important varieties.

While the ubiquitous Dung or Sacred Scarab Beetle *(Scarabaeus sacer)* is justly famous and assuredly the best known invertebrate from pharaonic Egypt, it was not the only species of beetle depicted in Egyptian iconography, nor was it the first to attract the attention of the ancient people of the Nile Valley. The Sacred Scarab makes a surprisingly late appearance in art and is only attested from the Sixth Dynasty onward. The Egyptologist Ludwig Keimer long ago cogently pointed out that well before the Sixth Dynasty, during the Gerzean Period (Naqada II) and continuing into the Old Kingdom, a type of click beetle (family Elateridae; Keimer thought it was probably the species *Agrypnus notodonta)* was often represented as well. This slender and elongated beetle frequently appears in the form of small amuletic charms, occurs as a hieroglyph, and was also the early sacred emblem of Neith, the goddess of war. The central element of this goddess's fetish was composed of a pair of large click beetles, transfixed by two arrows (fig. 128). An especially splendid amuletic necklace, consisting of an entire string of beetle pendants of hollow gold, was found in the late Fifth or

Fig. 129. (opposite) This detail is from a wall painting in the burial chamber of the tomb of Inherkha (no. 359) at Thebes, and shows a large Dung or Sacred Scarab Beetle, a creature linked to the morning sun-god Khepri, serving as the ornamental counterpoise to an elaborate menyet-necklace, a ceremonial object particularly associated with the goddess Hathor. Twentieth Dynasty.

Fig. 130. From the tomb-chapel of the 'Steward of the Divine Votaress' Pabasa (no. 279) at Thebes, this composition in painted sunk limestone relief illustrates a rarely represented aspect of ancient Egyptian rural life: beekeeping. The apiarists are busy harvesting the honey from the cylindrical beehives. Twenty-sixth Dynasty.

early Sixth Dynasty burial of a princess at Giza (tomb of shaft 294), and is now housed in the Egyptian Museum, Cairo. This piece is not only quite visually pleasing but would have afforded its wearer the magical protection of the goddess Neith. Also during the Old Kingdom another type of beetle, a brightly colored jewel beetle (Buprestidae) was represented in art, particularly in jewelry. This most beautiful family of beetles is

still often incorporated into jewelry designs today in some areas of the world.

A common sight in the Egyptian countryside is a Sacred Scarab, near a farmyard, with a ball of fresh animal dung. Since the ball it creates is much too large for it to fly with, the beetle, moving backward, slowly rolls it to a safe, underground location and consumes it there. Because the ancient Egyptians saw an analogy between the slowly rolling dung ball and the solar orb moving across the sky from east to west every day, the Sacred Scarab, from the Old Kingdom, became associated with the sun. The female Sacred Scarab also creates, in her hole in the ground, a pear-shaped ball, into which she lays her eggs and from which the larvae hatch and the young eventually emerge. This was noticed by the ancient Egyptians as well, but they misunderstood the species' reproductive process: in their eyes, the Dung Beetle possessed the unique capacity for spontaneous creation.

In Egyptian mythology, the Sacred Scarab became associated with the daily birth of the sun, personified as the god of the morning sun, Khepri, 'He who Came into Existence by Himself.' Thus, revered for its regenerative powers and linked with the life-giving sun, the Sacred Scarab developed into a tremendously popular and powerful symbol of the renewal and rebirth that was hoped for after death in the beyond (figs. 6, 129, pl. XXVI). The image of the Sacred Scarab epitomizes ancient Egypt for many. The beetle is unquestionably most widely known from the many thousands of small amulets, generally no more than a few centimeters in length, and fashioned from a range of materials, that are found in museums and private collections around the world. Scarabs served as good luck or protective amulets with inscriptions carved on their bases, as devices with texts or designs used to stamp sealings, as commemorative objects issued for important historical events, as elements of ornate jewelry, or as funerary amulets placed inside wrapped mummies. As divine creatures, some Sacred Scarabs were ritually mummified and buried during the Late Dynastic and Greco–Roman periods: the Egyptian Agricultural Museum, in the Cairo suburb of Dokki, exhibits several examples of such wrapped beetles buried in crudely-hewn and decorated limestone sarcophagi. The Metropolitan Museum of Art, New York, possesses a small bronze sarcophagus for a beetle from the Late

Dynastic Period, with a mean-looking Rhinoceros Beetle (*Oryctes nascicarnis*) resting on top of it.

Valued for its delicious honey, which was used as a sweetener in all kinds of tasty foodstuffs and as a key ingredient in medicines, perfumes, and unguents, as well as for its useful wax, the Honeybee (*Apis mellifera*) was taken full advantage of by the ancient Egyptians. According to one charming late myth, probably from the early Ptolemaic Period, when the sun-god Ra wept, his tears fell to the earth and sprang into Honeybees. For reasons that are not altogether certain, beginning with King Den in the First Dynasty and until the last of the Ptolemies, Egyptian monarchs bore the title 'He of the Sedge and Bee' as part of their royal titulary: this is usually translated as 'King of Upper and Lower Egypt,' the sedge being taken to represent Upper Egypt, the bee Lower Egypt. A hieroglyph of a bee was always used in the writing of this title (fig. 123). The Honeybee also had some associations with several other Egyptian deities, including the god Amun and the goddess Neith.

While honey had been gathered from the wild in the Egyptian countryside since time immemorial, this source was not sufficient to meet the ever-increasing demand for this greatly appreciated and versatile luxury product in the Dynastic period. Therefore, to supplement this source, from at least the mid-Fifth Dynasty onward, the Honeybee was domesticated and the ancient Egyptians developed a small but flourishing apiculture industry of some economic importance. Beekeeping first appears in a scene on a block of limestone relief from the fascinating 'chamber of the seasons' in the Fifth Dynasty sun temple of King Niuserre at Abu Ghurab, now in the Ägyptisches Museum, Berlin. Here, the various processes involved in harvesting honey from the busy hives are depicted, including apiarists pouring honey into large jars and sealing the filled containers, with

explanatory hieroglyphic captions written above the action. A small relief fragment of a similar episode is also known from the decoration that adorned the late Fifth Dynasty causeway of Wenis at Saqqara. Only one or two other instances of beekeeping are illustrated in Theban tomb-chapels during the New Kingdom, including that of the Eighteenth Dynasty vizier Rekhmire (no. 100), where the technique of fumigating the swarm of working bees with smoke in order to collect the honey from the hives is clearly indicated in the wall painting.

Perhaps the most instructive and best preserved of all beekeeping scenes from ancient Egypt, however, comes from rather late and is found in a painted sunk relief composition in the Twenty-sixth Dynasty tomb-chapel of the high official Pabasa (no. 279) at Thebes (fig. 130). Arranged in two registers, the lower section of the episode shows a row of eight horizontally placed beehive cylinders or tubes, probably made of simple mud and straw, which seem to be precisely the type still employed by modern apiarists in parts of Egypt. The insects, which are rendered disproportionately large, exit the hives, allowing the attendant (who more than likely blows smoke into the cylinders) access to the combs and honey. Above, more bees fly about and another beekeeper is pictured transferring the harvested honey into a large spouted vessel. Behind him are a number of lampstands, the purpose of which is unknown. The deceased owner, Pabasa, must have had a sweet tooth and wished to have a constant supply of honey in his stores throughout eternity. Another beekeeping episode is represented in the Twenty-sixth Dynasty Theban tomb-chapel of the high official Ankhhor (no. 414). We may also note here that there is some textual evidence from the Greco–Roman Period that apiarists in Egypt moved their hives by donkey from one district to another in order to take advantage of earlier or later flowering plants, exactly as their descendants were wont to do into this century. It

is not known whether this custom was in use during the time of the pharaohs, but it seems not improbable.

During the New Kingdom, generous dishes of honeycombs and jars of honey are carried by offering-bearers on many tomb-chapel walls, placed before the deceased to be enjoyed on their sumptuous funerary tables. From the 'annals' that Tuthmosis III had inscribed on the walls of Amun's great temple at Karnak during the Eighteenth Dynasty, we learn that the king received as tribute or obtained as booty from warfare some 734 jars of foreign honey from western Asia. Two small pottery jars found in the Eighteenth Dynasty tomb of Tutankhamun (no. 62) in the Valley of the Kings, bore hieratic labels that read "honey of good quality." Unfortunately, upon examination the jars proved to be empty except for a trace of dried residue adhering to the inside. Tremendous quantities of wild and domestically produced honey, many thousands of jars, are listed among the donations to various temples made by Ramesses III during his thirty-one year reign, and recorded in the great Harris papyrus of the Twentieth Dynasty. But in spite of its frequent appearance in art and references to it in textual sources, honey was almost certainly confined to the diet of the Egyptian well-to-do, except on special festive occasions, owing to its high cost. Beeswax was also a very valued commodity in ancient Egypt, used in medicine, mummification, metal casting, and as a key component of magical practices. This substance was apparently extensively used at mortuary temple complexes, because Ramesses III donated to his temple at Medinet Habu over six kilograms of beeswax in a single year.

The biblical account of the eighth plague (Exodus 10: 14–15) that was said to have been divinely brought upon Egypt in antiquity is familiar to most of us:

> And the locusts went up over all the land of Egypt, and rested in all the borders of Egypt;

Fig. 131. (opposite) This attractive scene of Nilotic animal life, carved in limestone relief, is from the tomb-chapel of the mastaba of the vizier Kagemni (LS 10) at Saqqara. It features a flowering clump of Pondweed on whose long stems a grasshopper, a frog, and a dragonfly have come to rest. Below the surface of the water, a unique detail shows a pair of Nile Crocodiles copulating in a rather human-like position. Sixth Dynasty.

Fig. 132. Chain with three large fly-shaped gold pendants, part of an honorific award for valor, bestowed upon Queen Ahhotep, perhaps in recognition of her role in the war of independence against the Hyksos rulers of Egypt. From the tomb of Queen Ahhotep at Thebes. Early Eighteenth Dynasty. THE EGYPTIAN MUSEUM, CAIRO.

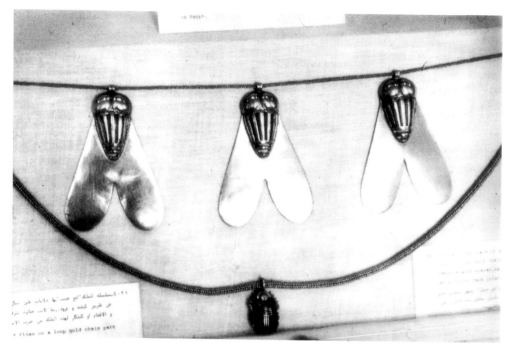

very grievous were they; before them there were no such locusts as they, neither after them shall be such. For they covered the face of the whole earth, so that the land was darkened; and they did eat every herb of the land, and all the fruit of the trees which the hail had left: and there remained not any green thing, either tree or herb of the field, through all the land of Egypt.

Indeed, the ancient Egyptians knew only too well the comparatively small grasshopper *(Schistocerca gregaria)* known in its migratory and gregarious phase as the Desert Locust. Massive swarms of voracious locusts, often consisting of as many as fifty billion individuals, have been known (and continue still) to do great damage, stripping bare essential agricultural crops and vegetation in North Africa, the Middle East, and elsewhere, causing considerable human suffering. In the spring of 1915, for instance, a vast plague of Desert Locusts swept through Palestine. Clouds of the insects flew overhead for five consecutive days, darkening the daytime sky, leaving droppings everywhere, and, with their ravenous appetites, causing significant destruction to the local crops and defoliating vegetation. Furthermore, the insects mated

and laid their eggs, and thirty or so days later, more very hungry locusts appeared.

The ancient Egyptians were painfully aware of the crop loss that can result from teeming numbers of this pest. A didactic text from the Ramesside Period, which relates the miseries of the farmer's lot while extolling that of the professional scribe, mentions that part of the lowly peasant's hardship was due to locusts: "Have you not recalled the condition of the cultivator faced with the registration of the harvest-tax after the snake has carried off one half and the hippopotamus has eaten up the rest? The mice abound in the field, the locust descends, the cattle devour. The sparrows bring want upon the cultivator."[31] During the Nineteenth Dynasty, in an inscription accompanying a scene of Ramesses II's famous battle of Kadesh on the first pylon of the Ramesseum at Thebes, the insect was used in a simile describing the king's foes, who were said to be so numerous that they covered the mountains and valleys like locusts.

In the extant pictorial record, only the solitary, shy, and docile grasshopper appears in Egyptian art. In tomb-chapels from the Old through New kingdoms, grasshoppers are often portrayed in a naturalistic setting, roosting on top of clusters of Papyrus umbels or on flowering stems of Pondweed in Nilotic swampland compositions (fig. 131, pl. ix). In the tomb-chapel of the Fifth Dynasty mastaba of Ptahhotep II (D 64) at Saqqara, a small vignette in a desert hunting scene depicts a hedgehog emerging from its burrow with a plump grasshopper in its mouth, about to consume the insect. A foreign grasshopper is represented as a curiosity amid the exotic fauna and flora that Tuthmosis III obtained from western Asia during the Eighteenth Dynasty and his artisans carved in relief upon the walls of the so-called 'botanical garden,' at the rear of his festival hall at Karnak temple (see chapter 8). A delightful decorative pattern of spirals, palmettes, grasshoppers, and bovine heads was combined in a pleasing manner to paint the burial chamber ceiling in the Eighteenth Dynasty tomb of Neferhotep (no. 50) at Thebes.

Certainly, the most noteworthy specimens of grasshoppers in all of ancient Egyptian art are two wonderful zoomorphic cosmetic boxes from the Eighteenth Dynasty: an especially magnificent and beautiful one fashioned from ivory and painted, evidently from a grand Theban tomb (pl. xxvii), the other fashioned in wood, which was found at Saqqara and is now in the Egyptian Museum, Cairo. Two pairs of movable wings form a cover for a hollow eye-makeup cavity inside their bodies. As on a small pottery vase, also in the Cairo Museum and probably dating from the same period as the two boxes, the form of this diminutive species has been closely observed and very successfully captured in a pleasing, stylized manner. It has been suggested that the shape of the grasshopper was selected for these objects because the cosmetics they once contained were derived predominantly from grasshopper oil. Although there is no proof that this was the case, it remains a distinct possibility, since the high-grade oil of grasshoppers

has been used for this purpose elsewhere. There is also no convincing evidence that the ancient Egyptians ate grasshoppers, a practice known from many other cultures. The insect does appear, though, as a motif on several limestone figured ostraca from the artisans' village at Deir al-Medina during the Ramesside era, which may hint that it was regarded as a food item: on one, a youth is pictured in the act of capturing a grasshopper with a net. And in the Twentieth Dynasty tomb-chapel of Ramose (no. 166) at Thebes, the deceased is presented with a wonderful bouquet of flowers that has a pair of tiny grasshoppers attached to it.

Even the pesky, mundane housefly (Muscidae) was accorded some symbolical significance by the ancient Egyptians. One indication of just how numerous houseflies were in ancient Egypt may be gleaned from the very frequent appearance of both men and women holding fly whisks in tomb decoration of all periods. A pair of ornamental horsehair fly whisks was included among the treasures and objects of daily use interred with Tutankhamun in his Eighteenth Dynasty tomb (no. 62) in the Valley of the Kings and now in the Egyptian Museum, Cairo, doubtless for his use in the fly-infested afterlife.

By at least the beginning of the Eighteenth Dynasty, the image of the common housefly had developed into an important military decoration, bestowed upon high-ranking soldiers, those who had distinguished themselves on the battlefield. The housefly's infamous behavior was equated with the talented and brave Egyptian soldier: quick, persistent, and difficult to wound, capture, or kill. These 'medals of valor' took the form of golden jewelry, a magnificent example of which is the gold chain with three large, stylized gold housefly pendants with bulging eyes presented to Queen Ahhotep during the reign of King Ahmose at the very beginning of the Eighteenth Dynasty, perhaps in recognition of her heroic efforts in freeing the country from the yoke of Hyksos domination by rallying the Theban forces at a critical moment in the war of liberation (fig. 132). In addition to these strikingly beautiful pieces, the housefly frequently occurs throughout pharaonic history as a common amulet, worn by both the living and the departed.

The ancient Egyptians were quite familiar with other varieties of flies as well. During the Old Kingdom, the dragonfly (order Odonata), easily identified by its long, slender body and double pairs of large wings, was something of a stock element of Papyrus swampland scenes (fig. 131). In a Ramesside Period text, the Egyptian official quoted earlier, still complaining of the hardships of his hellish post abroad, bemoans the wretched winged pests in this far-off locale: "There is the gnat at sunset and the midge at noon; the sand-fly stings and sucks at every vein."[32]

Finally, to conclude our survey of insect life in ancient Egypt, we must not forget that acme of grace and beauty, the colorful butterfly (order Lepidoptera), which enlivened so many swampland scenes (fig. 95, pls. V, XXIII, XXIV). Gently winging high above the stalks, or feeding on some herbage amid the huge umbels, butterflies are standard inhabitants of the lush backdrop of Papyrus pictured on the walls of Egyptian temples and tomb-chapels from the earliest age down to the Greco–Roman Period. Sometimes, when the bright coloring has been preserved, the insects can be identified at a glance as Egypt's Plain Tiger butterfly *(Danaus chrysippus)*. From the Old Kingdom onward, butterflies were also a recurrent decorative element of women's jewelry. During the Fourth Dynasty, Queen Hetepheres I, the mother of Cheops and wife of Snofru, possessed numerous fine silver bracelets with inlaid motifs representing schematic butterflies, which were found in her shaft-tomb (G 7000 X) at Giza and are now shared by the Egyptian Museum, Cairo, and the Museum of Fine Arts, Boston. Among the jewelry found in the burial of the Twelfth Dynasty princess Khnumet at Dahshur was a lovely gold butterfly pendant, also exhibited in the Cairo collection.

Chapter Eight

The Royal Menagerie

*T*he ancient Egyptians' interest in exotic creatures and rare, costly animal products from foreign lands reaches back at least to the Old Kingdom. The earliest firm evidence of the Egyptian interest in unusual animals is found in a scene from the Fifth Dynasty mortuary temple of King Sahure at Abusir. Part of the decoration of this grand edifice contains a remarkable composition, showing what is probably the successful return of an Egyptian maritime trading expedition to far-off Byblos on the Phoenician coast, in what is now Lebanon. The Egyptians would have been primarily interested in obtaining badly-needed coniferous

timber. But the mission seems also to have included a foray into the mountainous regions of the area, for pictured on a fragment of painted relief from the temple are several tethered Syrian Bears (*Ursus arctos syriacus*) from this region. The bears are portrayed along with tall-necked, single-handled jars of oil, characteristic of Syria, clinching the origin of both (fig. 133). If not actually trapped by the Egyptian party themselves, these captive beasts may have been among propitiatory gifts, or merely obtained through bartering with the local Asiatics. In any case, these magnificent bears were transported back to the Nile Valley, where they were a great novelty and served as objects of immense astonishment. Sahure must have thought highly of them to have his artisans depict them on

his temple. The large, stocky build and peculiar posture of these carnivores has been rendered with prodigious skill in this relief and is surely the product of direct observation of the living species. This is, by all means, a delightful little scene and ranks among the great masterworks of the ancient Egyptian animal genre.

Despite Herodotus's remark to the contrary (II, 67), bears are not indigenous to Egypt, and were known to the inhabitants of the Nile Valley only from specimens obtained from western Asia through trade, booty, or tribute. The Syrian Bear has long been thought to be extinct throughout its former range of the Middle East. Recent reports, however, maintain that it is still found in Kurdistan and possibly also in northern Syria. Its appearance in ancient

Fig. 133. Fragment of painted limestone relief showing parts of three wonderful Syrian Bears and a tall, single-handled, pottery vessel of Syrian manufacture. These exotic bears wear collars and are tethered by leashes to the ground. They are made all the more appealing by the expressions on their faces, which seem to betray the slightest grin. From the mortuary temple of King Sahure at Abusir. Fifth Dynasty. ÄGYPTISCHES MUSEUM, BERLIN.

Egyptian art is quite rare indeed, and is known from only approximately eight extant examples, the majority of them dating from the Eighteenth Dynasty, a period when the penchant for exotica peaked. Tame Syrian Bears, wearing collars and held on leashes by foreigners, are most often encountered during this period painted on the walls of Theban tomb-chapels. It seems clear that these exotic marvels were brought to Egypt for their curiosity value. Whether any of them were 'performing' bears, we have not the slightest hint. They are attested as trained entertainers in Egypt only during the Roman Period, as evidenced by a charming bronze

statuette of a dancing bear, now in the collections of the Brooklyn Museum.

Public zoological gardens as we know them did not exist in pharaonic Egypt; the first zoo known to us was an enormous collection of wild and domestic animals amassed by Ptolemy II Philadelphus in Alexandria during the Ptolemaic Period. It is clear, though, that royal menageries were established by a number of Egyptian monarchs during the Dynastic period. These were probably located in palace parks or perhaps on temple grounds. Here, unusual animals from Egypt and farther afield were collected and perhaps displayed as exotic wonders to courtiers and other visitors, stirring surprise and excited comments. Many other animal imports were destined

instead for the hunting reserves of the king and aristocracy. Some of these strange creatures entered Egypt as political gifts or tribute from rulers of other lands. Fellow potentates in other ancient Near Eastern kingdoms were also known occasionally to keep assortments of animals from distant countries for show. Receiving and possessing rare beasts was a matter of considerable royal prestige. There was also an extremely important underlying motivation for creating menageries, beside the general fascination with animals: in this array of captive exotic creatures, the Egyptian kings symbolically displayed their personal, political, and militaristic mastery over foreign countries through the domination of their faunas. As Egypt's power and influence

Fig. 134. Detail of painted limestone relief from a composition commemorating a sea-borne trip to the land of Punt in the mortuary temple of Queen Hatshepsut at Deir al-Bahari, Thebes. This scorpionfish is indigenous to the tropical waters the Egyptian expeditionary force visited. Eighteenth Dynasty.

197

Fig. 135. This painted limestone relief portrait is an exceedingly precise rendering of a Swordfish. It was encountered by the ancient Egyptians during the course of a maritime trip to the fabled African land of Punt (see also fig. 134). From the mortuary temple of Queen Hatshepsut at Deir al-Bahari, Thebes. Eighteenth Dynasty.

spread, so did the parade of animals imported from farther and farther away.

While ancient Egyptian hunting parks of the kind described in chapter 3 were generally stocked with endemic fauna, foreign imports were occasionally included in them as well. In an interesting hunting vignette at Saqqara on the causeway of Wenis, the last ruler of the Fifth Dynasty, the king's intrepid huntsmen are illustrated in pursuit of an exotic Syrian Bear and a Giraffe, in addition to the traditional Egyptian wildlife. The Giraffe had been well known in Egypt during the Predynastic Period (fig. 54, pl. I), but by this late time its numbers had no doubt already been very significantly reduced, if indeed it had not been entirely eradicated from its former range in the country. The appearance of a deer here, and the apparently unique depiction of a Roan, indicates that this was a collection of rare quarry. In the tomb-chapel of the Fifth

Dynasty mastaba of Ptahhotep II (D 64) at Saqqara, a fascinating relief scene pictures the return home of a desert hunting expedition, featuring the singular detail of a captured adult Lion and a Leopard, each imprisoned in a strong wooden cage, drawn on sledges by a gang of retainers (fig. 66). Perhaps these large felines were indeed destined for a royal menagerie or a hunting park, as some have suggested. On the other hand, the big cats may have been captured to serve as royal pets for the king at court and to accompany him into battle, although the training of the animals for this purpose would have been best accomplished with juvenile animals (see chapter 4).

During the Middle Kingdom, extrinsic and rare endemic faunas are only occasionally rendered in Egyptian art. Their absence may perhaps be an indication of the poor health of international trade in animals at this time. The few examples of unusual creatures pictured in artistic com-

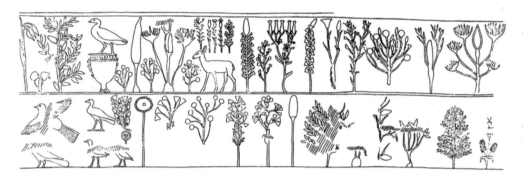

Fig. 136. *Drawing of a section of the remarkable relief decoration on a wall of the 'botanical garden' of Tuthmosis III at Karnak, depicting some of the exotic plants and animals that the king collected in western Asia and brought home during the twenty-fifth year of his reign. The learned Egyptologist Ludwig Keimer pronounced almost all of the plant specimens pictured by the artisans "purely fantastic." None of the birds shown in this drawing can be identified with certainty, but a Persian Gazelle might be depicted in the upper register. Eighteenth Dynasty.*

positions in this period are confined to Giraffes, deer, and Caracals in hunting scenes in tomb-chapels (fig. 35).

With the arrival of the New Kingdom, there was a renewed and much expanded interest in exotic wildlife and in rare, costly, imported merchandise. The Egyptian Empire, at its zenith and imperialistic height during the Eighteenth Dynasty, stretched from the Euphrates river in northern Syria all the way to the fourth cataract region in Upper Nubia. During this prosperous period in Egyptian history, a wide variety of foreign goods flowed into the country, including a stream of unfamiliar animals. It was also an era that saw an increased number of Egyptians traveling abroad. The walls of the southern half of the middle colonnade of the Eighteenth Dynasty mortuary temple of Queen Hatshepsut at Deir al-Bahari were decorated with lively and wonderful scenes, celebrating the events of her great sea-borne expedition to the remote and fabled land of Punt, which occurred during the eighth and ninth years of her reign. The primary purpose of this commercial voyage was to acquire aromatic trees, frankincense (*Boswellia* sp.), and Myrrh (*Commiphora myrrha*) for ceremonial use in Egyptian temples. The location of Punt has yet to be firmly established, but it is thought most likely to have occupied a considerable area of eastern Sudan, extending to the Red Sea and into northwestern Ethiopia. Punt was a lush, tropical land and Hatshepsut's artisans took painstaking care in capturing the region's exotic charm and character. This is especially evident in regard to the local fauna and flora,

which have been very closely observed and almost scientifically reproduced in the wall reliefs. These exquisite scenes constitute what Cyril Aldred once referred to as the first known example of an anthropological study of an alien culture. Wandering about the wood-and-mat beehive-shaped pile dwellings of the Puntite village that the expedition visited, which was situated amid a grove of tall palm trees, a variety of indigenous animal life was rendered: baboon, Giraffe, rhinoceros, cattle, dogs, donkeys, birds, and others. Of particular interest also is a whole range of faithfully illustrated fish and other marine animals of the Red Sea and Indian Ocean (figs. 134, 135). Among the treasure of marvelous rare and costly products from Punt triumphantly transported back to Egypt are thirty-one live Myrrh trees to be transplanted, as well as a collection of live exotic animals and animal products: cattle, baboons, monkeys, Leopards, Cheetahs, dogs, a Giraffe, a long-legged bird (probably an Ostrich), Leopard and/or Cheetah skins, elephant tusks, Giraffe tails, and Ostrich eggs and plumes. It would not be too speculative to suggest that some of these extraordinary creatures entered the menagerie of Hatshepsut. A few may even have become members of the royal household itself—a wall scene on the upper court of the Deir al-Bahari temple shows the queen's sumptuous retinue following behind the royal carrying-chair: fan bearers, servants, and grooms in charge of a pair of splendidly executed Cheetahs that have unfortunately now lost their color. These sleek, graceful felines are shown wearing collars and are led forward on leashes.

Fig. 137. Detail of limestone relief from the 'botanical garden' of Tuthmosis III at Karnak, showing a pair of birds surrounded by some of the strange, unidentifiable flora. The bird above is probably a swallow, the one below a diver, a type of bird not otherwise known in Egyptian iconography. Eighteenth Dynasty.

They were apparently the queen's pets and as such are the only recorded instance of Cheetahs being kept as 'household cats,' though one wonders whether King Akhenaten or a member of his family had a favorite Cheetah, since a tame one is delivered to him and Nefertiti and their six daughters by a delegation of Nubians in a scene in the Eighteenth Dynasty rock-cut tomb of Meryre II (no. 2) at al-Amarna.

Not to be outdone by his aunt and immediate predecessor, the great warrior-king Tuthmosis III also demonstrated an avid interest in exotica, devoting considerable space to this theme in the decorative program of a major temple. In two chambers set to the rear of his festival temple at Karnak, and conveniently referred to by Egyptologists today as the 'botanical garden,' Tuthmosis III had recorded, in delicate, low relief, the plants and animals he encountered while on a military campaign into western Asia during the twenty-fifth year of his reign. The strange fauna and flora are presented as a tribute to the powerful chief god of Thebes, Amun, whose cult was a major beneficiary of such triumphs. An accompanying inscription states that they are:

all plants that grow, all flowers that are in God's-Land [which were found by] his majesty when his majesty proceeded to Upper Rentenu [Palestine and Syria], to subdue [all] the countries, according to the command of his father Amun . . . . His majesty said: 'I swear, as Re [loves me] and as my father, Amun, favors me, all these things happened in truth . . . . My majesty hath done this from desire to put them before my father Amun, in this great temple of Amun, (as) a memorial forever and ever.'[33]

Discernible on the extant walls of the two small chambers is a collection that comprises approximately 275 specimens of plant life and fifty-two individual animals: thirty-eight birds, one tiny insect, and thirteen mammals. The 'botanical garden' would appear to be a kind of natural history museum in stone. While one may easily leap to the conclusion that Tuthmosis III was something of a savant with a genuine bent for botany and zoology, this need not have been the case. Nearly all the plants in the temple, some shown even with their root systems, seem to be purely fantastic forms and have defied repeated attempts at identification by modern botanists. This flora may have served only to indicate an environment as alien as possible (fig. 136).

The importance of the collection seems to have lain in its symbolical significance, the plants and animals of the conquered Asiatic lands—both true and strange, set before Amun—subtly representing the great god's power and dominion over these distant foreign soils.

Unlike the flora, much of the bird life depicted (at least from what can reasonably be determined in the absence of any preserved coloring) is similar to that traditionally pictured in Egyptian iconography for centuries (figs. 137–139). Some of the birds (at least those that can be firmly identified), such as the serpentine-necked Darter (*Anhinga rufa*), diver (*Gavia* sp.), and the parasitic Great Spotted Cuckoo (*Clamator glandarius*), are unique portraits in Egyptian art. These need not necessarily have been foreign species, though, since the Great Spotted Cuckoo exists in Egypt today, and the Darter and diver have been known to occur in the country at one time or other. A small gazelle pictured here has been tentatively identified as a Persian Gazelle (*Gazella subgutturosa*), which would make it a true import (fig. 136). Also prominently exhibited in the 'botanical garden' as exotic mar-

vels are several head of cattle of the two-tailed and three-horned variety! These may well be simply flights of the imagination, but they could represent common farmyard freaks, the kind well known to working large-animal veterinarians (fig. 140). Some of this unusual fauna could have been part of King Tuthmosis III's menagerie.

From the 'annals' that Tuthmosis III had inscribed on the walls of Amun's magnificent state temple at Karnak, we learn of other exotic animals that also arrived from western Asia as tribute during his reign, including a deer in year thirty-eight, and another creature that has elicited much comment from scholars over the years: a short passage in the 'annals' has been restored by the brilliant philologist Kurt Sethe to read that the king received from Syria "four birds that lay eggs every day." This has traditionally been interpreted as the earliest extant reference from ancient Egypt to the Red Junglefowl, better known to us today as the domestic chicken. The translation remains controversial, however, since the key word *ms* ('lay eggs') is missing from the original. But even if the restora-

Fig. 138. Carved relief illustration of a Darter on a wall in the 'botanical garden' of Tuthmosis III at Karnak. This singular picture is the only known depiction of this bird from ancient Egypt. The species' most arresting feature, an extremely attenuated neck with a pronounced kink, has been captured with total fidelity and bespeaks firsthand knowledge. Today the Darter is regarded as an accidental visitor to the Upper Nile Valley. Eighteenth Dynasty.

Fig. 139. From the 'botanical garden' of Tuthmosis III at Karnak, the birds in this attractively arranged group, on which the original coloring is no longer visible, cannot be identified with any degree of certainty. This underscores the difficulty in attempting to identify animal life depicted on poorly preserved Egyptian monuments. Eighteenth Dynasty.

tion is correct, it must remain an entirely open question whether the entry actually refers to Red Junglefowl.

The Red Junglefowl apparently arrived in Egypt comparatively late in history. It may have been introduced to the Nile Valley by way of Mesopotamia, where, through trading links with India (the original home of the species), the bird was already known by the time of the Third Dynasty of Ur (c.2113–2006 B.C.). The first unequivocal appearance of the chicken known to us from ancient Egyptian art takes the form of an attractive, but sparingly rendered, black ink drawing of a rooster on a limestone splinter, about the size of a human hand, found by Howard Carter in the course of Lord Carnarvon's excavations in the Valley of the Kings during the winter of 1920–21 (fig. 141). This figured ostracon is almost certainly the work of an observant artisan who lived during the Nineteenth Dynasty. There can be little doubt that the Red Junglefowl was imported into Egypt during the New Kingdom not for the table but as an extraordinarily rare prize, an object of marvel likely to have been exhibited with pride along with other exotic fauna in the royal menagerie.

We again meet a cockerel on a lovely embossed silver bowl from the late Nineteenth or early Twentieth Dynasty, now in the Metropolitan Museum of Art, New York. Then there is silence until the Thirtieth Dynasty, when we next encounter a rooster on a fragment of a finely decorated lintel from the tomb of Hapiu. On this relief, rather unexpectedly, the pert bird appears as a beloved pet sitting before its owner, who is enjoying the song of an old harper (fig. 142). Evidently even at this late date the bird was still considered unusual enough to warrant the privileged position of a pet. A pair of roosters is depicted a little later amid a myriad of offerings and victuals brought to the important dignitary and priest Petosiris on a wall in his tomb-chapel, which dates from the reign of the Macedonian king Philip Arrhidaeus, the half-brother of Alexander the Great, at Tuna al-Gebel. Thus it is only at the very close of the pharaonic period that the bird is attested as a food item in ancient Egypt. With the rise of the Ptolemaic Period, and in the centuries following, the chicken became a more abundant figure in the Egyptian farmyard: its image occurs more regularly in art and there is osteological evidence for the species from settlement sites at this time in the Nile Valley. By the Roman Period, there was a flourishing avicultural industry in Egypt centered around the chicken.

Far and away our greatest source of information on the vast array of exotic fauna and products that enriched Egypt during the New Kingdom are the Theban tomb-chapels of a number of noblemen and priests of the Eighteenth and Nineteenth Dynasties. The large and well preserved Eighteenth Dynasty tomb-chapel of Rekhmire (no. 100) at Thebes, which is on the itinerary of every tourist to the Theban necropolis, is particularly instructive (pls. XV, XVI). Rekhmire held the high office of vizier in 'the Southern City' (Thebes) during the reigns of Tuthmosis III and Amenhotep II, and apparently one of his functions in this capacity was to receive some of the foreign goods brought to the country. The walls of his tomb-chapel are lavishly adorned with some exceptional

and vibrant scenes of a cortège of tribute-bringers from the lands of Punt, Crete, Nubia, and Syria, bearing the rich produce and exotic merchandise of their respective countries, detailed in accompanying texts. In a striking series of long, painted registers, the chiefs of Punt are shown proffering, among a great many things, Leopard and/or Cheetah skins, elephant tusks, Ostrich eggs and plumes, and Giraffe tails. Live animals from Punt include a baboon, a Green Monkey, a Nubian Ibex, and a Cheetah. The Cretans are depicted presenting, among other things, a single elephant tusk. The Nubians' gifts include Ostrich plumes and eggs, elephant tusks, and various costly animal pelts. The tame animals they lead include a Leopard, a baboon, dogs, cattle with intentionally deformed horns, and a Giraffe with a little Green Monkey climbing up its long, spotted neck. The Syrians bring elephant tusks, a pair of fiery steeds, a skillfully rendered Syrian Bear, and the now-extinct Syrian

Fig. 140. Detail of a steer with two tails exhibited as an exotic curiosity on a wall in the 'botanical garden' of Tuthmosis III at Karnak. Other cattle in the collection are shown with three horns! These could be farmyard freaks. Eighteenth Dynasty.

Fig. 141. Figured limestone ostracon with a confident black ink drawing of a Red Junglefowl, a bird better known as our common chicken, the earliest known representation of this species from ancient Egypt. The spry rooster successfully conveys a feeling of the strutting gait so characteristic of its kind. This piece was discovered in the Valley of the Kings and was doubtless the product of one of the skilled artisans employed on the construction of the royal tombs of the New Kingdom with time to spare. Given the rarity of the subject matter, the artisan may have drawn it directly from life. Nineteenth Dynasty. THE BRITISH MUSEUM, LONDON.

Elephant. It would be safe to assume that a significant number of these exotic animals would have been exhibited in the royal menagerie. The arrival of a large Syrian delegation rendered in another Eighteenth Dynasty tomb-chapel at Thebes (no. 119), whose owner's name is now lost, records the appearance of a gift of an elegant Arabian Oryx. This handsome foreign antelope from western Asia would have been a very welcome addition to a pharaoh's collection of rare animals.

Theban tomb-chapel decoration amply testifies to the sophisticated Egyptians' taste for exotica during the New Kingdom. The processions of strange animals captured the imagination of the ancient Egyptians, who took obvious joy and wonder in their curious shapes, colorings, odors, and habits. This appreciation was shared by the community of artisans from the village of Deir al-Medina, and is reflected in the numerous well observed sketches of rare and unusual creatures they made—bat (fig. 113), bear, elephant, Lion, and others—on figured ostraca during the Ramesside Period.

In Predynastic times, the early ancient Egyptians knew the Gerenuk (*Litocranius*

walleri), a gazelle-like antelope, but this species had become locally extinct before the close of the Early Dynastic Period. However, in the Nineteenth Dynasty, during the reign of Ramesses II, the creature is pictured entering Egypt again, as part of Nubian tribute and spoils of war, carved on a wall of the rock-cut temple of Beit al-Wali in Lower Nubia. Pictured along with it is a host of other exotic creatures, including Beisa Oryx, Lion, Ostrich, cattle, Cheetah, monkey, and baboons. Many affluent ancient Egyptians, including royalty, kept pet monkeys, which had to be imported from the tropical southern lands (see chapter 4).

When excavated in the 1920s by the Egypt Exploration Society of London, the north palace in Akhenaten's short-lived capital city Akhetaten, 'Horizon of the Aten,' at al-Amarna in Middle Egypt, was found to be a self-contained royal residence. It included an open-air sun temple, gardens and courts, reception halls, and a domestic suite, complete with bedroom and bathroom. The excavators thought the palace unique in the ancient world because it also contained

Fig. 142. This rare representation of a rooster from the time of the pharaohs appears on a block of limestone relief, a fragment of a lintel from the tomb of Hapiu. It shows Hapiu seated before a musician, who plucks the strings of a large, angular harp. Between them sits a rooster, still an unusual bird in the Nile Valley. Its privileged position at Hapiu's feet indicates that the bird was his pet. From Heliopolis (?). Thirtieth Dynasty.
ÄGYPTISCHES MUSEUM, BERLIN.

what appeared to be a menagerie, with ponds, aviaries, and enclosures to house a variety of animal and bird life. The walls of some of these areas were painted with bright, charming themes drawn from nature. One large compound in the palace contained the remains of fourteen feeding-troughs around its mud-brick walls, with tethering rings for the beasts nearby. Carved in relief on the mangers are figures of cattle, Nubian Ibex, and Bubal Hartebeest. The most complete example of these features two large Nubian Ibex in sunk relief, standing before a manger containing fodder (fig. 43). The walls of one of the small chambers that opens onto a large garden court, the so-called 'green room,' portrays birds inhabiting a dense Papyrus marsh, a masterpiece of painting. While all these captive animals seem to be native species, more exotic forms were also kept during the Amarna Period. A block of relief from Akhenaten's temple of the Aten at Karnak portrays a grand house, in front of which are two caged Lions and, in a compound of the villa fringed with trees, gazelles or antelopes are seen feeding from mangers.

These might indeed be part of a private or royal menagerie.

An interest in foreign animals during Akhenaten's reign can also be glimpsed in the Amarna letters. This important archive of cuneiform diplomatic correspondences between Amenhotep III, Akhenaten, and Tutankhamun on the one hand and kings and vassals in Palestine, Syria, Mesopotamia, and Asia Minor on the other alludes to the royal presentation of gifts of friendship, some consisting of animals, especially horses, among fellow rulers. We are a little better informed about such exchanges later in Egyptian history. From Assyrian sources we know that during the Twentieth Dynasty, Ramesses XI, toward the end of his reign, sent a gift of a Nile Crocodile and a large monkey (baboon?) to Assur-bel-kala, the king of Assyria, while the latter was campaigning in western Asia. And in the Twenty-second Dynasty, during the reign of King Takelot II, an entry on Shalmaneser III's famous black obelisk discovered at Nimrud (Kalhu), on the Tigris river in modern Iraq, and now in the British Museum, London, asserts that this Assyrian king received tribute from Egypt in the form of exotic fauna: twin-humped camels (the Bactrian Camel was itself a curiosity even in Egypt), a rhinoceros, an antelope, elephants, and two varieties of monkeys. Another beast the Assyrian king received from Takelot II was described as a 'river-ox,' which may have been a Hippopotamus or a Water Buffalo *(Bubalus arnee)* (if the latter, this would itself have been an import into Egypt). These unusual creatures probably entered Assyrian menageries or hunting parks.

Archaeological excavations have been conducted in recent years by the Roemer- und Pelizaeus-Museum, Hildesheim, in the ruins of a royal palace at Piramesse, near Qantir, the Delta residence of the Ramesside kings during the Nineteenth and Twentieth Dynasties. An investigation of the animal remains recovered from an area of the site by Joachim Boessneck and Angela von den Driesch has revealed a rather interesting diversity of faunal elements. The species they identified from the palace location include African Elephant, Lion, Bubal Hartebeest(?), Roan, gazelle, horse, donkey, antelope, goat(?), Giraffe, Ostrich, Persian Fallow Deer, Nubian Ibex, Striped Hyena, and wild cattle (Aurochs). The presence of so many wild animals, several of which are also obvious exotic imports, came as something of a surprise to the investigators. The osteological evidence has been interpreted by the team as indicating the existence of a menagerie at the palace, a reasonable explanation. It seems, however, that these game animals could also be accounted for as the vestiges of a royal hunting park, as Wolfgang Decker has already pointed out. Indeed, one explanation need not necessarily exclude the other: conceivably, the animals could have served both functions. In any event, the bone remains surely attest to the continuing interest of pharaohs of the Ramesside Period in creatures from distant lands.

A model letter used in the instruction of young boys preparing to be professional

scribes, also of Ramesside date, concerns Nubian tribute. It gives an insight into the range of live animals, both wild and domestic, and other products that were probably regularly imported into Egypt from the southern lands:

> The fan-bearer on the right of the king, captain of troops and intendant of the foreign land of Kush, Psiur, speaks to him who protects his people. This letter is brought to you to the following effect: When my letter reaches you, you shall cause the tribute to be made ready in all its details, namely, oxen, younglings of long-horned cattle, short-horned cattle, gazelles, oryxes, ibexes and ostriches; their barges, their cattle-ferries and their *kr*-ships being ready to land (?); their skippers and their crews prepared and ready to set forth; much gold wrought into dishes, . . . ivory and ebony; ostrich feathers, . . . bread of Christ's-thorn fruit, . . . panther [Leopard and/or Cheetah] skins, gum, haematite, red jasper, amethyst, crystal, cats of Miw [Servals *(Felis serval)*?], a long-tailed monkey, baboons . . .[34]

The strangest and most ferocious beast the ancient Egyptians ever encountered was the rhinoceros, already a well-known and feared game animal during Predynastic times, appearing in a much-celebrated rock drawing on a sandstone cliff face near Silwa Bahari in Upper Egypt (fig. 30): a two-horned rhinoceros is shown in a hunting composition in the company of an African Elephant, an Ostrich, perhaps a Scimitar-horned Oryx, and possibly a Soemmering's Gazelle, being chased by a hunter with bow and arrows. Accurate ceramic models of rhinoceros horns have been discovered in a First Dynasty tomb (no. 3357) at Saqqara, probably placed there as apotropaic devices. The rhinoceros undoubtedly became extinct in Egypt quite early on, probably by the end of the Early Dynastic Period, and is now found only much further south, deep in modern Sudan.

Memory of the rhinoceros may have lived on in the Egyptian mind, however, because its appearance seems to be recalled once or twice in figures from reliefs and

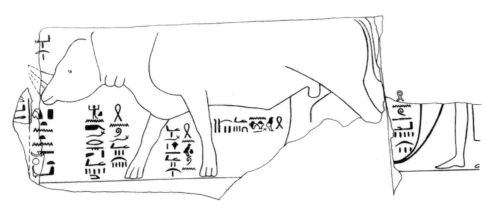

Fig. 143. Drawing of a damaged detail from a frieze of Nubian booty, carved in sunk relief, on a pylon of the temple dedicated to the war-god Montu at Armant, just south of Luxor. It shows an intriguing vignette of a live rhinoceros being brought to Egypt amid a procession of exotic animals and goods from the African hinterlands, restrained by a gang of men using ropes. Carved all around the mighty beast are inscriptions giving the dimensions of its massive body. Probably Nineteenth Dynasty.

paintings during the Old and Middle kingdoms, though these could be elephants. No positively identifiable representations occur until the Eighteenth Dynasty, when the rhinoceros first appears again as a native of the land of Punt, in Queen Hatshepsut's mortuary temple at Deir al-Bahari. A commemorative stela, erected by Tuthmosis III at the temple of the war-god Montu at Armant in Upper Egypt, vaunts the king's tremendous physical and hunting prowess, and relates what is probably a historical event during his first military campaign in Nubia: "He carried off a rhinoceros by shooting, in the southern country of Nubia."[35] Presumably the carcass and precious horn of the animal were taken back to Egypt to be displayed as the proud trophies of a young big-game hunter. In the same temple, a fascinating relief that has usually been dated to the Eighteenth Dynasty, but which on stylistic grounds should be assigned to the Ramesside Period, appears to go one better. Not to be outdone by his renowned warrior ancestor, an unknown king—more than likely the great Ramesses II—had carved upon a pylon at the temple an imposing scene depicting an adult rhinoceros in a procession of Nubian booty and tribute arriving in Egypt (fig. 143). This massive and dangerous game animal was captured alive and is being restrained by a gang of men using strong ropes. The rhinoceros appears to have been the object of vigorous examination, because the portrayal is made all the more intriguing by the inclusion of hieroglyphic captions carved all around it, briefly detailing its dimensions. This carefully observed and executed rendering represents the very apogee of the ancient Egyptians' 'scientific' inquisitiveness into exotic wildlife. The inscriptions measure the length of the horn as one cubit, one palm (sixty centimeters); the height of the foreleg as five and a half cubits (288 centimeters); the circumference of the foreleg as three cubits, five palms (two meters); the circumference of the foot as two cubits, one palm (112 centimeters); the circumference of the belly as thirteen cubits, two palms, two fingers (seven meters); and the circumference of the back leg as five cubits, three palms (285 centimeters).[36] There may have been a few further measurements, but there is a break in the relief, and if they existed they are now lost. When these dimensions are compared with those of a modern adult Black Rhinoceros (*Diceros bicornis*) or White Rhinoceros (*Ceratotherium simum*), the two African species, all but the considerably exaggerated height and girth are within reasonable parameters—and the anomalies in the record may be the result of our lack of understanding of precisely how the measurements were obtained. The transport of a live, fully grown, wild rhinoceros to Egypt from the southern hinterlands would have been a heroic feat, and its appearance hailed as a true rara avis, securing the animal a special place in the menagerie of any monarch.

With the advent of the Ptolemaic Period, there was an enormous surge in interest in the acquisition of rare and exotic animals, as well as in the study of their habits and behavior. There were also efforts to breed some of these creatures. Ptolemy II Philadelphus's establishment of a great royal zoo in Alexandria, of course, belongs to a wholly different cultural tradition, that of the Greco–Roman world, but is worth considering here because an immense wealth of African fauna and other wildlife from further afield entered Egypt at this time. Philadelphus's vast collection is best remembered for its appearance in his grand procession of extraordinary splendor, which he staged in Alexandria in the early 270s B.C. A long and detailed account of the pageant by the Rhodian historian Kallixeinos is preserved in the work of the Classical author Athenaeus (V, 197–208). The imposing procession featured tremendous numbers and varieties of beasts, which included asses, African and Asian elephants, goats, antelopes, oryxes, Bubal Hartebeest, Ostriches, Onagers *(Equus hemionus)*, horses, Dromedaries, Bactrian Camels, mules, dogs, parrots (order Psittaciformes), peacocks, Helmeted Guineafowl, pheasants (Phasianidae), sheep, cattle, a white bear (perhaps a rare albino rather than the Polar Bear [*Ursus maritimus*] it is usually identified as), Leopards, Cheetahs, Caracals, Giraffe, and a rhinoceros from Ethiopia! According to Diodorus Siculus (III, 36–37), Philadelphus's zoo also exhibited an astonishing snake over thirteen meters long, probably an African Rock Python, obtained from the swamps in the upper reaches of the Nile; and Aelian remarks (*De Natura Animalium* XVI, 39) that the collection also housed two great snakes from Ethiopia. This royal zoo, or remnants of it, may have survived into the reign of Ptolemy VIII Euergetes II (Physkon). Colossal numbers of elephants were also imported into Egypt during the Ptolemaic Period from eastern Sudan and Ethiopia, as well as from Asia, principally for use in warfare. The Ptolemies became some of the best known elephant-keepers in the ancient world, and many battles were waged deploying these noble giants.

The trade in exotic animals worked the other way too. Egypt played an important role during the Roman Period in supplying a considerable variety of its indigenous fauna for public and private animal collections throughout the Roman Empire, as well as for slaughter at the games and shows in the arena. As several authorities have observed, some of the decimation of large game animals in Egypt may be linked to this onerous practice, especially in the case of the Hippopotamus.

Chapter Nine

Animals in Humor and Wit

*T*he keen eye of gifted ancient Egyptian artisans observed a wide range of
humorous moments in the everyday pursuits of the lower classes of
society. Sometimes they included details of this jocularity, in picture and in word,
within the decorative program of tomb-chapels belonging to the wealthy and
socially superior. They would subtly poke fun at the coarse appearance, behavior,
and crude exclamations of the herders, fowlers, riverfolk, and common fieldhands.
Animals also figured prominently in this brand of quiet humor. The cries of a
young calf and its mother separated while fording a canal (frontispiece, pl. VIII),

Fig. 144. Drawing of a detail
from a wall painting in the
rock-cut tomb of the
nomarch Baket III (no. 15) at
Beni Hasan, showing a
country lad and a young calf
simultaneously drinking
milk from the udder of a
long-horned cow. The
mother cow is represented
affectionately licking her
offspring. Eleventh Dynasty.

Fig. 145. This small figured limestone ostracon bears a black and red ink sketch of a monkey climbing the trunk of a Doum Palm heavy with ripe nuts, one of its favorite foods. The beast is depicted sporting a girdle or halter tied around its waist, indicating that this is someone's domestic pet. Several Egyptologists have maintained that baboons such as this one were trained by the ancient Egyptians to harvest doum-nuts, dates, and figs from trees for their masters, as well as to perform other difficult work. This seems quite unlikely, however, and such motifs should be viewed for their 'aping' comic appeal. Probably from Deir al-Medina. Ramesside Period. Actual size. THE FITZWILLIAM MUSEUM, UNIVERSITY OF CAMBRIDGE.

a weeping cow who loses her precious milk—intended for her calf—to a herdsman (fig. 9), or a young peasant boy and a calf simultaneously sharing a drink from a cow's udder (fig. 144), strike the modern eye as welcome touches of levity in otherwise formal tomb compositions. In addition to their deep love of animals, the ancient Egyptians were by all means a fun-loving people who dearly appreciated a good laugh, and faunal images were a frequent vehicle for expressing what was considered funny.

The comic antics of beloved household pets, in particular, served as a constant source of inspiration for delightful, light-hearted episodes. We have seen (chapter 4) how tame monkeys and baboons were quite often depicted in Egyptian iconography clownishly behaving like human beings, helping with the vintage, directing ship-building, harvesting fruit from trees (fig. 145), scampering up a ship's mast and rigging, piloting a Nile vessel, yanking on the tail feathers of a Common Crane (fig. 71), and performing on musical instruments. This amusing and age-old genre found its widest and most creative expression in Egyptian art during the late Ramesside Period. Many hundreds of drawings rendered on small ostraca, and others found on fragments of three illustrated 'satirical' papyri, feature playful motifs of animal caricatures cast in quasi-human situations or revolving around a topsy-turvy animal world. A wide array of both wild and domestic creatures is represented in the faunal repertoire of this immensely appealing collection.

Ostraca—pottery shards and limestone chips—were very frequently used in ancient Egypt for writing and drawing as a cheap alternative to costly papyrus rolls. On average, these ostraca are usually about

Fig. 146. Drawing of a substantial portion of the famous Turin satirical papyrus, showing an assortment of animals undertaking various human activities. In the upper register, note the faunal musical ensemble, with a Lion on the lead vocal. Below, from the left, warrior mice attack a castle defended by cats, a crow climbs a ladder to the branches of a tree with a Hippopotamus in it gathering fruit in a basket, and an enraged duck or goose turns on a cat. Probably from Deir al-Medina. Ramesside Period. MUSEO EGIZIO, TURIN.

Fig. 147. Figured limestone ostracon with a black and red ink drawing of a monkey harpist, which wears a girdle tied round its waist, indicating that this is a tame household animal. Probably from Deir al-Medina. Ramesside Period. MUSÉES ROYAUX D'ART ET D'HISTOIRE, BRUSSELS.

the size of a human hand, but some examples of more than a meter in length are known. The Theban necropolis especially has yielded a tremendous quantity of them. Here, the cream-colored limestone of the mountain provided a wealth of handy and ready-made flakes for a variety of purposes. The highly skilled artisans of the royal gang of workers, who were employed by the state for the construction and decoration of the monumental sepulchers of the pharaohs in the Valley of the Kings, were quite fond of using ostraca as notepads for sketches, memorandums, letters, and copies of literary works among many other things. Excavations at Deir al-Medina, the site of the workers' walled village at the southern end of the Theban necropolis near the Valley of the Queens, have turned up thousands of them. They are datable from the Eighteenth through the Twentieth dynasties (and mostly to the Ramesside Period), the period when the artisans' community flourished and they were working

Fig. 148. Figured limestone ostracon with a humorous black and red ink drawing, showing a lively episode of an Egyptian tabby wielding a long staff and herding a flock of six ducks or geese. Above the birds, there is a nest filled with a clutch of eggs. The cat is equipped with a small bag of provisions suspended from the end of a long crook that it carries over its shoulder, just as shepherds frequently do in tomb-chapel decoration. From Deir al-Medina. Ramesside Period. THE EGYPTIAN MUSEUM, CAIRO.

Fig. 149. (opposite) This amusing detail is from a painted satirical papyrus dating from the Ramesside Period. It playfully illustrates a cat serving as a nursemaid to a baby mouse, which it tenderly holds, swathed in a shawl or a sling. The pair are shaded by a large fan, carried by a servant tabby following close behind. Purchased at Tuna al-Gebel, but probably originally from Deir al-Medina. THE EGYPTIAN MUSEUM, CAIRO.

on the royal tombs. The picture captured on such figured ostraca reveals an Egypt often considerably different to that presented in traditional art forms decorating tomb-chapel and temple walls. On these limestone flakes, the Egyptian artisans display a freedom of hand and imagination that is rarely met with in their official compositions, in which their artistic talents were restrained by strict conventions of representation, and the subject matter on the ostraca is often restricted to this medium. The standard of drawing, though, does vary and may range from mere childish doodlings to student trial pieces or fine studies deftly worked in anticipation of their execution in another medium elsewhere. Exotic and other unusual animal life, such as the Syrian Bear, bat (fig. 113), chicken (fig. 141), Giraffe, and African Elephant can be counted among the ranks of characters encountered on ostraca, but a

great many were clearly produced for the artisans' own personal amusement and pleasure, drawn perhaps to pass idle moments from their other work. It is in this last vein that we possess a sizable number of casual sketches in which the intent was clearly humorous or satirical. These rapidly created, concise images may even have been passed around to fellow workers on the job site, perhaps to share a good chuckle, then simply tossed away.

Three damaged Ramesside illustrated papyri, which probably all share a Deir al-Medina provenance, are now housed in museum collections in London, Turin, and Cairo, and each contains vignettes that are directly parallel to scenes on the informal, figured ostraca. Usually, the animals illustrated on the papyri and ostraca have adopted the roles, dress, and gestures of human beings, but often with an additional wrinkle: sometimes the natural order of the

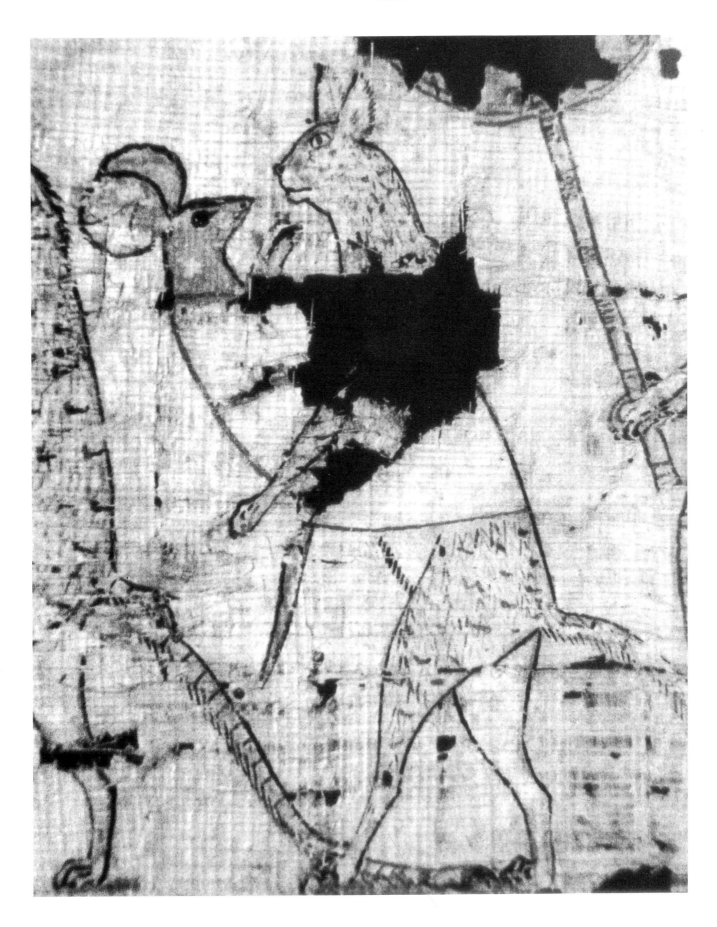

Fig. 150. A vignette from a painted satirical papyrus, in which a Lion and what is probably a Bubal Hartebeest play the board-game senet together. The match thus pits the hunter against the hunted. From the triumphant expression on the face of the Lion, things look bleak for the antelope. This scene seems to imitate a similar episode featuring human players in the Book of the Dead. Note too the presence of a large black crow in the lower lefthand corner, standing beside a basket of brightly colored fruit. Probably from Deir al-Medina. Ramesside Period. THE BRITISH MUSEUM, LONDON.

Fig. 151. This entertaining image of a mouse, wearing the long, pleated, flaring kilt of a well-to-do man, is drawn in black and red ink on a limestone ostracon. The mouse is depicted performing a juggling act with two balls. On the ground in front of him there is a wooden storage chest, where the balls were probably kept when not in use. Probably from Deir al-Medina. Ramesside Period. MEDELHAVSMUSEET, STOCKHOLM.

214

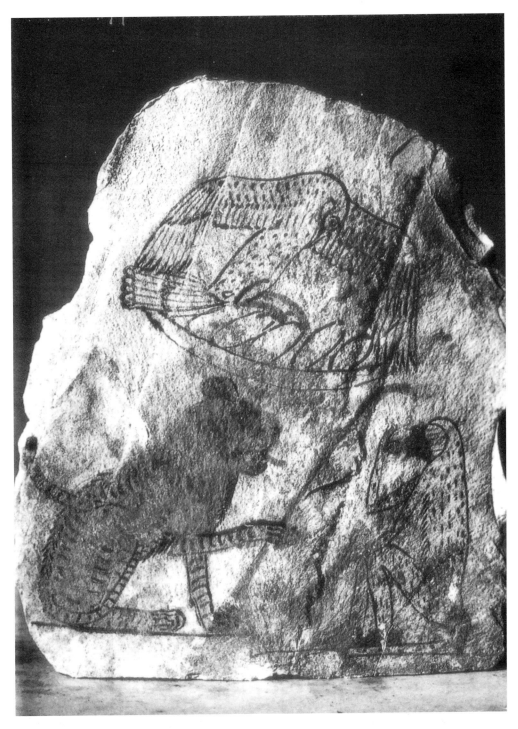

Fig. 152. Painted limestone ostracon featuring a baboon, representing the god Thoth, engaged in a lively conversation with a lioness, the goddess Tefnut. Above them, a bird, almost certainly a vulture, sits on its nest, which is filled with a clutch of eggs. This piece appears to offer firm evidence that some of the themes illustrated on figured ostraca may reflect religious stories, since these three animal characters relate to The Myth of the Eye of the Sun. From Deir al-Medina. Ramesside Period.
ÄGYPTISCHES MUSEUM, BERLIN.

species depicted is altered, so that humble servant cats must now wait upon the every need of well-heeled lady mice. Some of the more frequently recurring and entertaining themes in this corpus of material include: troupes of serenading animal musicians (figs. 146, 147), cats tending large flocks of domestic ducks or geese (fig. 148), cats who serve as nursemaids to infant mice (fig. 149), hyenas shepherding herds of goats, a Lion and an antelope playing the board-game *senet* together (fig. 150), a mouse juggling balls (fig. 151), baboons drinking beer under the shade of pavilions, cats administering corporal punishment to delinquent youths, and a crow ascending to the branches of a Sycamore Fig tree by means of a ladder, while a Hippopotamus

Fig. 153. Block of sandstone temple relief showing a satirical banqueting scene, with animals engaged in human roles. The precise interpretation of this composition remains somewhat obscure, but the presence of this very unusual relief in a sacred temple setting indicates that the scene must have had more than one layer of meaning attached to it. From al-Medamud. Twenty-fifth Dynasty. THE EGYPTIAN MUSEUM, CAIRO.

gathers ripe figs in a basket in the branches of the tree (fig. 146).

An especially favorite and always lively motif, which is best exemplified on the extraordinary papyrus now in the Museo Egizio, Turin, might have been entitled in antiquity 'The War of the Cats and Mice' (fig. 146). Here can be seen a fortress of cats besieged by an army of soldier mice, who are armed with bows and arrows or shields and long spears. A heroic warrior mouse rides toward the stronghold in a speeding chariot drawn by a pair of galloping dogs. This detail would seem to have been inspired by a scene of some Ramesside king charging the enemy. Other mice of the infantry are, in an instant, about to storm the high fortress walls with a ladder, and the cats seem ready to capitulate. All looks lost for the evil feline foes! Some other motifs seem to be directly parodying funerary themes depicted on the walls of tombs or in the *Book of the Dead* (fig. 150). One such scene occurs on the satirical papyrus in the British Museum, London, where a Lion is engaged in the rites of mummification on a dead donkey lying on a bier, while on a limestone ostracon in the

Museum of Art and Archaeology, the University of Missouri, Columbia, a crow and a Hippopotamus are portrayed standing on a weighing scale, similar to that known from the final judgment in the netherworld.

While no one can deny the amusing side of these illustrations, their precise meaning remains somewhat uncertain, owing to the absence of detailed explanatory accompanying texts. It has been suggested that this vein of humor may have served as trenchant wit, parody, or social satire directed against the aristocracy and the scenes in their splendid tomb-chapels, and may reflect the turmoil that Egyptian society was experiencing at the close of the Twentieth Dynasty. Another possibility that has been extensively studied by Emma Brunner-Traut is that the scenes may illustrate ancient Egyptian folk tales or fables, now lost, which featured stories centering around the actions of these highly animated creatures.

In any case, certain of these animal adventures must have had some degree of religious significance, in one way or other. This view is supported by at least one well-known Ramesside ostracon from Deir al-Medina, with a motif of three characters, a lioness, a baboon, and what is almost certainly a vulture on a nest filled with a clutch of eggs (fig. 152). The same trio is mentioned in the lengthy literary tale known as *The Myth of the Eye of the Sun*, preserved on several papyri from the second century A.D. The narrative of this work recounts the search for and the return of the goddess Tefnut, the daughter and 'eye' of the sun-god Ra, to Egypt after she fled south into Nubia. The god Thoth, in the guise of a baboon, persuades the lioness deity to return home, and in doing so relates several fables, one of which involves a vulture. That these animal actors occur together on the limestone fragment is evidence that the story, or a close variant of it, was already current in the late New Kingdom.

A mythological link of some sort must surely also account for the remarkable appearance of a 'satirical' scene carved on a block of wall relief from a temple at al-Medamud, which dates from the Twenty-fifth Dynasty (fig. 153). This improperly understood piece is made even more unusual by the fact that it has humans and animals appearing alongside each other. The relief portrays several animals at a festive banquet, featuring an elaborately dressed noblewoman mouse, with a fragrant flower in her hand, being served by a cat and a hound or jackal. Music for the grand affair is provided by a lute-playing crocodile, joined by a naked young woman on its back playing her angular harp. That a purely satirical or humorous composition would be included in the wall decoration of a sacred temple seems highly improbable, so clearly this episode held some additional level of meaning for the ancient Egyptians beyond the obvious comic appeal.

Notes

1 Smelik 1979, pp.225–26.
2 Breasted 1906, vol. 1, p.126, note (c).
3 Bourriau 1989, p.83.
4 Pritchard 1955, p.469.
5 Winter 1978, pp.27–28.
6 Sadek 1987, p.244.
7 Pritchard 1955, p.244.
8 Lichtheim 1980, p.73.
9 Lichtheim 1976, pp.186–87.
10 Hilzheimer 1932, p.418.
11 Lichtheim 1976, p.187.
12 Phillips 1948, p.[19].
13 Reisner 1936, p.97.
14 Caminos 1954, p.189.
15 Ebbell 1937.
16 Pritchard 1955, p.495.
17 Conway 1890, p.254.
18 te Velde 1988, p.130.
19 Hodjash and Berlev 1980, p.42.
20 Caminos 1954, pp.381–82.
21 Borghouts 1978, p.83.
22 Borghouts 1978, p.23.
23 Pritchard 1955, p.366.
24 Pritchard 1955, p.433.
25 Caminos 1956, p.7.
26 Lichtheim 1976, p.190.
27 Pritchard 1955, p.327.
28 Faulkner 1972, p.37.
29 Scott 1951, p.205.
30 Borghouts 1978, pp.77–78.
31 Caminos 1954, p.247.
32 Caminos 1954, pp.188–89.
33 Breasted 1906, Vol. 2, p.193.
34 Caminos 1954, p.438.
35 Pritchard 1955, p.244.
36 Mond and Myers 1940, Vol. 1, pp.159–60, 204; Cumming 1982, p.10.

Sources of the Illustrations

Oxford University Press: fig. 88 (drawing by N. M. Davies from J. G. Wilkinson MSS.; reproduced from Singer *et al.* 1954, p. 264, fig. 164). Museum of Fine Arts, Boston: fig. 91 (acc. no. 1977.619). S. M. Goodman: figs. 102, 107, 113. Petrie Museum of Egyptian Archaeology, University College London: fig. 105 (acc. no. UC. 14365). P. A. Clayton: fig. 132. E. Brunner-Traut: fig. 146 (from Brunner-Traut 1955, pl. III). The Werner Forman Archive, London: pls. I, II, IV, V, IX, X, XIII, XIV, XV, XVII, XIX, XXII, XXIII, XXIV, XXV, XXVI, XXVIII, XXIX, XXXIV, XXXV.

Figure 19 is reproduced from von Bissing 1956, pl. XIII. Figure 26 is reproduced from Wilkinson 1878, vol. 1, p. 237,

no. 70. Figure 66 is reproduced from Paget and Pirie 1898, pl. XXXIII. Figure 94 is reproduced from Steindorff 1913, pl. 113. Figure 97 is reproduced from Rosellini 1834, pl. VII. Figure 98 is reproduced from Wreszinski 1938, vol. 3, pl. 83(c). Figure 108 is reproduced from Boussac 1911, p. 63, fig. 10. Figure 114 is reproduced from Hassan 1936, pl. LI. Figure 117 is reproduced from Quibell 1908, pl. V. Figure 136 is reproduced from Wreszinski 1935, vol. 2, pl. 26.

Figs. 8, 9, 14, 40, 55, 56, 57, 61, 62, 68, 72, 74, 76, 77, 78, 80, 90, 99, 103, 109, 111, 116, 121, 129, 131, 134, 135, 137, 138, 139, 140, 141, 148, 149 and pls. III, VI, VII, VIII, XI, XII, XVI, XVIII, XX, XXI, XXX, XXXI, XXXII, and XXXIII are by Patrick Francis Houlihan.

Selected Bibliography

It is a pleasure to acknowledge that I have drawn considerable information for this book from the publications of the renowned German Egyptologist Dr. Ludwig (or Louis) Keimer (1893–1957), who specialized in the study of the fauna and flora of ancient Egypt. I have not cited individually the many valuable articles, reviews, and monographs of his that have been consulted. The interested reader is encouraged to refer to Keimer's complete (or nearly so) bibliography, for which, see his *Etudes d'égyptologie.* Fasc. 1 (Cairo: Imprimerie de l'Institut français d'archéologie orientale, 1940), pp. 2–11; and B. van de Walle, *Chronique d'Egypte* 33 (1958), pp. 74–78, 235. Further literature on specific species of animals and other related topics can be found in the comprehensive and indispensable *Lexikon der Ägyptologie,* vols. 1–7, ed. W. Helck, E. Otto, W. Westendorf (Wiesbaden: Otto Harrassowitz, 1975–92). In particular, see the many excellent entries on faunal subjects written by E. Brunner-Traut, P. Behrens, H. G. Fischer, D. Kessler, L. Kákosy, K. W. Butzer, and especially L. Störk.

Aldred, C. *The Development of Ancient Egyptian Art from 3200 to 1315 BC.* London: Alec Tiranti. 1968.
———. *Akhenaten and Nefertiti.* New York: The Brooklyn Museum and Viking Press. 1973.
———. *Egyptian Art in the Days of the Pharaohs 3100–320 BC.* New York and Toronto: Oxford University Press. 1980.
———. *The Egyptians.* Rev. edn. London: Thames and Hudson. 1988.
Altenmüller, H. *Darstellungen der Jagd im alten Ägypten.* Hamburg: Verlag Paul Parey. 1967.
Ancient Egypt: Discovering its Splendors. Washington, D.C.: The National Geographic Society. 1978.
Anderson, J. *Zoology of Egypt: Reptilia and Batrachia.* London: Bernard Quaritch. 1898.
———. *Zoology of Egypt: Mammalia.* Rev. by W. E. de Winton. London: Hugh Rees. 1902.
Andrews, C. *Ancient Egyptian Jewelry.* New York: Harry N. Abrams. 1991.
———. *Amulets of Ancient Egypt.* Austin: The University of Texas Press. 1994.
Les animaux dans l'Egypte ancienne: Le Louvre présente au Muséum de Lyon. Du 6 novembre 77 au 31 janvier 78. Lyon: Musée d'histoire naturelle de Lyon. 1977.
Anthony, D. *et al. Man and Animals: Living, Working and Changing Together.* Philadelphia: The University Museum, University of Pennsylvania. 1984.

Arnold, D. "An Egyptian Bestiary." *The Metropolitan Museum of Art Bulletin* (Spring 1995), pp. 1–64.

Baedeker, K. *Egypt and the Sûdân: Handbook for Travellers*. 8th edn. Leipzig: Karl Baedeker. 1929.

Bagnall, R. S. *Egypt in Late Antiquity*. Princeton: Princeton University Press. 1993.

Baines, J. and J. Málek. *Atlas of Ancient Egypt*. New York: Facts On File. 1980.

Beaux, N. *Le cabinet de curiosités de Thoutmosis III: Plantes et animaux du "Jardin botanique" de Karnak*. Louvain: Uitgeverij Peeters. 1990.

Behrens, H. "Neolithisch-frühmetallzeitliche Tierskelettfunde aus dem Nilgebiet und ihre religionsgeschichtliche Bedeutung." *Zeitschrift für ägyptische Sprache und Altertumskunde* 88 (1963), pp. 75–83.

Behrmann, A. *Das Nilpferd in der Vorstellungswelt der alten Ägypter*. Vol. 1. Bern and Frankfurt: Verlag Peter Lang. 1989.

Ben-Tor, D. *The Scarab: A Reflection of Ancient Egypt*. Jerusalem: The Israel Museum. 1993.

Bierbrier, M. *The Tomb-Builders of the Pharaohs*. London: British Museum Publications. 1982.

Bietak, M. *Avaris and Piramesse: Archaeological Exploration in the Eastern Nile Delta*. Rev. edn. London: The British Academy. 1986.

Blackman, A. M. *The Rock Tombs of Meir*. Vols. 1–2. London: The Egypt Exploration Fund. 1914–15.

Bodenheimer, F. S. *Animal and Man in Bible Lands*. Vols. 1–2. Leiden: E. J. Brill. 1960–72.

Boessneck, J. *Gemeinsame Anliegen von Ägyptologie und Zoologie aus der Sicht des Zooarchäologen*. Munich: Verlag der Bayerischen Akademie der Wissenschaften. 1981.

———, ed. *Die Münchner Ochsenmumie*. Hildesheim: Gerstenberg Verlag. 1987.

———, ed. *Tuna el-Gebel I: Die Tiergalerien*. Hildesheim: Gerstenberg Verlag. 1987.

———. *Die Tierwelt des alten Ägypten: Untersucht anhand kulturgeschichtlicher und zoologischer Quellen*. Munich: Verlag C. H. Beck. 1988.

Boessneck, J. and A. von den Driesch. *Studien an subfossilen Tierknochen aus Ägypten*. Munich: Deutscher Kunstverlag. 1982.

Bonnet, H. *Reallexikon der Ägyptischen Religionsgeschichte*. Berlin and New York: Walter de Gruyter. 1971.

Borchardt, L. *Das Grabdenkmal des Königs Śa3ḥu-Rē'*. Vols. 1–2. Leipzig: J. C. Hinrichs Verlag. 1910–13.

Borghouts, J. F. *Ancient Egyptian Magical Texts*. Leiden: E. J. Brill. 1978.

Boulenger, G. A. *Zoology of Egypt: The Fishes of the Nile*. Vols. 1–2. London: Hugh Rees. 1907.

Bourriau, J. *Pharaohs and Mortals: Egyptian Art in the Middle Kingdom*. Cambridge and New York: Cambridge University Press. 1989.

Boussac, P.-H. "Le canard à longue queue ou pilet, *Dafila acuta*, Linné." *Recueil de travaux relatifs à la philologie et à l'archéologie égyptiennes et assyriennes* 33 (1911), pp. 59–63.

Bowman, A. K. *Egypt after the Pharaohs: 332 BC–AD 642, from Alexander to the Arab Conquest*. Berkeley: The University of California Press. 1989.

Breasted, J. H. *Ancient Records of Egypt: Historical Documents from the Earliest Times to the Persian Conquest*. Vols. 1–5. Chicago: The University of Chicago Press. 1906–07.

Breasted, J. H., Jr. *Egyptian Servant Statues*. Washington, D.C.: Pantheon Books. 1948.

Brewer, D. J. *Fishermen, Hunters and Herders: Zooarchaeology in the Fayum, Egypt (ca. 8200–5000 bp)*. Oxford: BAR International Series. 1989.

Brewer, D. J. and R. F. Friedman. *Fish and Fishing in Ancient Egypt*. Warminster: Aris and Phillips. 1989.

Brewer, D. J., D. B. Redford, S. Redford. *Domestic Plants and Animals: The Egyptian Origins*. Warminster: Aris and Phillips. [1994.]

Brunner-Traut, E. "Ägyptische Tiermärchen." *Zeitschrift für ägyptische Sprache und Altertumskunde* 80 (1955), pp. 12–32.

———. *Die altägyptischen Scherbenbilder (Bildostraka) der deutschen Museen und Sammlungen*. Wiesbaden: Franz Steiner Verlag. 1956.

———. *Spitzmaus und Ichneumon als Tiere des Sonnengottes*. Göttingen: Vandenhoeck and Ruprecht. 1965.

———. *Egyptian Artists' Sketches: Figured Ostraka from the Gayer-Anderson Collection in the Fitzwilliam Museum, Cambridge*. Istanbul: Nederlands Historisch-Archaeologisch Instituut. 1979.

———. *Altägyptische Tiergeschichte und Fabel: Gestalt und Strahlkraft*. 7th edn. Darmstadt: Wissenschaftliche Buchgesellschaft. 1984.

———. "Die Stellung des Tieres im alten Ägypten." *Universitas* 40 (1985), pp. 333–47.

Burton, A. *Diodorus Siculus: Book I, a Commentary*. Leiden: E. J. Brill. 1972.

Butzer, K. W. "Environment and Human Ecology in Egypt during Predynastic and Early Dynastic Times." *Bulletin de la société de géographie d'Egypte* 32 (1959), pp. 43–88.

———. *Early Hydraulic Civilization in Egypt: A Study in Cultural Ecology*. Chicago and London: The University of Chicago Press. 1976.

Caminos, R. A. *Late-Egyptian Miscellanies*. London: Oxford University Press. 1954.

———. *Literary Fragments in the Hieratic Script*. Oxford: The Griffith Institute. 1956.

Capart, J. *Primitive Art in Egypt*. Rev. by A. S. Griffith. Philadelphia: J. B. Lippincott Company. 1905.

———. *Documents pour servir à l'étude de l'art égyptien*. Vols. 1–2. Paris: Editions du Pégase. 1927–31.

Capart, J. and M. Werbrouck. *Thebes: The Glory of a Great Past*. New York: The Dial Press. 1926.

———. *Memphis: À l'ombre des pyramides*. Brussels: Vromant and Company. 1930.

Carrington, R. "Animals in Egypt." *Animals in Archaeology*. A. Houghton Brodrick, ed. New York: Praeger Publishers. 1972. Pp. 69–89.

Carter, H. *The Tomb of Tut-ankh-Amen: Discovered by the Late Earl of Carnarvon and Howard Carter*. Vols. 1–3 (vol. 1 with A. C. Mace). New York: Cooper Square Publishers. 1963.

Černý, J. *Ancient Egyptian Religion*. London: Hutchinson's University Library. 1952.

Charron, A. "Massacres d'animaux à la Basse Epoque." *Revue d'égyptologie* 41 (1990), pp. 209–213.

Les chats des pharaons: "4000 ans de divinité féline." Exposition sous le haut patronage de Sa Majesté la Reine. Catalogue: 27 octobre 1989–25 février 1990. Brussels: Editions de l'Institut royal des sciences naturelles de Belgique. 1989.

Churcher, C. S. "Zoological Study of the Ivory Knife Handle from Abu Zaidan." *Predynastic and Archaic Egypt in The Brooklyn Museum.* W. Needler, ed. Brooklyn: The Brooklyn Museum. 1984. Pp. 152–68.

Clayton, P. A. *Chronicle of the Pharaohs: The Reign-by-Reign Record of the Rulers and Dynasties of Ancient Egypt.* London and New York: Thames and Hudson. 1994.

Cleopatra's Egypt: Age of the Ptolemies. Brooklyn: The Brooklyn Museum. 1988.

Clutton-Brock, J. *Domesticated Animals from Early Times.* Austin and London: The University of Texas Press and The British Museum (Natural History). 1981.

———. *Horse Power: A History of the Horse and the Donkey in Human Societies.* Cambridge: Harvard University Press. 1992.

———. "The Spread of Domestic Animals in Africa." *The Archaeology of Africa: Food, Metals and Towns.* T. Shaw *et al.*, eds. London and New York: Routledge. 1993. Pp. 61–70.

Conway, W. M. "The Cats of Ancient Egypt." *English Illustrated Magazine* 7 (1890), pp. 251–54.

Corteggiani, J.-P. *The Egypt of the Pharaohs at the Cairo Museum.* London: Scala Books. 1987.

Cumming, B. *Egyptian Historical Records of the Later Eighteenth Dynasty.* Fasc. 1. Warminster: Aris and Phillips. 1982.

Danelius, E. and H. Steinitz. "The Fishes and Other Aquatic Animals on the Punt-Reliefs at Deir el-Bahari." *Journal of Egyptian Archaeology* 53 (1967), pp. 15–24.

Darby, W. J., P. Ghalioungui, L. Grivetti. *Food: The Gift of Osiris.* Vols. 1–2. London and New York: Academic Press. 1977.

Dasen, V. *Dwarfs in Ancient Egypt and Greece.* Oxford: Clarendon Press. 1993.

D'Auria, S., P. Lacovara, C. H. Roehrig. *Mummies and Magic: The Funerary Arts of Ancient Egypt.* Boston: The Museum of Fine Arts, Boston. 1988.

Davies, N. de Garis. *Five Theban Tombs (being those of Mentuherkhepeshef, User, Daga, Nehemawäy and Tati).* London: The Egypt Exploration Fund. 1913.

———. "The Work of the Graphic Branch of the Expedition." *The Egyptian Expedition 1931–1932: Bulletin of The Metropolitan Museum of Art.* Supplement (Dec., 1932), pp. 23–29.

———. *Paintings from the Tomb of Rekh-mi-Rē' at Thebes.* New York: The Metropolitan Museum of Art. 1935.

———. *The Tomb of Rekh-mi-Rē' at Thebes.* Vols. 1–2. New York: The Metropolitan Museum of Art. 1943.

Davies, N. M. *Ancient Egyptian Paintings.* Vols. 1–3. Ed. by A. H. Gardiner. Chicago: The University of Chicago Press. 1936.

———. "Birds and Bats at Beni Hasan." *Journal of Egyptian Archaeology* 35 (1949), pp. 13–20.

Davies, N. M. and A. H. Gardiner. *Tutankhamun's Painted Box.* Oxford: The Griffith Institute. 1962.

Debono, F. and B. Mortensen. *The Predynastic Cemetery at Heliopolis: Season March–September 1950.* Mainz: Verlag Philipp von Zabern. 1988.

Decker, W. *Sports and Games of Ancient Egypt.* New Haven and London: Yale University Press. 1992.

Decker, W. and M. Herb. *Bildatlas zum Sport im alten Ägypten: Corpus der bildlichen Quellen zu Leibesübungen, Spiel, Jagd, Tanz und verwandten Themen.* Vols. 1–2. Leiden and New York: E. J. Brill. 1994.

del Francia, L. "Scènes d'animaux personnifiés dans l'Egypte pharaonique et copte. À propos d'une peinture de Baouit." *Acts of the Second International*

Congress of Coptic Study: Roma, 22–26 September 1980. T. Orlandi and F. Wisse, eds. Rome: C.I.M. 1985. Pp. 31–57.

Delvaux, L. and E. Warmenbol. *Les divins chats d'Egypte: Un air subtil, un dangereux parfum*. Louvain: Editions Peeters. 1991.

Derchain, P. *Rites égyptiens I: Le sacrifice de l'oryx*. Brussels: Fondation égyptologique Reine Elisabeth. 1962.

———. "Symbols and Metaphors in Literature and Representations of Private Life." *Royal Anthropological Institute News* 15 (August 1976), pp. 7–10.

de Wit, C. *Le rôle et le sens du lion dans l'Egypte ancienne*. Leiden: E. J. Brill. 1951.

Donadoni Roveri, A. M., ed. *Egyptian Museum of Turin: Egyptian Civilization, Daily Life*. Turin: Istituto Bancario San Paolo. 1988.

Drioton, E. and J. Vandier. *L'Egypte: Des origines à la conquête d'Alexandre*. 7th edn. Paris: Presses Universitaires de France. 1989.

Ebbell, B. *The Papyrus Ebers: The Greatest Egyptian Medical Document*. Copenhagen: Levin and Munksgaard. 1937.

Edel, E. and S. Wenig. *Die Jahreszeitenreliefs aus dem Sonnenheiligtum des Königs Ne-user-Re*. Tafelband. Berlin: Akademie-Verlag. 1974.

Edwards, I. E. S. *Treasures of Tutankhamun*. New York: Ballantine Books. 1978.

Egypt's Golden Age: The Art of Living in the New Kingdon 1558–1085 BC, Catalogue of the Exhibition. Boston: Museum of Fine Arts, Boston. 1982.

Elat, M. "The Economic Relations of the Neo-Assyrian Empire with Egypt." *Journal of the American Oriental Society* 98 (1978), pp. 20–34.

Emery, W. B. *Archaic Egypt*. Baltimore: Penguin Books. 1961.

Engelbach, R., ed. *Introduction to Egyptian Archaeology: With Special Reference to the Egyptian Museum, Cairo*. 3rd edn. ed. by D. Abou-Ghazi. Cairo: General Organization for Government Printing Offices. 1988.

Epstein, H. *The Origin of the Domestic Animals of Africa*. Vols. 1–2. Rev. by I. L. Mason. New York and London: Africana Publishing Corporation. 1971.

Erman, A. *Life in Ancient Egypt*. London: Macmillan and Company. 1894.

Faulkner, R. O. *The Book of the Dead*. New York: The Limited Editions Club. 1972.

Fay, B. *Egyptian Museum Berlin*. 4th edn. Berlin: Ägyptisches Museum der Staatlichen Museen Preussischer Kulturbesitz. 1990.

Fazzini, R. A. *Images for Eternity: Egyptian Art from Berkeley and Brooklyn*. Brooklyn: The Fine Arts Museums of San Francisco and The Brooklyn Museum. 1975.

Fazzini, R. A., R. S. Bianchi, J. F. Romano, D. B. Spanel. *Ancient Egyptian Art in the Brooklyn Museum*. New York and London: The Brooklyn Museum and Thames and Hudson. 1989.

Firmage, E. "Zoology (Fauna)." *The Anchor Bible Dictionary*. Vol. 6. D. N. Freedman, ed. New York and London: Doubleday and Company. 1992. Pp. 1109–1167.

Fischer, H. G. "A Fragment of Late Predynastic Egyptian Relief from the Eastern Delta." *Artibus Asiae* 21 (1958), pp. 64–88.

———. "A Scribe of the Army in a Saqqara Mastaba of the Early Fifth Dynasty." *Journal of Near Eastern Studies* 18 (1959), pp. 233–72.

———. *Ancient Egyptian Representations of Turtles*. New York: The Metropolitan Museum of Art. 1968.

———. "More Ancient Egyptian Names of Dogs and Other Animals." *Ancient Egypt in The Metropolitan Museum Journal Supplement: Volumes 12–13 (1977–1978)*. New York: The Metropolitan Museum of Art. 1980. Pp. 173–78.

———. "The Ancient Egyptian Attitude Towards the Monstrous." *Monsters and*

Demons in the Ancient and Medieval Worlds: Papers Presented in Honor of Edith Porada. A. E. Farkas, P. O. Harper, E. B. Harrison, eds. Mainz: Verlag Philipp von Zabern. 1987. Pp. 13–26.

———. *Ancient Egyptian Calligraphy: A Beginner's Guide to Writing Hieroglyphs.* 3rd edn. New York: The Metropolitan Museum of Art. 1988.

———. "Another Pithmorphic Vessel of the Sixth Dynasty." *Journal of the American Research Center in Egypt* 30 (1993), pp. 1–9.

Flower, S. S. "Notes on the Recent Mammals of Egypt, with a List of the Species Recorded from that Kingdom." *Proceedings of the Zoological Society of London* (1932), pp. 369–450.

Freed, R. E. *Ramses II: The Great Pharaoh and His Time, an Exhibition in the City of Denver.* Denver: The Denver Museum of Natural History. 1987.

Gaillard, C. "Les tâtonnements des égyptiens de l'Ancien Empire à la recherche des animaux à domestiquer." *Revue d'ethnographie et de sociologie* 3 (1912), pp. 329–48.

Gaillard, C. and G. Daressy. *La faune momifiée de l'antique Egypte.* Cairo: Imprimerie de l'Institut français d'archéologie orientale. 1905.

Gaillard, C., V. Loret, C. Kuentz. *Recherches sur les poissons représentés dans quelques tombeaux égyptiens de l'Ancien Empire.* Cairo: Imprimerie de l'Institut français d'archéologie orientale. 1923.

Gamer-Wallert, I. *Fische und Fischkulte im alten Ägypten.* Wiesbaden: Otto Harrassowitz. 1970.

Gardiner, A. H. *Egyptian Grammar: Being an Introduction to the Study of Hieroglyphs.* 3rd edn. London: Oxford University Press. 1957.

———. *Egypt of the Pharaohs: An Introduction.* Oxford: Oxford University Press. 1966.

Gazda, E. K., ed. *Karanis: An Egyptian Town in Roman Times. Discoveries of the University of Michigan Expedition to Egypt (1924–1935).* Ann Arbor: Kelsey Museum of Archaeology, The University of Michigan. 1983.

Ghalioungui, P. *The Physicians of Pharaonic Egypt.* Mainz and Cairo: Verlag Philipp von Zabern and Al-Ahram Center for Scientific Translations. 1983.

Ghoneim, W. *Die ökonomische Bedeutung des Rindes im alten Ägypten.* Bonn: Rudolf Habelt Verlag. 1977.

Gilbert, A. S. "Zooarchaeological Observations on the Slaughterhouse of Meketre." *Journal of Egyptian Archaeology* 74 (1988), pp. 69–89.

Goodman, S. M. "Victual Egyptian Bird Mummies from a Presumed Late 17th or Early 18th Dynasty Tomb." *Journal of the Society for the Study of Egyptian Antiquities* 17 (1987), pp. 67–77.

Goodman, S. M. and P. L. Meininger, eds. *The Birds of Egypt.* Oxford and New York: Oxford University Press. 1989.

Grimal, N. *A History of Ancient Egypt.* Oxford and Cambridge: Basil Blackwell. 1992.

El Habashi, Z. *Tutankhamun and the Sporting Traditions.* New York and Bern: Peter Lang. 1992.

Harpur, Y. *Decoration in Egyptian Tombs of the Old Kingdom: Studies in Orientation and Scene Content.* London and New York: KPI. 1987.

Harrison, D. L. *The Mammals of Arabia.* Vols. 1–3. London: Ernest Benn Limited. 1964–72.

Hart, G. *A Dictionary of Egyptian Gods and Goddesses.* London and Boston: Routledge and Kegan Paul. 1986.

Hartmann, F. *L'agriculture dans l'ancienne Egypte*. Paris: Librairies-Imprimeries Réunies. 1923.

Hassan, S. *Excavations at Gîza*. Vol. 2. Cairo: The Government Press. 1936.

———. *The Sphinx: Its History in the Light of Recent Excavations*. Cairo: The Government Press. 1949.

———. "The Causeway of *Wnis* at Sakkara." *Zeitschrift für ägyptische Sprache und Altertumskunde* 80 (1955), pp. 136–39.

Hayes, W. C. *The Scepter of Egypt: A Background for the Study of Egyptian Antiquities in The Metropolitan Museum of Art*. Vols. 1–2. New York: Harry N. Abrams. 1990.

Hecker, H. M. "A Zooarchaeological Inquiry into Pork Consumption from Prehistoric to New Kingdom Times." *Journal of the American Research Center in Egypt* 19 (1982), pp. 59–71.

Helck, W. and E. Otto. *Kleines Wörterbuch der Aegyptologie*. 3rd edn. Wiesbaden: Otto Harrassowitz. 1987.

Hendrickx, S. "Une scène de chasse dans le désert sur le vase prédynastique Bruxelles, M.R.A.H. E. 2631." *Chronique d'Egypte* 67 (1992), pp. 5–27.

Hepper, F. N. *Pharaoh's Flowers: The Botanical Treasures of Tutankhamun*. London: HMSO. 1990.

Hery, F.-X. and T. Enel. *Animaux du Nil, animaux de dieu*. Aix-en-Provence: Collection l'univers de l'Egypte pharaonique. 1993.

Hilzheimer, M. "Dogs." *Antiquity* 6 (1932), pp. 411–19.

Hoath, R. *Natural Selections: A Year of Egypt's Wildlife*. Cairo: The American University in Cairo Press. 1992.

Hodjash, S. I. and O. D. Berlev. "A Market-Scene in the Mastaba of *Ḏ3ḏ3-m-ꜥnḫ (Tp-m-ꜥnḫ)*." *Altorientalische Forschungen* 7 (1980), pp. 31–49.

———. *The Egyptian Reliefs and Stelae in the Pushkin Museum of Fine Arts, Moscow*. Leningrad: Aurora Art. 1982.

Hope, C. A. *Gold of the Pharaohs*. Sydney: International Cultural Corporation of Australia. 1988.

Hopfner, T. *Der Tierkult der alten Ägypter nach den griechisch-römischen Berichten und den wichtigeren Denkmälern*. Vienna: Alfred Hölder. 1913.

Hornung, E. "Die Bedeutung des Tieres im alten Ägypten." *Studium Generale* 20 (1967), pp. 69–84.

———. *Conceptions of God in Ancient Egypt: The One and the Many*. Ithaca: Cornell University Press. 1982.

———. *The Valley of the Kings: Horizon of Eternity*. New York: Timken Publishers. 1990.

Hornung, E. and E. Staehelin, eds. *Skarabäen und andere Siegelamulette aus Basler Sammlungen*. Mainz: Verlag Philipp von Zabern. 1976.

Houlihan, P. F. *The Birds of Ancient Egypt*. With S. M. Goodman. Warminster: Aris and Phillips. 1986.

———. "Some Remarks on Deer (Cervidae) in Ancient Egypt." *Journal of Egyptian Archaeology* 73 (1987), pp. 238–43.

———. "A Figured Ostracon with a Humorous Scene of Judgment." *MVSE: Annual of the Museum of Art and Archaeology, University of Missouri–Columbia* 25 (1991), pp. 30–35.

Houlihan, P. F. and S. M. Goodman. "Comments on the Identification of Birds Depicted on Tutankhamun's Embossed Gold Fan." *Journal of the Society for the Study of Egyptian Antiquities* 9 (1979), pp. 219–25.

Ikram, S. "Animal Mating Motifs in Egyptian Funerary Representations." *Göttinger Miszellen* 124 (1991), pp. 51–61.

James, T. G. H. *Egyptian Painting and Drawing in the British Museum*. London: British Museum Publications. 1985.

Janssen, J. J. *Commodity Prices from the Ramessid Period: An Economic Study of the Village of Necropolis Workmen at Thebes*. Leiden: E. J. Brill. 1975.

———. "The Economic System of a Single Village." *Royal Anthropological Institute News* 15 (August 1976), pp. 17–19.

Janssen, R. and J. Janssen. *Egyptian Household Animals*. Aylesbury: Shire Publications. 1989.

Jennison, G. *Animals for Show and Pleasure in Ancient Rome*. Manchester: Manchester University Press. 1937.

Jéquier, G. "La panthère dans l'ancienne Egypte." *Revue d'ethnographie et de sociologie* 4 (1913), pp. 353–72.

Joger, U. *The Venomous Snakes of the Near and Middle East*. Wiesbaden: Dr. Ludwig Reichert Verlag. 1984.

Junker, H. *The Offering Room of Prince Kaninisut*. Vienna: Kunsthistorisches Museum. 1931.

Kanawati, N. "Bullfighting in Ancient Egypt." *The Bulletin of the Australian Centre for Egyptology* 2 (1991), pp. 51–58.

Kayser, H. *Göttliche Tiere: Ein Bilderbuch aus dem Pelizaeus-Museum zu Hildesheim*. Hildesheim: Gerstenberg Verlag. 1951.

Kees, H. *Ancient Egypt: A Cultural Topography*. Ed. by T. G. H. James. London: Faber and Faber. 1961.

Keimer, L. See note above.

Keller, O. *Die antike Tierwelt*. Vols. 1–2. Leipzig: Verlag von Wilhelm Engelmann. 1909–13.

Kemp, B. J. *Ancient Egypt: Anatomy of a Civilization*. London and New York: Routledge. 1991.

Kessler, D. *Die heiligen Tiere und der König, Teil I: Beiträge zu Organisation, Kult und Theologie der spätzeitlichen Tierfriedhöfe*. Wiesbaden: Otto Harrassowitz. 1989.

Kessler, D. and A. Nureddin. "Der Tierfriedhof von Tuna el-Gebel: Stand der Grabungen bis 1993." *Antike Welt: Zeitschrift für Archäologie und Kulturgeschichte* 25 (1994), pp. 252–65.

Khairat, O. *Hunting in Ancient Egypt*. Cairo: Egyptian Shooting and Fishing Club. 1955.

Kitchen, K. A. *Pharaoh Triumphant: The Life and Times of Ramesses II, King of Egypt*. Warminster: Aris and Phillips. 1982.

———. *The Third Intermediate Period in Egypt (1100–650 BC)*. 2nd edn. Warminster: Aris and Phillips. 1986.

———. "The Land of Punt." *The Archaeology of Africa: Food, Metals and Towns*. T. Shaw *et al.*, eds. London and New York: Routledge. 1993. Pp. 587–608.

Klebs, L. *Die Reliefs des alten Reiches (2980–2475 v.Chr.); Die Reliefs und Malereien des mittleren Reiches (VII.–XVII. Dynastie ca. 2475–1580 v.Chr.); Die Reliefs und Malereien des neuen Reiches (XVIII.–XX. Dynastie, ca. 1580–1100 v.Chr.)*. Heidelberg: Carl Winters Universitätsbuchhandlung. 1915–34.

Köhler-Rollefson, I. "Camels and Camel Pastoralism in Arabia." *Biblical Archaeologist* 56 (1993), pp. 180–88.

Kosack, W. "Ein altägyptisches Hausbuch der Tiermedizin." *Armant: Deutsch Arabische Kulturzeitschrift* 3 (1969), pp. 172–87.

Kozloff, A. P., ed. *Animals in Ancient Art from the Leo Mildenberg Collection.* Cleveland: The Cleveland Museum of Art. 1981.

Kozloff, A. P. and B. M. Bryan. *Egypt's Dazzling Sun: Amenhotep III and His World.* Cleveland: The Cleveland Museum of Art. 1992.

Kuentz, C. "L'oie du Nil *(Chenalopex ægyptiaca)* dans l'antique Egypte." *Archives du muséum d'histoire naturelle de Lyon* 14 (1926), pp. 1–60.

Lacau, P. and H. Chevrier. *Une chapelle de Sésostris Ier à Karnak.* Planches. Cairo: Imprimerie de l'Institut français d'archéologie orientale. 1969.

Lane, E. W. *An Account of the Manners and Customs of the Modern Egyptians.* 5th edn., ed. by E. S. Poole. London: John Murray. 1860.

Lange, K. *Ägyptische Tierplastik.* Gütersloh: Sigbert Mohn Verlag. 1959.

Lange, K. and M. Hirmer. *Egypt: Architecture, Sculpture, Painting in Three Thousand Years.* 4th edn. London and New York: The Phaidon Press. 1968.

Lauer, J.-P. *Saqqara: The Royal Cemetery of Memphis, Excavations and Discoveries Since 1850.* New York: Charles Scribner's Sons. 1976.

Leca, A.-P. *The Egyptian Way of Death: Mummies and the Cult of the Immortal.* Garden City, N.Y.: Doubleday and Company. 1981.

Leclant, J. "Un parc de chasse de la Nubie pharaonique." *2000 ans d'histoire africaine: Le sol, la parole et l'écrit. Mélanges en hommage à Raymond Mauny, Professeur Honoraire à l'Université de Paris I.* Vol. 2. Paris: Société française d'histoire d'outre-mer. 1981. Pp. 727–34.

Leibovitch, J. *Ancient Egypt: An Easy Introduction to its Archaeology including a Short Account of the Egyptian Museum, Cairo, with a Description of Gîza and Saqqâra.* Cairo: Imprimerie de l'Institut français d'archéologie orientale. 1938.

Lhote, A. and Hassia. *Les chefs-d'œuvre de la peinture égyptienne.* Paris: Hachette. 1954.

Lichtheim, M. *Ancient Egyptian Literature: A Book of Readings.* Vols. 1–3. Berkeley and London: The University of California Press. 1973–80.

Littauer, M. A. and J. H. Crouwel. *Wheeled Vehicles and Ridden Animals in the Ancient Near East.* Leiden and Cologne: E. J. Brill. 1979.

————. *Chariots and Related Equipment from the Tomb of Tut'ankhamun.* Oxford: Griffith Institute. 1985.

Lloyd, A. B. *Herodotus, Book II: Introduction and Commentary 1–182.* Vols. 1–3. Leiden: E. J. Brill. 1975–88.

Lortet, L. C. and C. Gaillard. "La faune momifiée de l'ancienne Egypte." Série 1–5. *Archives du muséum d'histoire naturelle de Lyon* 8 (1903), pp. 1–205; 9 (1905), pp. 1–130; 10 (1907), pp. 1–104; 10 (1908), pp. 105–224; 10 (1909), pp. 225–336.

Loyrette, A.-M. "Les animaux dans l'Egypte ancienne." *Archeologia* 114 (1978), pp. 24–35.

Lurker, M. *The Gods and Symbols of Ancient Egypt: An Illustrated Dictionary.* Rev. by P. A. Clayton. London: Thames and Hudson. 1984.

The Luxor Museum of Ancient Egyptian Art: Catalogue. Cairo: The American Research Center in Egypt. 1979.

Macramallah, R. *Le mastaba d'Idout.* Cairo: Imprimerie de l'Institut français d'archéologie orientale. 1935.

Mahmoud, O. *Die wirtschaftliche Bedeutung der Vögel im Alten Reich.* Frankfurt and Bern: Verlag Peter Lang. 1991.

Malaise, M. "La perception du monde animal dans l'Egypte ancienne." *Anthropozoologica* 7 (1987), pp. 28–48.

Malek, J. *The Cat in Ancient Egypt.* London: British Museum Press. 1993.

————, ed. *Cradles of Civilization: Egypt — Ancient Culture, Modern Land*. Norman: The University of Oklahoma Press. 1993.

Malek, J. and W. Forman. *In the Shadow of the Pyramids: Egypt during the Old Kingdom*. Norman and London: The University of Oklahoma Press. 1986.

Manniche, L. *City of the Dead: Thebes in Egypt*. Chicago: The University of Chicago Press. 1987.

————. *Sexual Life in Ancient Egypt*. London and New York: KPI. 1987.

Manning, A. and J. Serpell, eds. *Animals and Human Society: Changing Perspectives*. London and New York: Routledge. 1994.

Marx, H. *Checklist of the Reptiles and Amphibians of Egypt*. Cairo: Special Publication United States Medical Research Unit Number 3. 1968.

Mason, I. L., ed. *Evolution of Domesticated Animals*. London and New York: Longman. 1984.

Maspero, G. *Guide to the Cairo Museum*. 5th edn. Cairo: Printing Office of the French Institute of Oriental Archaeology. 1910

————. *Egyptian Art: Studies*. London: T. Fisher Unwin. 1913.

Meeks, D. "Zoomorphie et image des dieux dans l'Egypte ancienne." *Le temps de la réflexion VII: Corps des dieux*. C. Malamoud and J.-P. Vernant, eds. Paris: Gallimard. 1986. Pp. 171–91.

Meinertzhagen, R. *Nicoll's Birds of Egypt*. Vols. 1–2. London: Hugh Rees. 1930.

Mekhitarian, A. *Egyptian Painting*. New York: Rizzoli International Publications. 1978.

Messiha, H. and M. A. Elhitta. *Mallawi Antiquities Museum: A Brief Description*. Cairo: General Organization for Government Printing Offices. 1979.

Michalowski, K. *Art of Ancient Egypt*. New York: Harry N. Abrams. 1968.

Miller, R. L. "Hogs and Hygiene." *Journal of Egyptian Archaeology* 76 (1990), pp. 125–40.

Moens, M.-F. "The Ancient Egyptian Garden in the New Kingdom: A Study of Representations." *Orientalia Lovaniensia Periodica* 15 (1984), pp. 11–53.

Mogensen, M. *La Glyptothèque Ny Carlsberg: La collection égyptienne*. Vols. 1–2. Copenhagen: Levin and Munksgaard. 1930.

Mond, R. and O. H. Myers. *Temples of Armant: A Preliminary Survey*. Vols. 1–2. London: The Egypt Exploration Society. 1940.

Montet, P. *Les scènes de la vie privée dans les tombeaux égyptiens de l'Ancien Empire*. Strasbourg: Librairie Istra. 1925.

————. *Isis: Or the Search for Egypt's Buried Past*. Geneva: Editions Ferni. 1977.

Moran, W. L., ed. *The Amarna Letters*. Baltimore and London: The Johns Hopkins University Press. 1992.

Moussa, A. M. and H. Altenmüller. *Das Grab des Nianchchnum und Chnumhotep*. Mainz: Verlag Philipp von Zabern. 1977.

Müller, H. W. *Ägyptische Kunstwerke, Kleinfunde und Glas in der Sammlung E. und M. Kofler-Truniger, Luzern*. Berlin: Verlag Bruno Hessling. 1964.

————. *Ägyptische Kunst*. Frankfurt: Umschau Verlag. 1970.

Murnane, W. J. *The Penguin Guide to Ancient Egypt*. Harmondsworth and New York: Penguin Books. 1983.

Muscarella, O. W., ed. *Ancient Art: The Norbert Schimmel Collection*. Mainz: Verlag Philipp von Zabern. 1974.

Nagel's Encyclopedia–Guide: Egypt. Geneva and Paris: Nagel Publishers. 1985.

Neufeld, N. "Apiculture in Ancient Palestine (Early and Middle Iron Age) within the Framework of the Ancient Near East." *Ugarit-Forschungen: Internationales Jahrbuch für die Altertumskunde Syrien-Palästinas* 10 (1978), pp. 219–47.

Newberry, P. E. *Beni Hasan*. Vol. 4. London: The Egypt Exploration Fund. 1900.

———. "The Pig and the Cult-Animal of Set." *Journal of Egyptian Archaeology* 14 (1928), pp. 211–25.

Nibbi, A. "Some Remarks on Ass and Horse in Ancient Egypt and the Absence of the Mule." *Zeitschrift für ägyptische Sprache und Altertumskunde* 106 (1979), pp. 148–68.

Nims, C. F. *Thebes of the Pharaohs: Pattern for Every City*. New York: Stein and Day Publishers. 1965.

Nowak, R. M. *Walker's Mammals of the World*. 5th edn. Vols. 1–2. Baltimore and London: The Johns Hopkins University Press. 1991.

Omlin, J. A. *Der Papyrus 55001 und seine satirisch-erotischen Zeichnungen und Inschriften*. Turin: Editioni d'Arte Fratelli Pozzo. 1973.

Osborn, D. J. and I. Helmy. *The Contemporary Land Mammals of Egypt (Including Sinai)*. Chicago: The Field Museum of Natural History. 1980.

Otto, E. *Beiträge zur Geschichte der Stierkulte in Aegypten*. Leipzig: J. C. Hinrichs Verlag. 1938.

———. "An Ancient Egyptian Hunting Ritual." *Journal of Near Eastern Studies* 9 (1950), pp. 164–77.

Paget, R. F. E. and A. A. Pirie. *The Tomb of Ptah-hetep*. London: Bernard Quaritch. 1898.

Paton, D. *Animals of Ancient Egypt*. Princeton: Princeton University Press. 1925.

Peck, W. H. and J. G. Ross. *Drawings from Ancient Egypt*. London: Thames and Hudson. 1978.

Pendlebury, J. D. S. *Tell el-Amarna*. London: Lovat Dickson and Thompson Publishers. 1935.

Perizonius, R., M. Attia, H. Smith, J. Goudsmit. "Monkey Mummies and North Saqqara." *Egyptian Archaeology: The Bulletin of the Egypt Exploration Society* 3 (1993), pp. 31–33.

Peterson, B. E. J. "Zeichnungen aus einer Totenstadt: Bildostraka aus Theben-West, ihre Fundplätze, Themata und Zweckbereiche mitsamt einem Katalog der Gayer-Anderson-Sammlung in Stockholm." *Medelhavsmuseet Bulletin* 7–8 (1973), pp. 1–141.

Phillips, D. W. *Ancient Egyptian Animals*. Rev. edn. New York: The Metropolitan Museum of Art. 1948.

Posener, G., S. Sauneron, J. Yoyotte. *Dictionary of Egyptian Civilization*. New York: Tudor Publishing Company. 1959.

Priese, K.-H., ed. *Ägyptisches Museum: Staatliche Museen zu Berlin, Stiftung Preussischer Kulturbesitz (Museumsinsel Berlin)*. Mainz: Verlag Philipp von Zabern. 1991.

Pritchard, J. B., ed. *Ancient Near Eastern Texts Relating to the Old Testament*. 2nd edn. Princeton: Princeton University Press. 1955.

Pusch, E. B. "Recent Work at Northern Piramesse. Results of Excavations by the Pelizaeus-Museum, Hildesheim, at Qantir." *Fragments of a Shattered Visage: The Proceedings of the International Symposium on Ramesses the Great*. E. Bleiberg and R. Freed, eds. Memphis: Memphis State University, Institute of Egyptian Art and Archaeology. 1991. Pp. 199–220.

Quibell, J. E. *Tomb of Yuaa and Thuiu*. Cairo: Imprimerie de l'Institut français d'archéologie orientale. 1908.

Quirke, S. and J. Spencer, eds. *The British Museum Book of Ancient Egypt*. New York: Thames and Hudson. 1992.

Ranke, H. *The Art of Ancient Egypt: Architecture, Sculpture, Painting, Applied Art.* Vienna: The Phaidon Press. 1936.

Reed, C. A. "Animal Domestication in the Prehistoric Near East." *New Roads to Yesterday: Essays in Archaeology, Articles from Science.* J. R. Caldwell, ed. London: Thames and Hudson. 1966. Pp. 178–209.

Reisner, G. A. "The Dog which was Honored by the King of Upper and Lower Egypt." *Bulletin of the Museum of Fine Arts, Boston* 34 (1936), pp. 96–99.

Retsö, J. "The Domestication of the Camel and the Establishment of the Frankincense Road from South Arabia." *Orientalia Suecana* 40 (1991), pp. 187–219.

Rice, E. E. *The Grand Procession of Ptolemy Philadelphus.* Oxford: Oxford University Press. 1983.

Ricke, H., G. R. Hughes, E. F. Wente. *The Beit el-Wali Temple of Ramesses II.* Chicago: The Oriental Institute of the University of Chicago. 1967.

Ridley, R. T. *The Unification of Egypt: As Seen Through a Study of the Major Knife-Handles, Palettes and Maceheads.* Deception Bay, Aus.: Shield Press. 1973.

Ritner, R. K. *The Mechanics of Ancient Egyptian Magical Practice.* Chicago: The Oriental Institute of the University of Chicago. 1993.

Rizkana, I. and J. Seeher. *Maadi III–IV.* Mainz: Verlag Philipp von Zabern. 1989–90.

Robins, G. "Ancient Egyptian Sexuality." *Discussions in Egyptology* 11 (1988), pp. 61–72.

———. "Problems in Interpreting Egyptian Art." *Discussions in Egyptology* 17 (1990), pp. 45–58.

Roeder, G. *Ägyptische Bronzefiguren.* Vols. 1–2. Berlin: Staatliche Museen zu Berlin. 1956.

Roemer- und Pelizaeus-Museum, Hildesheim. *Götter und Pharaohen: 29. Mai–16. September 1979.* Mainz: Verlag Philipp von Zabern. 1979.

Rommelaere, C. *Les chevaux du Nouvel Empire égyptien: Origines, races, harnachement.* Brussels: Connaissance de l'Egypte ancienne. 1991.

Rose, C. L. and E. Dietze. "Examination and Stabilization of Two Bull Mummies: Preserving Archaeological Evidence of Egyptian Rituals/Technology." *Technology and Conservation* 3 (Summer 1978), pp. 32–38.

Rosellini, I. *I monumenti dell' Egitto e della Nubia: Monumenti civili.* Atlas. Pisa: Presso N. Capurro. 1834.

Rowley-Conwy, P. "The Camel in the Nile Valley: New Radiocarbon Accelerator (AMS) Dates from Qasr Ibrîm." *Journal of Egyptian Archaeology* 74 (1988), pp. 245–48.

Rzóska, J., ed. *The Nile: Biology of an Ancient River.* The Hague: Dr. W. Junk B. V. 1976.

Saad, Z. Y. *The Excavations at Helwan: Art and Civilization in the First and Second Egyptian Dynasties.* Ed. by J. F. Autry. Norman: The University of Oklahoma Press. 1969.

Sadek, A. I. *Popular Religion in Egypt during the New Kingdom.* Hildesheim: Gerstenberg Verlag. 1987.

Saleh, M. and H. Sourouzian. *The Egyptian Museum Cairo: Official Catalogue.* Munich and Mainz: Prestel-Verlag and Verlag Philipp von Zabern. 1987.

Sauneron, S. "Some Newly Unrolled Hieratic Papyri in the Wilbour Collection of the Brooklyn Museum." *The Brooklyn Museum Annual* 8 (1966–67), pp. 98–102.

———. *The Priests of Ancient Egypt.* New York: Grove Press. 1960.

Säve-Söderbergh, T. *On Egyptian Representations of Hippopotamus Hunting as a Religious Motive.* Uppsala: Société Nathan Söderblom. 1953.

Scamuzzi, E. *Egyptian Art in the Egyptian Museum of Turin: Paintings, Sculpture, Furniture, Textiles, Ceramics, Papyri*. New York: Harry N. Abrams. 1965.

Schiff Giorgini, M. "Soleb: Campagnes 1961–63." *Kush: Journal of the Sudan Antiquities Service* 12 (1964), pp. 87–95.

Schmitz, B. *Vögel im alten Ägypten: Informationen zum Thema und Kurzführer durch die Ausstellung*. Hildesheim: Roemer- und Pelizaeus-Museum. 1987.

Schneider, H. D. and M. J. Raven. *De Egyptische oudheid: Een inleiding aan hand van de Egyptische verzameling in het Rijksmuseum van Oudheden te Leiden*. The Hague: Rijksmuseum van Oudheden te Leiden. 1981.

Schoske, S., B. Kreissl, R. Germer. *"Anch" Blumen für das Leben: Pflanzen im alten Ägypten*. Munich: Staatliche Sammlung Ägyptischer Kunst. 1992.

Schulman, A. R. "Egyptian Representations of Horsemen and Riding in the New Kingdom." *Journal of Near Eastern Studies* 16 (1957), pp. 263–71.

———. "Chariots, Chariotry and the Hyksos." *Journal of the Society for the Study of Egyptian Antiquities* 10 (1980), pp. 105–153.

Schweitzer, U. *Löwe und Sphinx im alten Ägypten*. Glückstadt: J. J. Augustin. 1948.

Scott, N. E. "The Metternich Stela." *Bulletin of The Metropolitan Museum of Art* 9 (1951), pp. 201–217.

Shafer, B. E, ed. *Religion in Ancient Egypt: Gods, Myths, and Personal Practice*. Ithaca and London: Cornell University Press. 1991.

Silverman, D. P. "Pygmies and Dwarves in the Old Kingdom." *Serapis: The American Journal of Egyptology* 1 (1969), pp. 53–62.

Simpson, W. K. *The Offering Chapel of Sekhem-ankh-Ptah in the Museum of Fine Arts, Boston*. Boston: Museum of Fine Arts, Boston. 1976.

Singer, C., E. J. Holmyard, A. R. Hall, eds. *A History of Technology*. Vol. 1. Oxford: The Clarendon Press. 1954.

Smelik, K. A. D. "The Cult of the Ibis in the Graeco–Roman Period, with Special Attention to the Data from the Papyri." *Studies in Hellenistic Religions*. M. J. Vermaseren, ed. Leiden: E. J. Brill. 1979. Pp. 225–43.

Smelik, K. A. D. and E. A. Hemelrijk. "'Who knows not what monsters demented Egypt worships?' Opinions on Egyptian Animal Worship in Antiquity as Part of the Ancient Conception of Egypt." *Aufstieg und Niedergang der Römischen Welt: Geschichte und Kultur Roms im Spiegel der neueren Forschung, Principat*. Vol. 17(4). W. Haase, ed. Berlin and New York: Walter de Gruyter. 1984. Pp. 1852–2000, 2337–57.

Smith, H. S. "Animal Domestication and Animal Cult in Dynastic Egypt." *The Domestication and Exploitation of Plants and Animals*. P. J. Ucko and G. W. Dimbleby, eds. London: Gerald Duckworth. 1969. Pp. 307–314.

———. *A Visit to Ancient Egypt: Life at Memphis and Saqqara (c. 500–30 BC)*. Warminster: Aris and Phillips. 1974.

Smith, W. S. *A History of Egyptian Sculpture and Painting in the Old Kingdom*. 2nd edn. London and Boston: Museum of Fine Arts, Boston. 1949.

———. *Country Life in Ancient Egypt*. 2nd edn. Boston: Museum of Fine Arts, Boston. [1954].

———. *Ancient Egypt as Represented in the Museum of Fine Arts, Boston*. 4th edn. Boston: Beacon Press. 1961.

———. *Interconnections in the Ancient Near East: A Study of the Relationships Between the Arts of Egypt, the Aegean, and Western Asia*. New Haven and London: Yale University Press. 1965.

————. *The Art and Architecture of Ancient Egypt*. Rev. by W. K. Simpson. Harmondsworth and New York: Penguin Books. 1981.

Spencer, A. J. *Death in Ancient Egypt*. Harmondsworth and New York: Penguin Books. 1982.

————. *Early Egypt: The Rise of Civilisation in the Nile Valley*. London: British Museum Press. 1993.

Steindorff, G. *Das Grab des Ti*. Leipzig: J. C. Hinrichs Verlag. 1913.

————. "The Magical Knives of Ancient Egypt." *Journal of the Walters Art Gallery* 9 (1946), pp. 41–51, 106–107.

Störk, L. *Die Nashörner: Verbreitungs- und kulturgeschichtliche Materialen unter besonderer Berücksichtigung der afrikanischen Arten und des altägyptischen Kulturbereiches*. Hamburg: Verlag Born. 1977.

Strouhal, E.. *Life of the Ancient Egyptians*. Norman: The University of Oklahoma Press. 1992.

Terrace, E. L. B. and H. G. Fischer. *Treasures of the Cairo Museum: From Predynastic to Roman Times*. London: Thames and Hudson. 1970.

te Velde, H. "A Few Remarks Upon the Religious Significance of Animals in Ancient Egypt." *Numen: International Review for the History of Religions* 27 (1980), pp. 76–82.

————. "Some Remarks on the Mysterious Language of the Baboons." *Funerary Symbols and Religion: Essays Dedicated to Professor M. S. H. G. Heerma van Voss on the Occasion of His Retirement from the Chair of the History of Ancient Religions at the University of Amsterdam*. J. H. Kamstra, H. Milde, K. Wagtendonk, eds. Kampen: J. H. Kok. 1988. Pp. 129–39.

————. "Some Egyptian Deities and their Piggishness." *Intellectual Heritage of Egypt: Studies Presented to László Kákosy by Friends and Colleagues on the Occasion of His 60th Birthday*. U. Luft, ed. Budapest: Studia Aegyptiaca XIV. 1992. Pp. 571–78.

Thausing, G. and H. Goedicke. *Nofretari: A Documentation of Her Tomb and its Decoration*. Graz: Akademische Druck und Verlaganstalt. 1971.

Thomas, E. *The Royal Necropoleis of Thebes*. Princeton: Privately published. 1966.

Thompson, D. J. *Memphis under the Ptolemies*. Princeton: Princeton University Press. 1988.

Tooley, A. M. J. "Coffin of a Dog from Beni Hasan." *Journal of Egyptian Archaeology* 74 (1988), pp. 207–211.

Toynbee, J. M. C. *Animals in Roman Life and Art*. Ithaca: Cornell University Press. 1973.

Trigger, B. G., B. J. Kemp, D. O'Connor, A. B. Lloyd. *Ancient Egypt: A Social History*. Cambridge: Cambridge University Press. 1983.

Uerpmann, H.-P. *The Ancient Distribution of Ungulate Mammals in the Middle East: Fauna and Archaeological Sites in Southwest Asia and Northeast Africa*. Wiesbaden: Dr. Ludwig Reichert Verlag. 1987.

van Buren, E. D. *The Fauna of Ancient Mesopotamia*. Rome: Pontificium Institutum Biblicum. 1939.

Vandersleyen, C. *Das alte Ägypten*. Berlin: Propyläen Verlag. 1985.

van de Walle, B. *L'humour dans la littérature et dans l'art de l'ancienne Egypte*. Leiden: Nederlands Instituut voor het Nabije Oosten. 1969.

————. *La chapelle funéraire de Neferirtenef*. Brussels: Musées royaux d'art et d'histoire. 1978.

Vandier, J. *Manuel d'archéologie égyptienne*. Vols. 1–6. Paris: Editions A. et J. Picard. 1952–78.

———. *Musée du Louvre: Le département des antiquités égyptiennes. Guide sommaire*. 5th edn. Paris: Editions des Musées Nationaux. 1973.

Vandier d'Abbadie, J. *Catalogue des ostraca figurés de Deir el Medineh*. Fasc. 1–5 (Fasc. 5 by A. Gasse). Cairo: Imprimerie de l'Institut français d'archéologie orientale. 1936–86.

———. "Les singes familiers dans l'ancienne Egypte (Peintures et bas-reliefs)." *Revue d'égyptologie* 16 (1964), pp. 147–77; 17 (1965), pp. 177–88; 18 (1966), pp. 143–201.

von Bissing, F. W. "La chambre des trois saisons du sanctuaire solaire du roi Rathourès (V dynastie) à Abousir." *Annales du service des antiquités de l'Egypte* 53 (1956), pp. 319–38.

von Droste zu Hülshoff, V. *Der Igel im alten Ägypten*. Hildesheim: Gerstenberg Verlag. 1980.

Walker, R. E. "The Veterinary Papyrus of Kahun: A Revised Translation and Interpretation of the Ancient Egyptian Treatise Known as the Veterinary Papyrus of Kahun." *The Veterinary Record* 76 (1964), pp. 198–200.

Ward, W. A. *Studies on Scarab Seals*. Vol. 1. Warminster: Aris and Phillips. 1978.

Weeks, K. R. "Art, Word, and the Egyptian World View." *Egyptology and the Social Sciences: Five Studies*. K. R. Weeks, ed. Cairo: The American University in Cairo Press. 1979. Pp. 59–81.

Wendorf, F. and R. Schild. *Cattle-Keepers of the Eastern Sahara: The Neolithic of Bir Kiseiba*. Ed. by A. E. Close. Dallas: Southern Methodist University Press. 1984.

———. "Are the Early Holocene Cattle in the Eastern Sahara Domestic or Wild?" *Evolutionary Anthropology* 3 (1994), pp. 118–28.

Werbrouck, M. *Musées royaux d'art et d'histoire: Département égyptien. Album*. Brussels: Fondation égyptologique Reine Elisabeth. 1934.

Westendorf, W. *Painting, Sculpture, and Architecture of Ancient Egypt*. New York: Harry N. Abrams. 1968.

Wiedemann, K. A. *Der Tierkult der alten Ägypter*. Leipzig: J. C. Hinrichs Verlag. 1912.

Wildung, D. *Nilpferd und Krokodil: Das Tier in der Kunst des alten Ägypten*. Munich: Staatliche Sammlung Ägyptischer Kunst. 1987.

Wilkinson, C. K. and M. Hill. *Egyptian Wall Paintings: The Metropolitan Museum of Art's Collection of Facsimiles*. New York: The Metropolitan Museum of Art. 1983.

Wilkinson, J. G. *The Manners and Customs of the Ancient Egyptians*. Vol. 1–3. Rev. by S. Birch. London: John Murray. 1878.

Wilkinson, R. H. *Reading Egyptian Art: A Hieroglyphic Guide to Ancient Egyptian Painting and Sculpture*. London and New York: Thames and Hudson. 1992.

Willoughby, K. L. and E. B. Stanton, eds. *The First Egyptians*. Columbia: The McKissick Museum, The University of South Carolina. 1988.

Winkler, H. A. *Rock-Drawings of Southern Upper Egypt*. Vols. 1–2. London: The Egypt Exploration Society. 1938.

Winlock, H. E. *Models of Daily Life in Ancient Egypt from the Tomb of Meket-Rē' at Thebes*. Cambridge: Harvard University Press. 1955.

Winter, E. *Der Apiskult im alten Ägypten*. Mainz: Verlag Philipp von Zabern. 1978.

Wreszinski, W. *Atlas zur altägyptischen Kulturgeschichte*. Vols. 1–3. Leipzig: J. C. Hinrichs Verlag. 1923–38.

Wulleman, R., M. Kunnen, A. Mekhitarian. *Passage to Eternity*. Knokke: Mappamundi. 1989.

Yoyotte, J. *Treasures of the Pharaohs: The Early Period, the New Kingdom, the Late Period*. Geneva: Editions d'Art Albert Skira. 1968.

Zahran, M. A. and A. J. Willis. *The Vegetation of Egypt*. London and New York: Chapman and Hall. 1992.

Zeuner, F. E. *A History of Domesticated Animals*. New York: Harper and Row Publishers. 1963.

Ziegler, C., C. Barbotin, M.-H. Rutschowscaya. *The Louvre: Egyptian Antiquities*. London: Scala Books. 1990.

Ziegler, C., J.-M. Humbert, M. Pantazzi. *Egyptomania: Egypt in Western Art, 1730–1930*. Paris and Ottawa: Editions de la Réunion des Musées Nationaux and the National Gallery of Canada. 1994.

Index of Common Names

Index of Scientific Names

General Index